# ESSENTIAL WORDS FOR THE

**Third Edition**

**TOEFL**®

## Test of English as a Foreign Language

**Steven J. Matthiesen, M.A.**
Johns Hopkins University
Baltimore, Maryland, USA

**BARRON'S**

Definition on page 31 copyright © 1992 by Houghton Mifflin Company. Reprinted by permission from the AMERICAN HERITAGE DICTIONARY OF THE ENGLISH LANGUAGE, THIRD EDITION.

Thesaurus entry on page 34 from WEBSTER'S NEW WORLD THESAURUS by Charlton Laird, copyright © 1985. Used by permission of the publisher, Simon & Schuster, New York.

*All inquiries should be addressed to:*
Barron's Educational Series, Inc.
250 Wireless Boulevard
Hauppauge, New York 11788
**http://www.barronseduc.com**

Library of Congress Catalog Card No. 2003062820

International Standard Book No. 0-7641-2025-5

**Library of Congress Cataloging-in-Publication Data**
Matthiesen, Steven J.
    Essential words for the TOEFL, test of English as a foreign language / Steven J. Matthiesen. — 3rd ed.
        p.    cm.
    ISBN 0-7641-2025-5
    1. Test of English as a Foreign Language—Study guides.
2. English language—Textbooks for foreign speakers. 3. English language—Examinations—Study guides. 4. Vocabulary—Examinations—Study guides. I. Matthiesen, Steven J. II. Title.

PE1128.S735   2004
428'0076—dc22                                    2003062820

PRINTED IN THE UNITED STATES OF AMERICA
9 8 7 6 5 4 3 2 1

To

Guadalupe and Stephanie

# CONTENTS

# Introduction

# SUCCESS ON THE TOEFL

**What vocabulary is necessary to score high on the TOEFL?**
How can I improve my vocabulary for this important test?
How can I be a better TOEFL test taker?

*Essential Words for the TOEFL* answers these questions and provides you with a proven plan for improving your English vocabulary while also preparing you for the TOEFL. The words and practice questions that appear throughout this book will help you to maximize your understanding of words that will likely appear in every section of the TOEFL. Important information about how to maximize your score on the TOEFL is given in addition to vocabulary building hints and exercises. By following the program and mastering the words in this book, you will be ready to earn a higher score on the TOEFL.

*Essential Words for the TOEFL* is a product of an extensive study of more than 2,000 TOEFL vocabulary questions from dozens of different TOEFL tests administered during recent years. A list of all TOEFL vocabulary was made and the number of times each word was tested was counted. The word each tested word was associated with was identified. Words that appeared as incorrect answers were also identified and counted. The result is this little book of words that you should know before you take the TOEFL.

## RECENT CHANGES IN THE TOEFL

Prior to 1995 Section 3 of the TOEFL, Vocabulary and Reading Comprehension, contained 60 items. In 1995 the 30-question vocabulary subtest was eliminated. Instead, vocabulary items were taken from the stimulus passages used to test reading comprehension. The total number of questions in Section 3 was reduced to 50. The number of vocabulary items was reduced to between 14 and 17 per TOEFL, and the format of the vocabulary items was changed. Thus, vocabulary items now account for between 25 percent and 34 percent of the score on Section 3.

Beginning in July 1998, when the computer-based TOEFL came into existence, the vocabulary questions changed format again. Now, instead of identifying which of four choices is the correct synonym for a word in the text, the test taker is usually asked to locate another word in the text that means the same as the word whose meaning is being tested. Currently, both a paper version and a computer-delivered version of TOEFL exist. Individuals taking the TOEFL in certain countries and those taking the Institutional TOEFL take the older paper version of TOEFL. Everyone else takes the computer-delivered version.

While the words tested on both versions are the same, the format of the vocabulary questions differs. This book gives you practice with both formats. It also anticipates further changes in TOEFL by including practice questions that encompass whole phrases or word combinations.

## MAXIMIZING YOUR VOCABULARY POTENTIAL— A DESCRIPTION OF THIS PROGRAM

This book is divided into seven chapters. This introduction gives you basic information about their contents and how to use the book. Let's look at the seven chapters.

### Getting to Know the TOEFL

Chapter 1 describes the complete TOEFL test and gives you sample questions from each part. The questions are explained in detail and test-taking strategies for each section are given. The paper version and the computer version of TOEFL are described and compared.

### Understanding the TOEFL Reading Section

Chapter 2 gives you a complete description of the vocabulary questions that appear on Section 3 of the TOEFL. This chapter contains a detailed analysis of the kinds of words that are tested on the TOEFL. It illustrates both the paper and computer formats for vocabulary questions, and it gives you important strategies and hints to follow when taking either version of the TOEFL.

### Improving Your TOEFL Vocabulary

Chapter 3 gives you a plan for studying vocabulary. You should use the plan when studying the words in this book.

## Building Your Vocabulary

Chapter 4 helps you to build your TOEFL vocabulary through the study of "roots, prefixes, and suffixes." These are the parts of words that add meaning. Roots, prefixes, and suffixes appear often in the English language.

## Important Vocabulary Building Tools

Two useful tools in any vocabulary building program are the dictionary and thesaurus. Chapter 5 explains how to use both and introduces you to the kind of information that each contains.

## The Essential TOEFL Vocabulary

Barron's TOEFL Vocabulary Building Program is explained in Chapter 6. The carefully selected words that appear on the list are important for all TOEFL test takers. An explanation of the program is given, including how to study the list, how to understand the words and how to follow the program from beginning to end. Thirty carefully developed vocabulary lessons follow the explanation. Each lesson ends with practice questions like those that appear on both the paper and computer-based TOEFL.

## The Practice Test (Computer-Based Format)

Chapter 7 contains a complete practice test for Section 3 of the TOEFL. The test contains both reading comprehension and vocabulary questions that closely follow the new format of the computer-based TOEFL. This is followed by a key of correct answers, and information on how to convert your number of correct answers to a score on the TOEFL scale. Both the old scale for the paper version of the TOEFL and the new scale for the computer-based version are included, so you will be able to convert your score to either scale. Chapter 7 is followed by an alphabetical index of the 450 essential words taught in this book. The page on which each word is introduced is indicated next to the word.

## A Final Word

Among the thousands of vocabulary words TOEFL test makers can choose from, this book presents the words that are most likely to appear often. By mastering the words in this book and learning the roots, prefixes, and suffixes that make up other words related to them, you will be well prepared for the vocabulary tested on the TOEFL. Furthermore, by following these TOEFL test-taking strategies, you will be on your way to a higher score on the TOEFL in general, and Section 3 of the TOEFL in particular.

# CHAPTER 1

# GETTING TO KNOW THE TOEFL

## WHAT IS THE TOEFL?

The TOEFL is a comprehensive English language examination required by more than 3,000 colleges and universities in the United States, Canada, and other parts of the world. In addition, foreign born professionals frequently need a TOEFL score for certification to practice their profession in the United States or Canada.

## PAPER AND COMPUTER-BASED TOEFLs

From 1964 to 1998 the TOEFL was administered in only a paper version. Examinees marked their answers with a pencil on an answer sheet. In 1998, the Educational Testing Service (ETS), which prepares the TOEFL, and Sylvan Learning Systems, which administers the computer-based TOEFL, began offering the TOEFL on computer. Today, nearly everyone who takes the TOEFL takes the computer version of the test. However, the paper-based version is still offered in some parts of the world, chiefly Asia, to supplement computer-delivered administrations as demand requires.

Examinees in the United States, Canada, Europe, Latin America, Africa, the Middle East, Australia, New Zealand, and most other countries, began taking the computer version of TOEFL in 1998. Examinees taking the Institutional TOEFL in any country continue to take the paper version. Because the computer-based version includes items that are similar to those found in the paper-based test, and because the Institutional TOEFL is still offered on paper only, people preparing to take the TOEFL are advised to become familiar with both versions.

Although the two versions of the TOEFL are similar, the computer-based version is slightly different from the paper version. Both differences and similarities are discussed below. Because the computer-based TOEFL is an adaptation of the paper TOEFL, we begin with a description of the paper TOEFL and then discuss how the computer-based version differs from it.

In addition to these versions of the TOEFL, an entirely new TOEFL test is under development. If the development process goes according to plan, the new test will be significantly different from either of these two versions now on the market. While little is known about what form it will finally take, a few broad changes can be delineated. They are discussed at the end of this chapter (A Word About the Future).

## THE PAPER TOEFL

The paper TOEFL is a timed test that consists of the three sections listed below.

| Section 1 | Listening Comprehension | 50 questions 35 minutes |
|---|---|---|
| Part A | Short Dialogs | 30 questions |
| Part B | Short Presentations and Extended Conversations | 20 questions |
| Section 2 | Structure and Written Expression | 40 questions 25 minutes |
| | Structure | 15 questions |
| | Written Expression | 25 questions |
| Section 3 | Reading Comprehension | 50 questions 55 minutes |

## SECTION 1: LISTENING COMPREHENSION

This section of the TOEFL tests your ability to understand spoken American English. After you hear taped conversations you will answer questions.

## Short Dialogs

Part A contains short dialogs between two people followed by a question about what the people said in their conversation. The people may have different purposes for speaking to each other. A speaker may give advice, apologize, or ask for information. Generally, key information is found in the second speaker's sentence. You will need to understand the meaning of the conversation and also the context, such as the time or place in which it could occur. The correct choice is that which directly answers the question.

YOU WILL HEAR:

| (Man) | Did you get to go shopping last night? |
|-------|----------------------------------------|
| (Woman) | They'd already locked the doors by the time I got there. |
| (Man) | What does the woman mean? |

YOU WILL SEE:

(A) She arrived in time to shop.
(B) She was too late.
(C) She locked the doors.
(D) She had to buy the door.

The correct choice is (B). Since the doors were locked when she arrived, she could not have gone shopping. Note that the other choices use words heard in the conversation. Choices that contain such words are usually not correct. Part A contains samples of informal American English. Idiomatic expressions and two-word verbs are common in this part.

## Extended Conversations/Minitalks

In Part B you will hear extended conversations between two or more people or a short presentation by one person. Usually, there are two extended conversations and three short presentations. TOEFL program publications refer to these short presentations as Minitalks. The English in this section is generally more formal and academic, typical of English conversations or lectures that take place in a university or college setting. After each conversation or short presentation, there are between three and five (usually four) spoken questions about its content. Choose your answer from among the four choices that appear in your test booklet.

The extended conversations and short presentations, are preceded by an introductory statement that tells you the context for the conversation. Pay particular attention to this information as it orients you for what follows. Look at the example of a minitalk below.

YOU WILL HEAR:

Listen to this talk by a tourist guide.

Man: Good morning ladies and gentlemen. Welcome to this tour of one of the nation's most important cities, Chicago. Before we begin, I'd like to give you some background information that will make the tour more enjoyable for you. The city was founded in 1837. Its strategic location on Lake Michigan quickly made it

3

the center of commerce for the midwest section of the country. It currently is the third largest metropolitan area in the United States. The city's site is generally level, built mostly on a glacial plain. The narrow Chicago River extends one mile inland from Lake Michigan, where it splits, dividing the city into North, West, and South sides. Chicago's weather is subject to rapid changes, but generally the climate is cold and windy in the winter, and hot and humid in the summer.

Woman: What gave Chicago an advantage over other midwestern cities?

YOU WILL SEE:

(A) Its level site.
(B) Its location on Lake Michigan.
(C) Its large population.
(D) Its location along the Chicago River.

According to the Minitalk, (B) would be the correct choice. Remember that you will not have a written copy of the speaker's presentation or conversation and you will hear it only once. You must concentrate on details, such as names, dates, and the main idea of the selection that you hear. Do not read the choices as you listen to the talk. Listen carefully and try to remember what you hear.

## SECTION 2: STRUCTURE AND WRITTEN EXPRESSION

This section contains two types of questions, both designed to test your ability to recognize correct style and grammar in written English. The sentences are academic; ones that you typically find in college-level texts, journals, and encyclopedias. The sentence topics include the social sciences, physical and life sciences, and the humanities.

### Structure

The Structure questions test your ability to recognize correct structure and word order. These questions consist of a sentence with one or more words missing. You must make the choice that best completes the sentence. Here is an example of this type of question.

You will see:

> _____ a short time after the Civil War, Atlanta has
> become the principal center of transportation, commerce,
> and finance in the southeastern United States.
>
> (A) While rebuilt
> (B) It was rebuilt
> (C) Rebuilt
> (D) When rebuilt

The correct choice is (C). The other choices make the sentence incorrect or awkward.

## Written Expression

The Written Expression questions test your ability to recognize errors in grammar or expression. These questions consist of complete sentences with four underlined words or phrases. You must identify the underlined part of the sentence that needs to be changed in order to make the sentence correct. An example follows.

You will see:

> The Navajo Indians <u>have displayed</u> a <u>marked</u> ability to
>                                 (A)                    (B)
> incorporate aspects of other cultures <u>into</u> a changing,
>                                                          (C)
> <u>flexibility</u> life-style.
>     (D)

The correct choice is (D). _Flexibility_, an adverb, appears where an adjective must occur. In addition to inappropriate parts of speech, be sure to check for missing words and extra words that are inappropriate for the context.

## SECTION 3: READING COMPREHENSION

Good reading skills and an ample vocabulary are keys to doing well on all sections of the TOEFL. In this section of the TOEFL these skills are specifically tested. Many TOEFL test takers complain that they do not have enough time to carefully answer all questions in this section. It is very important that you follow the instructions in this book, so that you will use all the allotted time to your advantage.

## Reading Comprehension Items

Your ability to read and understand college-level reading material is tested on this part of the TOEFL. You will find five or six reading passages, each followed by nine to eleven questions. You must work quickly and efficiently. Here is a sample passage.

YOU WILL SEE:

      A lens has one or more curved surfaces that refract, or bend, light rays passing through it to form an image on a surface beyond the lens. Examples of such surfaces are the retina of the eye or a movie screen. The distance
(5)  from the lens to the focal plane is known as focal length. In cameras, telescopes, and similar devices, the lens is turned on a screw-thread mounting to adjust the focal length. This action allows focusing of images of objects at various distances. In the human eye, focal length is
(10)  adjusted by muscles that alter the lens curvature. Light rays of different colors are bent by varying degrees as they pass through a curved surface. This causes a distortion of the image, known as chromatic aberration. In cameras, sharp images are obtained by arranging two or
(15)  more lenses so that the aberration of one cancels out the aberration of another. Such an arrangement of lenses is called an achromatic lens.

YOU WILL SEE:

According to the passage, what is focal length?

(A) A curved surface that refracts light.
(B) The distance from the focal plane to the lens.
(C) Adjustment by the muscles that alters lens curvature.
(D) The degree that light rays of different colors are bent by the lens.

This is a factual question. The information needed to answer this question is directly stated in the text. Choice (B) is the correct answer. Some questions will ask you to draw conclusions based on material in the passage, others will ask about the main idea of a selection. Some may even ask what information does not appear in the passage.

## Vocabulary Items

The vocabulary questions on this section test your English vocabulary. There are between 12 and 17 questions focusing on specific words from the reading passage. Each word is taken from a specific line in the text; the line is referred to in the question. You must choose the word that has the same meaning from among the four choices given. Here's an example from the above text.

YOU WILL SEE:

**The word "distortion" in lines 12 and 13 is closest in meaning to**

**(A)** classification.
**(B)** deformation.
**(C)** reaction.
**(D)** reflection.

The word that is the closest in meaning to the tested word, *distortion,* is Choice (B). Further hints for vocabulary questions can be found in Chapter 2.

On the computer-based TOEFL, this type of vocabulary item can also occur. However, in the computer-based TOEFL, you are normally told to click on to a word or phrase in the passage that is closest in meaning as the bold word **distortion**. In this case, the word *aberration* in line 13 and in line 15 has about the same meaning as **distortion**. If you click on either occurrence of *aberration*, your answer is counted as correct.

## Cohesion Items

Another type of question that is used to test reading comprehension is called Cohesion. Cohesion occurs when elements of a passage are linked to other elements. Cohesion allows the author to refer to previously mentioned information, and it allows the reader to keep previously mentioned information in mind while continuing to read the passage. To understand cohesion when it is used one must understand the passage. Thus, TOEFL uses cohesion to test reading comprehension. Cohesion items typically test object pronouns (it, they, them) and demonstrative pronouns (this, these, those). Here is an example of a question that involves cohesion.

YOU WILL SEE:

**The word "This" in line 13 refers to**

**(A)** surface.
**(B)** adjusting.
**(C)** light.
**(D)** bending.

The word that **"This"** refers to is *bending*, Choice D. A typical version of the TOEFL will contain about five such items, or an average of one per passage.

## THE COMPUTER-BASED TOEFL

The computer-based TOEFL differs slightly in presentation format, in item format, and mostly in response format. The major differences between the paper and computer-based TOEFL are found in Section 1.

## Listening

On the computer-based TOEFL stimuli will come to you through headphones, not through a test tape as is the case with the paper TOEFL. On the computer-based TOEFL, you will both see and hear each question; on the paper TOEFL, you only hear the question. Following the question, the answer choices appear on the screen; the question stays on the screen until you have made your response. For multiple-choice items, each option is preceded by an oval [○], instead of the letters (A), (B), (C), or (D).

The computer-based TOEFL uses a greater variety of response types. For example, there may be more than one correct answer and you will be asked to click on the oval next to all correct answers. Whenever there is more than one correct answer, you will be told how many correct answers you should identify. To see an example, reread the Minitalk about Chicago on pages 3 and 4. Then answer the following question:

What can be inferred about the weather in Chicago?  (Click on 2)
- ○ It is influenced by a glacier.
- ○ Summers are unpleasantly warm.
- ○ The wind is usually accompanied by cold.
- ○ It is very dry during the winter months.
- ○ It is temperate and stable.

In the above example, you would click on the oval to the left of the second and third statement.

Sometimes a response format is visual. In that case, you click on the correct visual with your mouse. Sometimes a response will involve matching. In that case, you must classify each new piece of information you are given into three or four categories, according to classifications or distinctions you learned when reading the stimulus. You do this with your mouse.

**Dialogs**. Dialogs on the computer-based TOEFL are sometimes slightly longer than on the paper TOEFL, but they are still followed by a single question. In the dialogs, each stimulus is supported by a visual that represents the two people talking. The visual will tell you if the speakers are men or women. Otherwise, do not become distracted by the people in the visual. Only listen to what they are saying. The visuals are of no help to you in answering the questions.

**Extended Conversations and Minitalks**. On the computer-based TOEFL, you may be told both the context and the topic of the conversation. The extended conversations typically involve a main presenter who gives the information, and one or two other persons who ask questions of the main presenter. All speakers are pictured on the screen. Each stimulus is normally followed by three or four questions on what was said.

On the computer-based TOEFL, Minitalks also include an introduction that tells you who is speaking and the topic. Going back to the Minitalk on Chicago, the introduction might be as follows:

"Listen to a tour guide as he tells a group of visitors about the city of Chicago."

In computer-based TOEFL Minitalks, the presentations usually simulate a lecture by a professor who is using visuals. The professor and the visuals are depicted on the screen. Using your mouse, you answer each question, after it is asked.

## Structure and Written Expression

Structure and Written Expression is nearly identical in the paper and computer-based versions. The only difference is that in the computer-based version you click on the correct option with your mouse, whereas in the paper version you darken the option with a pencil on your answer sheet.

## Reading

On the computer-based TOEFL, Section 3 continues to contain 50 items, and most of the questions are multiple-choice. Unlike Sections 1 and 2, which are adaptive, Section 3 is a fixed-length test. (Adaptive means that the test questions and length may vary from one examinee to another.) The Reading section is essentially identical in content to the paper TOEFL.

In the Reading section, you first read the passage, which normally involves more than one full screen. After you have finished reading one screen, you will use the scroll bar to view the rest of the passage. The computer will not give you the questions until you have finished scrolling through the passage. At this point, click on **Proceed**. Then, you will see the passage on the left and the question on the right side of the screen. In this section, you can go back to a previous question by clicking on **Prev**.

There are some new response formats in the Reading section. These involve clicking on a word, phrase, or sentence. Vocabulary items are usually tested by asking you to click on another word in the text that means the same thing as a bold word. Sometimes you will be asked to click on a sentence or group of sentences where the answer to a particular question can be found. Sometimes, you may be asked to insert a sentence into the text. On Cohesion items, you will be asked to click on the word or phrase in the bold part of the passage that the cohesion word refers to. After you click on the word or phrase, it will darken.

## THE TEST OF WRITTEN ENGLISH

A Test of Written English (TWE)—requiring a short essay—was included in many, but not all, administrations of paper versions of the TOEFL. The TWE tests your ability to respond to topics that you may find on typical college-level writing assignments. It will test your ability to express yourself as well as your organizational skills. The TWE is not administered with the Institutional TOEFL. The score on this test is reported separately from your overall TOEFL score.

The TWE is now integrated into the computer-based TOEFL and thus forms part of all administrations of the computer-based test. Since it is not a separate test, it is no longer called the Test of Written English; rather, it is called Writing, and the task is simply referred to as an *essay*. The score on the essay is incorporated into the score for Section 2, where it counts as one half of the score. Thus, your score on the essay counts as one-sixth of your total score on the TOEFL. In addition, your essay score is reported separately on your TOEFL score report, so that colleges and universities can judge the adequacy of your writing ability. The essay can either be handwritten on an answer sheet or typewritten directly into the computer at most administrations, though clearly the latter writing method now predominates.

On the computer-based TOEFL, you can cut, paste, insert, and delete, just as if you were composing the document on the computer. Thus, if you are used to writing on a computer, it is probably to your advantage to write your essay on the computer.

## SOME HELPFUL HINTS FOR BOTH VERSIONS OF TOEFL

Obtain your free copy of the *TOEFL Bulletin* and the *TOEFL Sampler* (for the computer-based TOEFL only) and study the practice items they contain. Pay particular attention to the directions for each section.

On all parts of the TOEFL, be sure to answer every question. Do not leave any question unanswered. On multiple-choice items, if you must guess, choose Choice (B) or (C), since they are slightly more likely to be the correct choice than (A) or (D).

On the computer-based TOEFL, remember that some multiple-choice questions may have more than one correct answer, particularly if the question deals with factual information presented as a series in the stimulus text. A box under the question will tell you if you should click on more than one option. For example, the box may say "Click on 2 answers."

On the computer-based TOEFL, sample items are given before each section of the test. Since there is no time limit for this "tutorial," take as much time as you need to familiarize yourself with these sample items.

The **Time** display will remain on when you have only five minutes left. If you finish before time is up, use the **Prev** icon to go back and review your answers to vocabulary items. If you finish before the **Time** display comes on, click on the **Time** icon to learn how much time you have left.

Because the computer-based TOEFL employs a greater variety of response formats, always read the directions for each item carefully. Ask yourself: "What am I to do here?"

Watch your time! Both the paper and computer-based TOEFLs are timed. The amount of time available is stated at the beginning of each section. If you are taking the paper TOEFL, be sure to wear a watch and be aware of the time you have remaining in each section. Regardless of whether you are taking the paper or computer-based version, you should become familiar with the directions and examples for each section before you take the test. When you are told to begin, go directly to the first question. When time has expired on a section, you may not return to it. Work quickly and accurately. If it seems obvious that you will not finish a section of the paper version of TOEFL within the time limit, GUESS answers (B) or (C).

On the computer-based TOEFL, you are only penalized for not finishing Section 3 (Reading). If you do not finish Sections 1 and 2 in the time allotted, you are scored only on the basis of the questions you have answered.

In the Reading section of the computer-based TOEFL, you may go back and change your answers. However, don't waste time doing this unless you are fairly sure you have made a mistake. If you finish early, check your answers to the vocabulary items, as these do not require comprehension of the entire passage. Change your answer if you find a better one.

If you ordinarily use a computer in your studies or work, and you have a choice as to whether to take the paper or computer-based TOEFL, take the computer-based version.

Prepare yourself for the test. In addition to this book, Barron's *How to Prepare for the TOEFL* provides you with practical hints, tapes with sample questions, model tests, and a grammar review to help you maximize your TOEFL score.

## A WORD ABOUT THE FUTURE

The new TOEFL scheduled to appear in 2005 will probably be longer and more comprehensive. For one thing, all four skills will be assessed—listening, reading, writing, *and* speaking. Since TOEFL has never previously tested speaking, this represents a major change in the test's structure and scope. Furthermore, the test will be integrative—that is to say, reading and listening input will be included in the tests of writing and speaking. More precisely, examinees will first listen to a conversation and/or read a short passage. Then, they will be asked to either write or speak—describe, synthesize, compare, make a decision, or express a viewpoint—about the material they have just heard or read. Finally, the test will involve new reading, listening, and writing tasks. For example, examinees may be asked to evaluate the "purpose" content of utterances they hear, they may be asked to apply what they have read, new writing tasks may be introduced, and vocabulary items will likely include whole phrases as well as individual words. Some of these changes are explored in some detail in the *LanguEdge* courseware TOEFL has put on the market.

# CHAPTER 2

# UNDERSTANDING THE TOEFL READING SECTION

Developing a good English vocabulary is the most important way to prepare for the vocabulary you will see on the TOEFL. It is also a good way to prepare for the test generally. In addition to developing a good English vocabulary, it is very important to know the kind of vocabulary you will see on the TOEFL and to understand how it is tested.

The Reading section (or Reading Comprehension, as it is called on the paper version) makes up Section 3 of the TOEFL. This section contains 50 questions. It is important for you to remember that your general vocabulary is tested in all sections of the TOEFL. However, it is in this section of the TOEFL where your knowledge of specific vocabulary items is tested.

Passages from which vocabulary questions are drawn are written in a formal, academic style, typical of most college- or university-level texts and journals. The topics of these passages are those that a first-year college student in North America would be likely to encounter. The topics come from such areas as the natural sciences, business, liberal arts, and the social sciences. Some passages contain references to North American places and personalities. Others will refer to historical events and may include dates. It is important for you to understand that your knowledge of these North American places and personalities is never tested on the TOEFL. You do not have to be familiar with the content of the passages to be successful on this section of the TOEFL.

## SAMPLE QUESTIONS

The following passage and the questions that follow are used to illustrate and discuss the Reading Comprehension, Cohesion, and Vocabulary questions that you will find in Section 3.

(5)

(10)

(15)

Through a somewhat controversial process, Hawaii was the last territory to become a state. In 1842, the United States recognized the Kingdom of Hawaii as an independent country. In subsequent years, Americans and other foreign groups moved to the islands. They began to influence local politics. In 1887, Hawaiian King Kalakaua gave the United States exclusive rights to use Pearl Harbor as a naval base in exchange for certain trading privileges. After the King died, his sister, Queen Liliuokalani, followed him to the throne. In 1894, a bloodless revolution led by American businessmen removed her from office. She was replaced by Stanford B. Dole. With the support of the Americans running the local government, Hawaii became a U.S. territory in 1900. In 1959, the U.S. Congress approved legislation permitting Hawaii to convert to statehood. Shortly afterwards, Hawaiians voted almost 17 to 1 in favor of statehood, thereby allowing it to become the fiftieth state.

1. What does the passage mainly discuss?
   Ⓐ Democracy in Hawaii
   Ⓑ The history of Hawaiian monarchs
   Ⓒ The evolution of Hawaii's political status
   Ⓓ American military control in Hawaii

On the computer-based TOEFL you would click on the oval next to the third option. On the paper TOEFL, you darken the oval containing the letter (C) on your answer sheet.

2. The word "controversial" in line 1 is closest in meaning to
   Ⓐ adversarial.
   Ⓑ remarkable.
   Ⓒ gratifying.
   Ⓓ debatable.

This type of vocabulary item is typically used on the paper TOEFL. However, the TOEFL test makers are free to include it on computer-based versions of TOEFL also. The correct response is (D).

3. Look at the word "They" in line 5. What word or phrase does it refer to?

Ⓐ The United States
Ⓑ Americans and other foreign groups
Ⓒ In subsequent years
Ⓓ The islands

This is a Cohesion item. It tests whether you understand what **they** refers to. In the paper TOEFL, you would see four options and mark the letter of the correct option on your answer sheet, (B). On the computer-based TOEFL, using your mouse, you would highlight the phrase **Americans and other foreign groups**.

4. Look at the phrase "in exchange for" in line 8. In saying that the United States got exclusive access to Pearl Harbor "in exchange for certain . . . privileges," the author means the United States

Ⓐ traded access to its markets for a naval base in Hawaii.
Ⓑ offered to rent the land it needed for a base in Hawaii.
Ⓒ absorbed Hawaii by granting it membership in the union.
Ⓓ was excluded by the Hawaiian king from Hawaiian markets.

This is a whole phrase item. It tests whether you can separately understand the words in a group and then assemble them to arrive at an understanding of their meaning as a group. One clue to the meaning of this phrase is the word *exchange*. Since you are already familiar with exchanging money or exchanging addresses, you can probably guess that this has something to do with a two-way transfer—in this case, the right to use some land in Hawaii for access to U.S. markets. Once you have pieced together the larger context, it is easier to see that **traded access to its markets for a naval base in Hawaii,** (A), is the phrase to highlight.

5. Look at the word "permitting" in line 15. What other word in the last two sentences is closest in meaning to "permitting?"

You would click on the word **allowing** in the last line. This vocabulary item format can only be used in the computer-based TOEFL. In the paper version, four possible synonyms for **allowing** would be given, as in question 2 above.

**6. Look at the word "convert" in line 16. What other word or phrase in the last two sentences is closest in meaning to "convert?"**

You would click on the word **become** in the last line. This vocabulary item format can only be used in the computer-based TOEFL. In the paper version, four possible synonyms for **convert** would be given, as in question 2 above.

**7. Look at the phrase "in favor of" in line 17. In saying that "Hawaiians voted almost 17 to 1 in favor of statehood," the author means that they**
   Ⓐ  supported independence.
   Ⓑ  voted against statehood.
   Ⓒ  wanted to join the union.
   Ⓓ  became a favorite resort.

Here, you would click on **wanted to join the union,** (C). The word **favor** is a good clue to the meaning of the whole phrase, as are the adjoining phrases **voted almost 17 to 1** and **allowing it to become the fiftieth state.** These phrases strongly suggest that a vote had been taken and that the Hawaiians supported statehood by the margin given. Therefore, **in favor of** must indicate a positive vote, or formal support for a particular proposition or candidate.

## STRATEGY FOR THE PAPER TOEFL

On the paper TOEFL, each TOEFL vocabulary item refers you to a word (or phrase, such as a two-word verb) in a specific line of the passage. You are then asked to identify a synonym for that word. These choices are marked by the letters: (A), (B), (C), and (D). *You must identify the word among the choices that is closest in meaning to the word in quotation marks.* Words that are very close or identical in meaning are called **synonyms.** Now go back and examine question 2 above again.

This question is typical of vocabulary items on the paper TOEFL. The topic is from U.S. history and the question contains a single word in quotation marks. The correct answer is (D), debatable. **Debatable** is a synonym for **controversial.** As in this example, the word you select is the one that best matches the meaning of the word in quotation marks. Note that all four of the choices make sense in the sentence and that they make use of other information given in the passage. Vocabulary questions are written so that the context of the sentence or the passage seldom helps you to determine the meaning of the word. Therefore, you must know the word in order to make the correct choice.

Because the context will not help you, you should simply look at the quoted word and choose its synonym from among the four choices. It is best for you to use this strategy because it will prevent frustration and save time. You will need this time for the Reading Comprehension questions. If you do not know the word tested or can't determine its synonym, choose (B) or (C) as your answer. On the TOEFL, (B) and (C) answers tend to be used slightly more than (A) and (D). Also remember that answer choices that contain the same prefix or suffix, or are pronounced like the underlined word, are seldom the correct answers.

Note that Choice (A), adversarial, has sounds and letters similar to **controversial**. Such words are not usually the correct choice; they are often used to distract you. Unless you are sure of the answer do not choose these words.

Let's see how to use our strategy with a sample item. Look at question 2 again, noting the word in quotation marks. Do not reread the line referred to or the paragraph that contains it. Instead, read the four choices and make your selection of the best synonym.

**This is an example of how you should read vocabulary items.**

+ + + + + + + "controversial" + + + + + + + + + + + + + + +

+ + + + + + + + +

**(A) adversarial**
**(B) remarkable**
**(C) gratifying**
**(D) debatable**

You should pay attention only to the word in quotation marks and the choices that follow. If you know the meaning of the word and recognize the synonym, there is no need to read the context in which it is used. If you do not know the meaning of the quoted word, you must make an educated guess about its synonym. The context will not usually help you to determine the correct choice. All of the choices from the example above fit into the original context.

**Through a somewhat *adversarial* process, Hawaii was the last territory to become a state.**

**Through a somewhat *remarkable* process, Hawaii was the last territory to become a state.**

**Through a somewhat *gratifying* process, Hawaii was the last territory to become a state.**

**Through a somewhat *debatable* process, Hawaii was the last territory to become a state.**

17

These sentences show that the context does not help you to determine the meaning of the word being tested. If you simply cannot decide on the answer, you can refer to the sentence in which it is used. In the case of the phrasal examples above, there may be some clues in the context that can help you figure out the meaning of the phrase, as shown above. It may also help you to remember any previous experience you have had with the word. However, you are always better off ignoring the context if you know the answer, and you should not waste a lot of time analyzing contextual information. If you cannot make sense of any of the clues available in the context, or recall the phrase from another context, simply take a guess and move on.

Essential Words gives you additional practice in ignoring the context of vocabulary items on the paper TOEFL through the matching exercises that are found in each lesson. In these exercises, you  are given a word followed by four possible synonyms. Your task is to mark the letter of the correct synonym. The following matching exercise uses the example previously introduced.

**Controversial**
**(A)** **adversarial**
**(B)** **remarkable**
**(C)** **gratifying**
**(D)** **debatable**

REMEMBER

- Do not waste time rereading the context in which the word is used. Look only at the word in quotation marks and search for a synonym among the answer choices.
- Analyze words quickly. Spending too much time studying word roots, prefixes, and suffixes can cause you to misuse valuable time.
- Work quickly, but carefully. You should try to spend only 30 seconds on each vocabulary question.
- Words that contain similar sounds and spelling are usually not the correct answer.
- Always answer every question. If you must guess, choose (B) or (C) as your answer. Your score on Section 3 is based solely on the number of correct answers.

## STRATEGY FOR THE COMPUTER-BASED TOEFL

**Finding the answer**. On the computer-based TOEFL, most questions will refer you to two or three highlighted sentences in the passage. You must click on the one word that is closest in meaning to the tested word.

As soon as you see the bold word in the question, try to think of one or more synonyms. Then look for any of those synonyms in the highlighted sentences as you read them.

If you don't find a synonym, focus on the meaning of the word in the context in which it is used. Do you know the meaning of the word? If not, try to guess it. Then look for words with similar meanings in the highlighted text.

Focus on the structure of the word and its context. What part of speech is the word—noun, verb, adjective, adverb, etc? Now look for other words in the same part of speech.

Is the word followed by a noun, verb, preposition, adjective, or adverb? Look for other words followed by the same part of speech. Remember, a pronoun may substitute for a noun.

Usually, the synonym will be in the same part of speech. If you have identified a synonym that is not in the same part of speech, look again at the highlighted sentences. If you don't find a synonym that could be substituted in the context of the tested word, then click on the word that is closest in meaning but is not in the same part of speech.

On the computer-based TOEFL you may find some multiple-choice vocabulary items like those on the paper TOEFL. If you do, use the same strategies you would for the paper TOEFL. Specifically, you should ignore the context of the underlined word, at least initially, and try to find the best synonym without referring to the context.

**Timing and checking**. You have 55 minutes to complete this section. Some test takers report that they do not have enough time to complete the reading questions, so you should work quickly. If you follow the strategies in this book you will have adequate time to complete the Reading section of the TOEFL.

Five minutes before the end of this section, the time display will appear. This shows you how much time you have left. If you finish early, use the **Prev** icon to go back to successive vocabulary items and check your answers. Because vocabulary items on the computer-based TOEFL typically allow you to choose one word among all the words in two or more sentences, it is easy to carelessly make an error on vocabulary items. Checking your responses will allow you to identify and correct any errors. Also, because vocabulary items do not require you to reread and comprehend the entire passage, they can be checked more rapidly than reading comprehension items. After you have checked your responses to the vocabulary items, if you still have time, beginning with the first passage, check your answers to the reading comprehension and cohesion items.

**Answer all items**. Sections 1 and 2 are adaptive. This means that your score on these sections is based on the difficulty of the items you answer correctly, rather than on the number of correct answers. Section 3 is the only section of the computer-based TOEFL that is not adaptive. Because of this, your score on Section 3 is based solely on the number of questions you answer correctly. Therefore, answer every question, even if you have to guess.

# CHAPTER 3

# IMPROVING YOUR TOEFL VOCABULARY

## READ A LOT

One of the best ways to build your vocabulary is to read authentic English language material. You should read material that a college student would read. Examples of such material are newspapers, college textbooks, encyclopedia articles, magazines, and academic books. Any material that has an academic theme will help you to get used to the kinds of words and the style of writing you will find on the TOEFL. Reading articles on a variety of topics of interest to you will help you to develop your vocabulary. Pay attention to new groups of words, expressions, and phrases you encounter in your reading. Take advantage of resources— teachers, native speakers of English—to learn their meanings.

## MAKE FLASH CARDS

As you are reading, you will find new words that you will want to learn. One good way to learn words is to make flash cards. Use small cards made of thick paper. The cards should be small enough to fit in your pocket. On one side write the new word or group of words, then on the back write a synonym, a word or words that mean the same. For example, expressions such as "run a risk" and "take a chance" are similar in meaning: they are synonyms. You may also want to note the meaning of the words you put on your flash cards. Review these cards as often as you can, perhaps with a friend who is preparing for the TOEFL. You will be able to build a large "sight vocabulary" by using this method. Do not be concerned if you are unable to actually use these words in conversations you have in English. With time, they will become a part of your active vocabulary. The ability to use new words is not as important as your ability to recognize new words and their meanings.

## MAKE WORD LISTS

Another good way to learn new words is to make word lists. Many students use a small notebook especially for this purpose. When you discover a new word, or group of words, add it to a list of words to be learned. On one side

21

of the page, list the new words. To the right of this list, write synonyms for the new words. Study the words by covering the synonyms, looking at the new word, and recalling the synonyms. It is also useful to reverse the process so that you practice both the new words and their synonyms.

## LEARN WORDS FROM OLD TOEFLs

Learn words that have been tested on previous TOEFLs. The underlined words on previous TOEFL tests are sometimes tested again, but they frequently appear among the four choices presented as synonyms for new words that are tested. You can find words to put on your flash cards or word lists on any TOEFL tests that you have. TOEFL tests can be found in the TOEFL test kits available from the Educational Testing Service.

## LEARN THE WORDS IN THIS BOOK

*Include all of the words listed in this book on your cards and lists.* These words have been carefully selected, and many will appear on the TOEFL.

You should learn prefixes, suffixes, and word roots. For a list of them, see Chapter 4. Suggestions for studying word roots, suffixes, and prefixes can be found in that chapter.

## LEARN TO USE A THESAURUS

Become familiar with a thesaurus. A thesaurus is a dictionary of synonyms. When you find a word that you don't know, look it up in the thesaurus. Note a synonym for the word on a card or a word list. If you find a synonym, but still don't know the meaning of the word, look it up in an English language dictionary. *If you can't find the word in the thesaurus, it will not be tested on the TOEFL.* The TOEFL tests only those words that have a variety of synonyms. For more information about the use of a thesaurus, see Chapter 5.

---

### VOCABULARY BUILDING STRATEGIES

- Read often. Choose material that is written for college-level readers.
- Make flash cards of new words with synonyms and practice them often.
- Make word lists of new words with synonyms and practice them often.
- Learn words that have been tested on previous TOEFLs.
- Learn word roots, prefixes, and suffixes found in Chapter 4
- Study the list of 450 essential words in Chapter 6 of this book.

---

# CHAPTER 4

# BUILDING YOUR VOCABULARY

## DEVELOPING WORD ATTACK SKILLS

When readers find an unfamiliar word in a sentence they are sometimes able to determine its meaning by reading the other words in the sentence. The other words give the "context" that allows readers to make an educated guess about the meaning of an unfamiliar word.

Words fit into contexts in two ways. One is purely grammatical: The *form* of the word is grammatically correct for its position in the sentence. For example, you know that the space between "the" and "student" belongs to an adjective, so you know that "brilliant" fits into that space correctly, while "brilliance," which is a noun, does not.

However, we already know that on TOEFL vocabulary questions all of the possible answers fit the grammatical context of the sentence. Therefore, the degree of success you will have on this part of the TOEFL depends upon whether you understand a word's *meaning* as well as its form. That in turn depends upon how well you can understand its parts and how well you can read its context for clues to its meaning. In this chapter, you will learn how to determine the meaning of a word by studying its parts.

Many English words consist of more than one part. Let's examine three important parts you should know in order to improve your vocabulary.

### Word Roots

Many words in English contain Latin and Greek roots. These roots convey the basic meaning of the word and they occur repeatedly throughout the language. Knowing these roots will help you to determine the meaning of words with which you are not familiar. Below is a list of common roots and their general meanings.

Learning these roots will help you to recognize the basic meaning of hundreds of English words. Let's look at the word *manufacture*. Manufacture is a combination of two root words, *manu* and *fact*. Using the list below, we can see that *manu* means "hand" and *fact* means "make" or "do." Therefore, we can infer the meaning "make by hand."

Let's look at another example, *biography*. Again, using the list below, we see that *bio* means "life" and *graph* "write." Therefore, we can conclude that the word's meaning relates to the "writing of a life," the written story of a person's life.

## How to Study Word Roots

There are several ways to study word roots. One effective way is to make a flash card for each one. On this card write the root and a word containing the root. Also, write the meaning of the root and a synonym for the example word on the back of the card. As you practice with the cards, first identify the meaning of the root, then the word containing the root. Next, give a synonym for that word. As you study the roots, set aside those you have learned and concentrate only on those roots and synonyms that you have not learned. Save all of the cards for review.

Make word lists. When you read English material, make lists of words that contain the roots that you have studied in this section of the book. Identify the root and look up the word in a thesaurus. Write the meaning of the root and a synonym of the word. This method will help you to identify root words and synonyms on the TOEFL.

| Root | Meaning | Example |
|------|---------|---------|
| belli | war | rebellion |
| biblio | book | bibliography |
| bio | life | biology |
| cosm | order | microcosm |
| cycl | circle | cyclone |
| dic | two | dichotomy |
| dict | word | dictate |
| duc | carry, lead | conducive |
| duct | carry, lead | conduct |
| fac | do, make | facsimile |
| fact | do, make | manufacture |
| fect | do, make | perfect |
| form | shape | uniform |
| fort | strong | fortify |
| geo | earth | geography |
| gram | write | telegram |
| graph | write | autograph |
| homo | same | homophone |
| log | speech, study of | dialog |
| logy | speech, study of | analogy |
| man | hand | manage |
| manu | hand | manual |
| mater | mother, home | maternity |
| matri | mother, home | matriarch |
| medi | middle | mediocre |
| miss | send | dismiss |
| mit | send | submit |
| multi | many | multiply |
| nom | name | nominate |
| nym | name | synonym |
| pater | father | paternal |
| pathy | feeling, suffering | sympathy |
| patri | father | patriarch |
| ped | foot | pedal |
| port | carry | transport |
| scend | climb | ascend |
| scrib | write | scribble |
| script | written language | postscript |
| secut | follow | consecutive |
| sent | feel | consent |
| sequ | follow | subsequently |
| tact | touch | contact |
| tempor | time | contemporary |
| tract | pull, draw out | attractive |
| vene | come, go | convene |
| vent | come, go | advent |
| vers | turn | reverse |
| vert | turn | convert |
| voc | voice, call | vocal |
| vok | voice, call | revoke |
| volu | turn, roll | convoluted |
| volve | turn, roll | involve |

## Prefixes

Prefixes are the second important part of words. A prefix is a part of a word that is attached to the beginning of a word root. A prefix adds meaning to the base word. Thus, if you know the meaning of the prefix, you will be better prepared to determine the meaning of the word. Knowing both prefixes and word roots will unlock the meaning of thousands of English words.

There are many prefixes in English. The list below contains some of the most common prefixes found on the TOEFL.

| Prefix | Meaning | Example |
| --- | --- | --- |
| ante | before | anterior |
| anti | against, not in favor | anticipate |
| auto | self | autonomous |
| bi | two | biased |
| circum | circle, around | circumvent |
| co | with, together | coherent |
| col | with, together | collect |
| com | with, together | complex |
| con | with, together | condense |
| de | down, reverse | decline |
| dis | no, not | disregard |
| e | out, from | emit |
| ex | out, from | eject |
| im | no, not | improper |
| in | in | inactive |
| inter | between, among | interact |
| ir | no, not | irrelevant |
| micro | small, tiny | microscopic |
| mis | wrong, bad, not | mistake |
| mono | one | monotone |
| non | not | nonsense |
| post | after | postpone |
| pre | before | preconception |
| prim | first | primary |
| pro | for, in favor of | promote |
| re | again | recover |
| sub | under | submit |
| sup | under | supposition |
| trans | across, over | transmit |
| tri | three | triple |
| ultra | excessive | ultrasonic |
| un | no, not | undeniable |
| uni | one | unique |

Let's examine the word *contact*. We can determine from the list of prefixes that *con* means "with." Upon further examination of the word, we see the word root *tact* means "touch." Without knowing the exact meaning of the word, we can guess that the word is related to "touch" and "with." Indeed, *contact* conveys the meaning of communication with another person. Referring to the root words and prefixes in this chapter we can ascertain that *autobiography* means "self, life, and write," or the story of a person's life written by that same person.

You can approach your study of prefixes with the same method you are using to learn word roots. Make a flash card for each of the prefixes. On this card write the prefix and a word containing the prefix. Write the meaning of the prefix and a synonym for the example word on the back of the card. As you practice with the cards, first identify the meaning of the prefix, then the word containing the root. Next, give a synonym for that word. Save all of the cards for review.

Make word lists. When you read English material, make lists of words that contain the prefixes you recognize. Identify the prefix and look up the word in a thesaurus. Write the meaning of the prefix and a synonym for the word. This method will help you to identify words with prefixes and synonyms on the TOEFL.

## Suffixes

The final word part is the suffix. A suffix is added to the end of a word. Similar to a prefix, a suffix adds meaning to the root word. However, the meaning is often grammatical, telling us the tense or the function of the word. Seldom does it change the actual meaning of the word in the way that prefixes do. Suffixes are attached to verbs, nouns, and adjectives. There are not many suffixes on this part of the TOEFL, and you may already know many of them from your grammar study. Nevertheless, you should become familiar with all the English suffixes in the lists here.

## ADJECTIVE SUFFIXES

| Suffix | Meaning | Example |
|--------|---------|---------|
| able | capable of | affordable |
| ant | tendency to | dominant |
| ative | tendency to | innovative |
| ent | tendency to | persistent |
| etic | relating to | sympathetic |
| ful | full of | harmful |
| ible | capable | discernible |
| ical | relating to | identical |
| less | without | harmless |
| ous | full of | famous |
| ness | a quality of being | kindness |
| ry | occupation | ministry |
| ship | condition or state | citizenship |
| some | tendency to | bothersome |
| y | a quality of being | arbitrary |

## NOUN SUFFIXES

| Suffix | Meaning | Example |
|--------|---------|---------|
| ary | place | library |
| ation | process | population |
| cule | small | minuscule |
| dom | state of being | wisdom |
| er | one who does | teacher |
| ery | occupation | dentistry |
| hood | state of being | manhood |
| ist | one who does | geologist |
| less | without | careless |
| ly | like, similar to | manly |
| ment | state of being | contentment |
| ness | state of being | happiness |
| ous | full of | enormous |
| ship | state of being | citizenship |

## ADVERB SUFFIXES

| Suffix | Meaning | Example |
|--------|---------|---------|
| ly | the way | predictably |
| ways | the way | sideways |
| wise | the way | otherwise |

## VERB SUFFIXES

| Suffix | Meaning | Example |
|--------|---------|---------|
| ade | process of | persuade |
| ate | to make | accentuate |
| en | to make | broaden |
| er | process of | shelter |
| ize | to make | emphasize |

# CHAPTER 5

# IMPORTANT VOCABULARY BUILDING TOOLS

## THE DICTIONARY

For students of English as a Second Language, a good English dictionary is essential. It is a source of valuable information and if it is used correctly, the dictionary will serve as a useful tool toward your goal of English fluency.

There are many types of dictionaries that a student may consider, including collegiate, learner's, unabridged, and bilingual dictionaries.

For more advanced students, collegiate or college dictionaries are preferred. In addition to the standard word entries, collegiate dictionaries often contain separate sections that contain abbreviations, foreign expressions used in English, and biographical listings. Some may also contain geographical listings.

Highly recommended are learner's dictionaries. This type of dictionary is specifically written for students of English as a foreign language. Definitions are written in a clear, easy to understand English. These dictionaries often anticipate learner's questions with special explanatory sections. They also use a standard phonetic alphabet to indicate the pronunciation of the entries.

Unabridged dictionaries are the most comprehensive, but not practical for second language learners because of their size and detail. These dictionaries are often found in the reference sections of libraries on special tables to accommodate their size and weight. An unabridged dictionary is an excellent source for determining the historical development of words, examples of sentences that demonstrate proper usage, antonyms, and synonyms.

A bilingual dictionary that contains words in your native language and English should be avoided. Often these dictionaries are incomplete and give only basic native language equivalent words. These words are frequently out of date or inappropriate for the context of the sentence in which you want to use the unknown words. Therefore, entries in bilingual dictionaries can be misleading. In fact, they can actually cause you to make mistakes. It is worthwhile for English language students to switch to a learner's dictionary as soon as possible, or to use it in conjunction with a bilingual dictionary. You will find that your vocabulary will increase faster by using an English language dictionary.

## What You Can Learn

A dictionary gives you the information required to choose the best word for your needs. A typical dictionary entry contains the correct spelling of a word, followed by the word written in a phonetic alphabet. The word is separated by syllables. This helps you to determine where to separate it at the end of a line. Following the phonetic spelling of the word, its part

word are given in a numeri-
: that shows the proper use
s list the meanings of words
ing to the oldest meaning,
meaning to the latest mean-
on, you should read all the
hat meets your needs. Some
ith the same general mean-
posite meaning. Some dictio-
velopment of the word that
nages to its origin.
ntries listed in alphabetical
e words appear at the top of
e left is the first entry of the
s the last entry on the two
etermine if the word you are
s on the two pages.

**max • i • mum** (măk′sə-məm) ... **-mums** or **-ma** (-mə). *Abbr.* max. **1.a.** The greatest possible quantity or degree. **b.** The greatest quantity or degree reached or recorded; the upper limit of variation. **c.** The time or period during which the highest point or degree is attained. **2.** An upper limit permitted by law or other authority. **3.** *Astronomy.* **a.** The moment when a variable star is most brilliant. **b.** The magnitude of the star at such a moment. **4.** *Mathematics.* **a.** The greatest value assumed by a function over a given interval. **b.** The largest number in a set. **—maximum** *adj. Abbr.* **max.** **1.** Having or being the greatest quantity or the highest degree that has been or can be attained: *maximum temperature.* **2.** Of, relating to, or making up a maximum: *a maximum number in a series.* [Latin, from neuter of *maximus*, greatest.]

As we see, the word entry is for the word *maximum*. By examining the word entry, we can determine that it contains three syllables; each syllable being separated by the mark •, max•i•mum. The word is followed by a phonetic spelling of the word inside parentheses, (măk′sə-məm). At the bottom of every page of the dictionary, you will find a pronunciation key that will give you the speech sounds of the symbols. Following the pronunciation, you will find a part of speech label. Here are the traditional speech labels found in most dictionaries.

## WORD LABELS

| abbr. | abbreviation | n. | noun |
|-------|-------------|------|-----------|
| adj. | adjective | pl. | plural |
| adv. | adverb | prep. | preposition |
| ant. | antonym | pron. | pronoun |
| arch. | archaic | sing. | singular |
| conj. | conjunction | syn. | synonym |
| interj. | interjection | tr. | transitive |
| intr. | intransitive | v. | verb |

Following the pronunciation entry for the word maximum, an *n.* and the plural forms (identified by the abbreviation *pl.*) *pl. -mums*, or *-ma* appear. According to the labels, these abbreviations mean that the word is a noun and its plural can be formed two ways, by replacing the last syllable mum with *mums* (maximums) or *ma* (maxima). The plural forms are followed by the abbreviation of the word, identified by Abbr. *max.* Each definition of the word is marked by a number.

In many dictionaries, the order of the definitions reflects the frequency of use of each meaning of the word. The definitions that follow the first definition reflect more specialized uses. Your dictionary will explain the order in which the meanings are presented. When the numbered definition has closely related meanings, they are marked with *1.a.*, *b.*, and *c.* as in the example above. Also note that words with specialized definitions in academic disciplines are identified. In the sample entry, there are two specialized uses of the word maximum, one in *Astronomy*, *3.a* and *b.*, and another in *Mathematics*, *4.a.* and *b.* After all meanings of the noun form are defined, the entry continues with the definition of the adjective form. The last item of the entry gives the derivation, or word origin, inside brackets [ ].

Please note that several styles of usage are normally indicated in a dictionary entry. These styles are typically identified in the following ways:

| | | |
|---|---|---|
| Nonstandard | — | Words that do not belong to any standard educated speech |
| Informal | — | Words that are often used in conversation and seldom in formal writing |
| Slang | — | Usually a highly informal word that is often figurative in use. Its meaning is usually short-lived |
| Vulgar | — | A word that is taboo or not socially acceptable in most circumstances |
| Obsolete | — | A word that is no longer in common usage |
| Archaic | — | A word that was in common usage, but now rarely used |
| Rare | — | Words that have never been common in the language |
| British | — | Words that are in common usage in British English |
| Regional | — | Words that are used in a limited geographical area |

## THE THESAURUS

A *thesaurus* is a collection of words with similar meanings, usually presented in alphabetical order. These words are called *synonyms*. A thesaurus is useful when you must change a word to another word with a similar meaning. Many thesauruses list whole phrases in addition to single words. For example, one well-known thesaurus contains more than 330,000 words *and* phrases in over 1,000 categories. Thus, it provides useful information about how words group or combine in the language as well as clues to their meanings and synonyms.

The entries in a thesaurus typically contain the synonyms in most frequent to least frequent occurrence. In a modern thesaurus, guide words also appear at the tops of pages. Their function is the same as that of the guide words in dictionaries, indicating the first and last words of the pages. All words on the page appear in alphabetical order. Not all words have synonyms, yet almost all words on the TOEFL are words with many synonyms. Therefore, regular use of a thesaurus will build your vocabulary and help you to prepare for the TOEFL.

Most of the same word labels used in dictionaries appear in a thesaurus. Many entries do not specify the difference between adjective and adverb, since the same forms can often appear both as an adjective and adverb. The abbreviation *mod.* is used to mark such a word. Let's examine an entry for the word *maximum.*

> **maximum**, *mod.* –*Syn.* supreme, highest, greatest: see best 1.
> **maximum**, *n.* – *Syn.* supremacy, height, pinnacle, preeminence, culmination, matchlessness, preponderance, apex, peak, greatest number, highest degree, summit, nonpareil; see also climax. –*Ant.* minimum*, foot, bottom.

There are two entries for this word. The abbreviation *mod.* in the first entry indicates that the word could be used as a modifier of other words. Following this, *syn.* indicates that synonyms for the the word follow. At the end of the listing appears the suggestion see *best 1*. This suggestion refers us to the first entry for the word *best* if we wish to see more words with meanings related to *maximum.*

The second entry gives the synonyms for the noun form of the word. The *n.* indicates that the word is used as a noun, and *syn.* indicates that synonyms follow. This entry also refers the reader to the word *climax* for additional words related to *maximum.* At the end of the entry, antonyms, marked with the label *ant.*, are listed.

The dictionary and thesaurus are two powerful learning tools that you should have for reference. They are essential for a good vocabulary building program. In addition, many publishers offer idiom dictionaries and phrase books that can be useful in learning word combinations commonly used in academic settings. Instructional material focusing on idioms and phrases is available on line at numerous sites catering to ESL and EFL students. When you study such material, be sure to focus on academic vocabulary, not slang. Slang does not appear on the TOEFL. Often, slang will be indicated as such in a dictionary or thesaurus. Some academic words have phrasal equivalents. A few examples are listed below:

| **Single Word** | **Phrasal Synonym** |
| --- | --- |
| adjust | straighten out |
| endanger | put in jeopardy |
| clandestine | in disguise |
| settle | take root |
| vague | ill-defined |

As a general rule, single words are preferable to phrases in formal academic style when both options are available. However, the use of phrases is still correct. Sometimes the words in phrases are so closely associated with each other that they are written with a hyphen, as in *ill-defined* above. Hyphens are also used to link word sequences that might otherwise appear ungrammatical.

# CHAPTER 6

# THE ESSENTIAL TOEFL VOCABULARY

This chapter contains 30 lessons. Each lesson contains entries for 15 key TOEFL words. Following the entries, there are 10 matching exercises. At the end of each lesson, there are 11 TOEFL-like vocabulary questions that contain most of the words in each lesson. Six of these are entitled **Paper TOEFL Test Questions** and five are entitled **Computer-Based Test Questions**. The last question in the first series is a phrase-type question like the ones that are discussed in Chapter 1. All of these TOEFL-like questions are an excellent vocabulary review as well as an excellent preparation for the vocabulary section of the TOEFL.

You should study the lessons in order. For example, after studying lesson 1, go directly to lesson 2. Do not study lessons out of order. The book is designed to provide systematic review of words in previous lessons. By studying the lessons out of order, you will be defeating the review system.

Let's examine a sample entry to see the kinds of information you will learn.

| **intricate** | *adj.* having many parts; finely detailed |
|---|---|
| *adv.* intricately<br>*n.* intricacy | *syn.* complex |

The *intricate* design of the vase made it a valuable piece for her collection.

I cannot begin to understand all of the *intricacies* of modern automobile motors.

The entry features the word *intricate*. Directly under the word, you will find other forms of the same word. These words have the same general meaning; they represent the different parts of speech of the word. For each of the forms, the part of speech is given. The following abbreviations for parts of speech are used in the word entries:

| adj. | → | adjective |
| adv. | → | adverb |
| conj. | → | conjunction |
| v. | → | verb |
| n. | → | noun |

In the case of *intricate*, the adjective form, **adj.**, is presented as the key word. Other forms of the entry, *intricately*, and *intricacy* are listed below the main entry.

The key word is then defined in clear, easy to understand English. In this example, we see that *intricate* means *something having many parts* or *something that is finely detailed*.

Under the definition you will find a synonym for the key word. The synonym is a word that has the same or a similar meaning and it is marked with the letters *syn*. In the example above, the synonym given for *intricate* is *complex*.

Below the synonym, there are two sentences that show the usage of two different forms of the word. The sentences are rich in context, that is, the words surrounding the key word tend to support and clarify the meaning of the key word. Let's look at the two sentences in the example.

**The *intricate* design of the vase made it a valuable piece for her collection.**

**I cannot begin to understand all of the *intricacies* of modern automobile motors.**

The key word will *always* appear in the first sentence. The key word sentence is followed by a second sentence illustrating the use of one of the related words, but with a different part of speech. If no related words are given, then the second sentence serves as another illustration of the meaning of the key word.

Some word forms are not included in the entries. These are words that are not in common usage and not likely to appear on the TOEFL.

The word entries provide you with all the information that you need to build a powerful TOEFL vocabulary.

## STUDYING THE WORD ENTRIES

To learn vocabulary efficiently, you must have a study plan and follow it carefully. The following plan has been useful to many students who are building their TOEFL vocabulary.

Plan to spend at least an hour studying the words in each lesson of this book. Do not study words that you already know.

*Read*
First, read the 15 entries of the lesson carefully, including the definition, different forms, synonym, and example sentences. It is important for you to associate the key word with its meaning and synonym. These are the three most important parts of the word entry.

*Reread*
Next, read each word entry again. Look up unfamiliar words that appear in the example sentences. This time when you study the entry we suggest that you cover the key word, then look at the meaning and its synonym. Then identify the key word. When you are able to identify the key word, reverse the process by identifying the covered synonym. Finally, cover everything in the entry, except the meaning, and identify the key word and its synonym.

*Find the Synonyms*
You are now ready for the matching exercise at the end of the word list. Let's look at a typical matching question.

1. **intricate**
   (A) **functional**
   (B) **complex**
   (C) **predominant**
   (D) **inordinate**

The purpose of the question is to test your knowledge of synonyms, a key skill for the TOEFL. You will see four choices. In this example, you must choose the synonym for the word *intricate*. The correct answer is **(B) complex**. Nearly all the words that appear as answer choices are key words introduced in the same and previous lessons. Check your answers by referring to the Answer Key found at the back of this book.

You are now ready to test your skill on actual TOEFL-like questions. Let's look at the following test question.

The <u>intricate</u> design of the building's facade is typical of buildings of the nineteenth century.
(A) **functional**
(B) **accurate**
(C) **standard**
(D) **complex**

This test question is typical of the questions on the vocabulary section of the TOEFL. You must choose the word that has the same or similar meaning as the underlined word in the sentence. Most TOEFL questions do not use the word in context-rich sentences. Therefore, as we learned in Chapter 2, you will probably not be able to determine the meaning of the word by reading the sentence. Therefore, look directly to the under-lined word and do not read the sentence. Look for its synonym among the four choices. The correct answer is **(D) complex**. Most of the answer choices for the test questions at the end of each lesson are key words introduced in that lesson.

After you have studied the 15 words and their synonyms, and com-pleted the practice exercises, make flash cards. On one side of the card, write the key word and its related forms. On the other side of the card, write its synonym. Review these cards several times during the weeks before your TOEFL test session. If you are preparing for a specific TOEFL test date, make a study schedule based on how much time you have before the TOEFL. For example, if you have six weeks before your test date, plan to study five lessons each week

Be sure that you organize your cards. It is suggested that you orga-nize your cards by alphabetical order of the **synonyms** or by the **lesson number**. Keep two groups of cards; one group for the words you have learned, the second group for those words you need to learn. Review the second group more often than the first group of words that you already know.

As your vocabulary grows, return to the exercises and test questions in each lesson.

By following this study plan you will be better prepared for the impor-tant day when you hear the words "You may now open your TOEFL test booklet."

## ANSWERING PHRASAL QUESTIONS

**One** phrase-type question is provided in each of the book's 30 lessons. Each question contains a short passage that illustrates the use of a vocabulary item in combination with other words that it is often grouped with. For example, *densely* is a word that appears as a single item in one of these lessons, but it is often combined with the word *populated* to form the phrase *densely populated*. Therefore, *densely populated* is treated as a whole phrase in one of the phrasal questions in the book. It is always useful to learn the meanings of single words, but it is also important to learn how these words combine with other words in com-mon word pairs or word groups.

In answering these questions, it is helpful to use what you already know about the words in isolation and to keep a few simple strategies in mind. Let's look more closely at the *densely populated* example.

First, you should read the passage carefully. A lot of what you need to know about the word in combination and the meaning of the whole phrase is already available in the passage itself. In this case, you know that the phrase has something to do with the distribution of people in a particular country: Some live close together in cities, while others live far apart in the countryside. Therefore, you have a sense of what the words mean in combination because you understand the general meaning of the passage that illustrates and defines them.

Understanding the general meaning and the phrase's context is probably enough for you to come up with the right answer to the practice question in this book:

> **In stating that the Netherlands is *densely populated*, the author means that its**
>
> **(A) people are very unevenly distributed.**
> **(B) population is the largest in Europe.**
> **(C) population is the largest per square kilometer.**
> **(D) cities are the largest cities in Europe.**

Without going much further, you can probably guess that the best answer here is **(C)** since it comes the closest to saying that the country as a whole contains a lot of people without saying that it contains more than any other country in Europe. However, there are other steps you can take just to be sure.

You can also take a look at the entry for the target word, in this case *densely*. Notice that the word is an adverb. This means that it limits or modifies an adjective and a verb; in this instance, it tells you *how heavily populated* a particular European country is—how many people it contains per square kilometer. Other word combinations or phrases fall into other categories. For example, some contain verbs followed by prepositions (*conforms to*), some contain nouns preceded by prepositions (*on impulse*), and some contain nouns preceded by adjectives (*crushing blow*). In other words, try to use as much information about a word's form or part of speech as you can in arriving at its meaning, and specifically at an understanding of its relationship with the other words around it.

Finally, recall any other instance of the phrase you have heard or seen. For example, you may discover that you have already encountered the phrase in your reading—in developing your awareness of vocabulary through extensive reading—and you may have recorded it on one of your flash cards. These phrases have been chosen because they are commonly used in the language. For that reason, you are likely to come across them in a variety of contexts. Their frequent use is also the reason why understanding these words in combination can give you a deeper and more general understanding of the language as a whole.

## Word Combinations in This Book

The table that follows includes the word combinations and phrases highlighted in the book's 30 vocabulary lessons.

In the first column on the left, you can see grammatical information about each word combination's part of speech. For example, *disapprove of* is described as a verb because it fills that role in an English sentence:

**Sheila *disapproves of* students who make a lot of noise.**

In the third column, the chapter in which each word combination is found is specified. Finally, an illustrative sentence is given in the fourth column.

The table will help you learn new phrases and word combinations, as will general strategies for learning new words in combination wherever you find them.

## Word Combinations in This Book
(See the second column for lesson number)

---

| VERBS | | Example |
|---|---|---|
| **disapprove of** | 1 | Many communities now disapprove of cell or car phone use. |
| **(see an) advantage in** | 2 | Many people can see an advantage in moving to big cities. |
| **conform to** | 3 | A chameleon changes color to conform to its surroundings. |
| **(be) determined to** | 4 | Many residents are determined to .restrict the movement of deer. |
| **(be) reported to** | 12 | They were reported to have powers that protected them from attack. |
| **take the initiative** | 20 | The center forward takes the initiative and moves the ball forward. |
| **react to** | 21 | The colorant reacts to the presence of acid by turning red. |
| **account for** | 22 | Scientists seek to account for patterned circles in grain fields. |
| **(be) renowned for** | 23 | The orchestra is especially renowned for its violin players. |
| **(be) peculiar to** | 24 | Water storage is peculiar to a class of animals called ruminants. |
| **(be) open to interpretation** | 26 | Historical facts about the Pyramids are open to interpretation. |

| ADJECTIVES + NOUNS | | |
|---|---|---|
| **intriguing question** | 5 | Where human life first arose is still an intriguing question. |
| **crushing blow** | 8 | The airplane's invention was a crushing blow for ballooning. |
| **face-to-face encounters** | 13 | Lack of eye contact is a sign of disrespect in face-to-face encounters. |
| **heightened awareness** | 16 | Heightened awareness has led to worry about greenhouse gases. |
| **gradual decrease** | 17 | A gradual decrease will not stimulate spending or employment. |

---

| ADJECTIVES + NOUNS (continued) | | Example |
|---|---|---|
| balanced view | 18 | TV news rarely gives a balanced view of people, products, and events. |
| curative powers | 28 | A substance with curative powers would actually kill bacteria. |

**ADVERBS + ADJECTIVES**

| comparatively easy | 6 | It is comparatively easy to switch off some Internet sites. |
|---|---|---|
| densely populated | 9 | The Netherlands is the most densely populated country in Europe. |
| exceptionally talented | 10 | Relatively few children are exceptionally talented musically. |
| fundamentally sound | 14 | NASA is confident that spacecraft are fundamentally sound. |
| perilously close | 15 | The world came perilously close to losing the panda in the 1980s. |
| aptly named | 27 | The ship was aptly named after the Titans, who ruled the universe. |
| prominently displayed | 29 | The electronic bar code is not prominently displayed on a product. |
| severely punished | 30 | In some countries, high-speed driving is severely punished. |

**PREPOSITIONS + NOUNS**

| to its core | 7 | Patients view the medical profession as selfish to its core. |
|---|---|---|
| on impulse | 25 | Psychology has explored why purchases are made on impulse. |

**COMPARATIVE ADJECTIVE**

| more prevalent than | 11 | Sports utility vehicles are more prevalent than compact cars. |
|---|---|---|

**PHRASAL PREPOSITION**

| in opposition to | 19 | There is growing sentiment in opposition to sea bass fishing. |
|---|---|---|

# LESSON 1

- abroad ▪ abrupt ▪ acceptable ▪ acclaim ▪ actually
- adverse ▪ advice ▪ attractive ▪ autonomous
- disapproval ▪ disruptive ▪ haphazardly ▪ ideal
- persistent ▪ wide

---

**abroad**      *adv.* to or in another country

                    *syn.* overseas; internationally

Louis Armstrong often traveled *abroad*.

Living *abroad* can be an educational experience.

**abrupt**      *adj.* quick; without warning

*adv.* abruptly      *syn.* sudden
  *n.* abruptness

There was an *abrupt* change in the weather.

After the incident everyone left *abruptly*.

**acceptable**      *adj.* allowable or satisfactory

  *v.* accept      *syn.* permissible
*adv.* acceptably
  *n.* acceptability
*adj.* accepting

The idea was *acceptable* to everyone.

The registrar *accepted* more applicants than he should have.

**acclaim**      *n.* enthusiastic approval; applause

*adj.* acclaimed      *syn.* praise
  *n.* acclamation

Isaac Stern has won *acclaim* abroad.

*Acclaimed* authors often win Pulitzer Prizes.

**actually**      *adv.* being in existence, real or factual

*adj.* actual      *syn.* truly

They were *actually* very good soccer players.

The *actual* time allotted to complete the test is two hours.

43

**adverse**

adv.  adversely
n.   adversity
n.   adversary

*adj.*  displeasing, objectionable, or bad

*syn.*  unfavorable

*Adverse* weather conditions made it difficult to play the game.

His indecision *adversely* affected his job performance.

**advice**

v.   advise
adj.  advisable
n.   advisability

*n.*  a recommendation given by someone not associated with the problem or situation

*syn.*  suggestion

Good *advice* is hard to find.

It is not *advisable* to stay up late the day before a test.

**attractive**

v.   attract
n.   attraction
n.   attractiveness
adv.  attractively

*adj.*  calling attention to; pleasing; creating interest; pretty

*syn.*  appealing

The idea of working four, ten-hour work days was *attractive* to the employees.

The major *attraction* of the show was a speech by the president.

**autonomous**

adv.  autonomously

*adj.*  by itself; with no association

*syn.*  independent

Mexico became an *autonomous* state in 1817.

Although working closely with the government, all businesses function *autonomously*.

**disapproval**

v.   disapprove
adv.  disapprovingly

*n.*  the act of disagreeing; not giving approval

*syn.*  objection

Their *disapproval* of the plan caused the experiment to be abandoned.

The students *disapproved* of the plan of study.

**disruptive**

v.   disrupt
n.   disruption
adv.  disruptively

*adj.*  causing confusion and interruption

*syn.*  disturbing

Frequent questions during lectures can be *disruptive*.

The storm caused a *disruption* in bus service.

**haphazardly**     *adv.*   having no order or pattern; by chance

*adj.*   haphazard     *syn.*   arbitrarily; carelessly
*n.*   haphazardness

It was obvious that the house was built *haphazardly*.

Susan completed the assignment in a *haphazard* way.

**ideal**     *adj.*   having no flaw or mistake; excellent

*adv.*   ideally     *syn.*   perfect
*n.*   ideal

The beach is an *ideal* place to relax.

Candidates for the job should *ideally* have five years experience in similar positions.

**persistent**     *adj.*   continuous; refusing to give up; firm in
*v.*   persist              action or decision
*n.*   persistence     *syn.*   constant
*adv.*   persistently

The attorney's *persistent* questioning weakened the witness.

Her *persistence* earned her a spot on the team.

**wide**     *adj.*   extending over a large area

*adv.*   widely     *syn.*   broad
*n.*   wideness

Pine forests are found over a *wide* area of the Pacific Northwest.

The senator has traveled *widely*.

## MATCHING

Choose the synonym.

1. widely
   - (A) broadly
   - (B) abroad
   - (C) secretly
   - (D) truly

2. autonomous
   - (A) independent
   - (B) sudden
   - (C) international
   - (D) abrupt

3. advice
   - (A) acclaim
   - (B) attention
   - (C) suggestion
   - (D) praise

4. attractive
   - (A) appealing
   - (B) adverse
   - (C) arbitrary
   - (D) perfect

5. disapproval
   - (A) attraction
   - (B) attention
   - (C) objection
   - (D) persistence

6. haphazardly
   - (A) suddenly
   - (B) secretly
   - (C) carelessly
   - (D) constantly

7. constant
   - (A) disruption
   - (B) acceptable
   - (C) abrupt
   - (D) persistent

8. perfect
   - (A) attractive
   - (B) ideal
   - (C) actual
   - (D) abrupt

9. unfavorably
   - (A) attractively
   - (B) haphazardly
   - (C) acceptably
   - (D) adversely

10. disturbing
    - (A) perfect
    - (B) disruptive
    - (C) persistent
    - (D) attractive

## LESSON 1—MULTIPLE-CHOICE TEST QUESTIONS

1. A customs union is an organization of **autonomous** countries that agree that international trade between member states is free of restrictions. They place a tariff or other restriction on products entering the customs union from nonmember states. One of the best known customs unions is the European Common Market, formerly called the European Union.

   The word **autonomous** in the passage is closest in meaning to

   Ⓐ massive
   Ⓑ acclaimed
   Ⓒ prosperous
   Ⓓ independent

2. The search to hide natural body odors led to the discovery and use of musk. Musk is a scent used in perfumes. It is obtained from the sex glands of the male musk deer, a small deer native to the mountainous regions of the Himalayas. The odor of musk, penetrating and **persistent**, is believed to act as an aphrodisiac. In animals, musk serves the functions of defining territory, providing recognition, and attracting mates.

   The word **persistent** in the passage is closest in meaning to

   Ⓐ attractive
   Ⓑ disruptive
   Ⓒ constant
   Ⓓ ideal

3. Until the late ninteenth century all rubber was extracted **haphazardly** from trees found in the jungles of South America. It was expensive and the supply was uncertain. However, during the 1860s the idea of transporting rubber trees to the British colonies in Asia was conceived. This led to the larger-scale cultivation of rubber trees on organized plantations.

   The word **haphazardly** in the passage is closest in meaning to

   Ⓐ carelessly
   Ⓑ secretly
   Ⓒ constantly
   Ⓓ dangerously

4. Some animals' coloration uses bold, **disruptive** markings to scare predators. Other animals have color patterns that blend with their surroundings. Such coloration serves for protection, to attract mates, or to distract enemies. Called cryptic coloration, it uses the animal's living place, habits, and means of defense. Cryptic coloration may blend an animal so well with its environment that it is virtually invisible.

The word **disruptive** in the passage is closest in meaning to

&#9398; disturbing
&#9399; distinctive
&#9400; brilliant
&#9401; unfavorable

5. Cognitive approaches to therapy assume that emotional disorders are the result of irrational beliefs or perceptions. The mind may interpret an event as scary or calming, happy or sad. The emotionally disordered person may perceive **adverse** events as personal failures. Cognitive psychotherapies seek to make the patient aware of the irrationality of this perception and to substitute more rational evaluations of such events.

The word **adverse** in the passage is closest in meaning to

&#9398; monotonous
&#9399; threatening
&#9400; inoffensive
&#9401; unfavorable

6. Increasingly, authorities are uneasy about teenagers who drive while talking on the telephone. For many, phone use and driving are perfectly compatible; others are more easily distracted, especially while listening to music. The growing number of accidents associated with phone use also supports this claim. Many communities now **disapprove of** these phones so much that they have forbidden anyone of any age to use them while driving.

In stating that many communities now **disapprove of** these phones, the author means that they

&#9398; fully endorse their popularity.
&#9399; condemn or oppose their use.
&#9400; favor their use only by adults.
&#9401; agree to their unrestricted use.

## LESSON 1—COMPUTER-BASED TEST QUESTIONS

1. Fans are used to circulate air in rooms and buildings, and for cooling and drying people, materials, or products. Even though air circulated by a fan is comforting, no fan **actually** cools the air. Only devices such as air conditioners can truly affect changes in air temperature.

   Find the word in the passage closest in meaning to the word **actually.**

2. Tornadoes strike in many areas of the world, but nowhere are they as frequent or as devastating as in the United States. A vast "tornado belt," where sudden shifts in climatic conditions are commonly experienced, embraces large portions of the Great Plains of the United States and the southeastern portion of the country. Tornadoes pose the greatest threats to these areas, which are especially vulnerable to **abrupt** changes in weather conditions.

   Find the word in the passage closest in meaning to the word **abrupt.**

3. For women in the 1920s, freedom in dress reflected their new freedom to take up careers. Only a small percentage of women pursued such opportunities, but the revolutionary change affected the types of clothes worn by most women. For example, trousers became **acceptable** attire for almost all activities. This milestone in the fashion world made it permissible for women to relinquish standard, formal modes of dress in favor of more stylish and comfortable clothing.

   Find the word in the passage closest in meaning to the word **acceptable.**

4. The National Film Board of Canada was established in 1939 to produce films that reflect Canadian life and thought, and to distribute them both domestically and abroad. By winning praise and awards from film festivals around the world, it has earned international **acclaim** for the artistic and technical excellence of its work.

   Find the word in the passage closest in meaning to the word **acclaim.**

5. In the 1700s, overseas assignments were particularly prized by diplomats. Among the most famous government officials of the era was Benjamin Franklin, who traveled **abroad** frequently. He became the first American minister to France. For seven years he acted as diplomat, purchasing agent, recruiting officer, loan negotiator, and chief of intelligence. His fame made him the main representative of the United States in all of Europe.

Find the word in the passage closest in meaning to the word **abroad.**

# LESSON 2

- advanced ∎ advantage ∎ advent ∎ agile ∎ albeit
- allow ∎ appealing ∎ celebrated ∎ contemporary
- distribute ∎ encourage ∎ energetic ∎ frail ∎ refine
- worthwhile

---

**advanced**
*v.* advance
*n.* advancement

*adj.* ahead of current thought or practice; forward thinking; new

*syn.* progressive

*Advanced* technology is changing the world.

His *advancement* to captain came unexpectedly.

**advantage**
*adv.* advantageously
*adj.* advantageous

*n.* something that may help one to be successful or to gain something

*syn.* benefit

Is there any *advantage* in arriving early?

He was *advantageously* born into a rich family.

**advent**

*n.* the coming or appearance of something

*syn.* arrival

With the *advent* of computers, many tasks have been made easier.

The newspapers announced the *advent* of the concert season.

**agile**
*adv.* agilely
*n.* agileness
*n.* agility

*adj.* able to move in a quick and easy way

*syn.* nimble

Deer are very *agile* animals.

She moved *agilely* across the stage.

**albeit**

*conj.* in spite of the facts, regardless of the fact

*syn.* although

His trip was successful, *albeit* tiring.

*Albeit* difficult at times, speaking another language is rewarding.

**allow**

*n.* allowance
*adj.* allowable
*adv.* allowably

*v.* to agree to let something happen, to not interfere with an action

*syn.* permit

Arthur's natural agility will *allow* him to excel in sports.

The extra money *allowed* us to stay abroad another day.

**appealing**

*v.* appeal
*n.* appeal
*adv.* appealingly

*adj.* attractive or interesting

*syn.* alluring

Working abroad is *appealing* to many people.

Through his speeches, the candidate *appealed* to the voters.

**celebrated**

*adj.* acclaimed; well-known and popular

*syn.* renowned

The *celebrated* pianist will be giving a concert this weekend.

San Francisco is *celebrated* for its multicultural makeup.

**contemporary**

*n.* contemporary

*adj.* modern, up-to-date, or (*n.*) a person living at the same time as another person

*syn.* current

*Contemporary* architecture makes very good use of space.

Cervantes was a *contemporary* of Shakespeare.

**distribute**

*n.* distribution

*v.* to divide among people or to give out

*syn.* dispense

Many publishers *distribute* their newspapers directly to homes in their area.

The *distribution* of seeds is very quick with this new machine.

**encourage**

*n.* encouragement
*adj.* encouraging
*adv.* encouragingly

*v.* to give courage or hope to someone

*syn.* inspire

Even though the runner finished second, he was *encouraged* by his performance.

His teacher gave him the *encouragement* that he needed to learn the material.

**energetic**

*n.* energy
*adv.* energetically

*adj.* full of life, action, or power ✓
*syn.* vigorous

Sam hasn't been as *energetic* as he usually is.
There's a lot of *energy* in these batteries.

**frail**

*n.* frailty

*adj.* weak in health or in body ✓
*syn.* fragile

The *frail* wings of the newborn bird could not lift it off the ground.
One of the *frailties* of human beings is laziness.

**refine**

*n.* refinement
*adj.* refined

*v.* to make pure; to improve
*syn.* perfect (verb)

Factories must *refine* oil before it can be used as fuel.
A squirt of lime juice is the perfect *refinement* to cola.

**worthwhile**

*adj.* value in doing something
*syn.* rewarding

It was *worthwhile* waiting ten hours in line for the tickets.
It's *worthwhile* to prepare for the TOEFL.

## MATCHING

Choose the synonym.

1. inspire
   - (A) celebrate
   - (B) attract
   - (C) encourage
   - (D) appeal

2. advantage
   - (A) benefit
   - (B) persistence
   - (C) nimbleness
   - (D) allure

3. fragile
   - (A) modern
   - (B) famous
   - (C) allowable
   - (D) frail

4. contemporary
   - (A) timing
   - (B) current
   - (C) well-known
   - (D) perfect

5. appealing
   - (A) refined
   - (B) encouraging
   - (C) alluring
   - (D) popular

6. renowned
   - (A) unknown
   - (B) celebrated
   - (C) adverse
   - (D) disapprove

7. worthwhile
   - (A) rewarding
   - (B) acceptable
   - (C) agile
   - (D) permitted

8. vigorous
   - (A) attractive
   - (B) beautiful
   - (C) energetic
   - (D) advantageous

9. refine
   - (A) persist
   - (B) value
   - (C) perfect
   - (D) divide

10. distribute
    - (A) disappoint
    - (B) disrupt
    - (C) discourage
    - (D) dispense

**LESSON 2—MULTIPLE-CHOICE TEST QUESTIONS**

1.  Over the years, investigators have evaluated the local folklore of areas where sightings of the **celebrated** Abominable Snowman have been reported. The same scientists have collected physical evidence, such as footprints, body parts, and photographs, but this evidence remains unconvincing. In 1960 the renowned mountaineer Sir Edmund Hillary of New Zealand conducted an investigation of the reports of the creature, but found no evidence of its existence.

    The word **celebrated** in the passage is closest in meaning to

    (A) elusive
    (B) ambiguous
    (C) renowned
    (D) indistinct

2.  Exercises that demand total body involvement improve and maintain fitness. The most effective way to feel more mentally alert and **energetic** is to engage in aerobic activity at least three times a week for thiry minutes. Such activities may include jogging, running, swimming, dancing, and fast walking.

    The word **energetic** in the passage is closest in meaning to

    (A) vigorous
    (B) frail
    (C) agile
    (D) appealing

3.  Most people do not appreciate the importance of packaging. Packages maintain the purity and freshness of their contents and protect them from elements outside. If the contents are harmful, corrosive, or poisonous, the package must also protect the outside environment. A package must identify its contents, which facilitates **distribution** of the product.

    The word **distribution** in the passage is closest in meaning to

    (A) usage
    (B) disruption
    (C) dispensing
    (D) advertising

4. A **contemporary** issue among psychologists is the activation or cause of emotion, its structure or components, and its functions and consequences. Each of these aspects can be considered from a biosocial view. Generally, biosocial theory focuses on the neurophysiological aspects of emotions and their roles as organizers of cognition and motivators of action.

The word **contemporary** in the passage is closest in meaning to

- Ⓐ current
- Ⓑ acclaimed
- Ⓒ contemptuous
- Ⓓ favored

5. The early artists of the Hudson River school were Thomas Doughty, Asher Durand, and Thomas Cole. They found the wilderness in the Hudson River valley **appealing**. Although these painters studied in Europe, they first achieved a measure of success at home, and chose the common theme of the remoteness and splendor of the American interior.

The word **appealing** in the passage is closest in meaning to

- Ⓐ annoying
- Ⓑ ongoing
- Ⓒ spectacular
- Ⓓ alluring

6. Recent polls suggest that fewer people see an **advantage in** moving to the city than they used to. There was a time when cities attracted country dwellers like powerful magnets: cities had more jobs, better schools, more services. Today, people often see pollution, crime, stress, and unemployment where they once saw opportunity. Instead of advantages, they see disadvantages in uprooting their families for the uncertainty of urban life.

In stating that fewer people see an **advantage in** moving to the city, the author means that fewer people

- Ⓐ consider cities a poor option
- Ⓑ prefer to relocate to big cities
- Ⓒ take a positive view of cities
- Ⓓ view city life as advantageous

**LESSON 2—COMPUTER-BASED TEST QUESTIONS**

1.  The arrival of television in the 1950s marked an important turning point in the entertainment world. This development created vast new entertainment choices for people who lived within the signal areas of TV stations. Later, with the **advent** of satellite and cable TV, almost everyone, regardless of location, was able to participate in this explosion of entertainment choices.

    Find the word in the passage closest in meaning to the word **advent**.

2.  Passerines form the dominant avian group on earth today. They are regarded as the most highly evolved of all birds and occur in abundance. Passerines are nimble, small to medium-sized land birds. Humans have long enjoyed passerines for their songs and their almost infinite variety of colors, patterns, and behavioral traits. Many passerines are considered to be quite **agile**. Among the most energetic of them is the swallow, whose small body is designed for effortless maneuvering.

    Find the word in the passage closest in meaning to the word **agile**.

3.  The United States is a major consumer of shrimp. In the United States, shrimping is permitted only during specific predetermined seasons. For example, in Mississippi tidal waters, shrimping is **allowed** only from October to May. The development of freezing techniques in the 1940s permitted shrimping to expand considerably, making it a global operation. The United States now imports frozen shrimp from more than 60 countries.

    Find the word in the passage closest in meaning to the word **allowed.**

4.  The eating habits of tadpoles are of interest to many scientists. One curious observation made by those who study the diets of these creatures is that, **albeit** the majority of tadpoles are vegetarian, a small subpsecies is carivorous. Although scientists have known this fact for many years, they are still unable to explain this difference.

    Find the word in the passage closest in meaning to the word **albeit.**

5. **Advanced** scientific disciplines, such as genetic engineering and computer science, are exploding with possibilities. As a result of progress brought about by new technologies, many methods to detect and treat disease are sure to be developed. These progressive technologies will change the course of modern medical history.

Find the word in the passage closest in meaning to the word **advanced.**

# LESSON 3

■ alter ■ analyze ■ ancient ■ annoying ■ anticipate
■ conform ■ detect ■ enrich ■ intensify ■ intolerable
■ observe ■ ongoing ■ propose ■ restore ■ vital

**alter**
*v.* altered
*n.* alteration
*adj.* alterable
*adv.* alterably

*v.* to change or make different

*syn.* modify

Will the storm *alter* its course and miss the coast?

Gloria hasn't *altered* her plans to return to school.

**analyze**
*v.* analyzed
*n.* analysis

*v.* to study something carefully; to separate into parts for study

*syn.* examine

Scientists must *analyze* problems thoroughly.

*Analysis* of the substance confirms the presence of nitrogen.

**ancient**

*adj.* something from a long time ago; very old

*syn.* old

Archaeologists analyze *ancient* civilizations.

Dave found an *ancient* Roman coin.

**annoying**
*n.* annoyance
*v.* annoy
*adv.* annoyingly

*adj.* a slight bother; disturbing to a person

*syn.* bothersome

Mosquitos can be an *annoying* part of a vacation at the beach.

She *annoyed* her parents by coming home late.

**anticipate**
*adj.* anticipatory
*n.* anticipation

*v.* to think about or prepare for something ahead of time

*syn.* predict

No one can *anticipate* the results of the games.

They planned their vacation with *anticipation*.

**conform**
*n.* conformity
*n.* conformist

*v.* to follow established rules or patterns of behavior

*syn.* adapt

You must *conform* to the rules or leave the club.

She has always been a *conformist*.

**detect**
*n.* detection
*n.* detective

*v.* to find out; to observe something

*syn.* notice

He *detected* a smile on his girlfriend's face.

They are the best *detectives* on the police force.

**enrich**
*n.* enrichment
*adj.* enriching

*v.* to make rich; to make something of greater value

*syn.* enhance

The fine arts *enrich* our lives.

The discovery of oil was an *enrichment* for the country.

**intensify**
*n.* intensity
*adj.* intense
*adj.* intensive
*adv.* intensely
*adv.* intensively

*v.* to make stronger in feeling or quality

*syn.* heighten

The importance of the test will sometimes *intensify* the nervousness of the students.

The chess match was played with great *intensity*.

**intolerable**
*n.* intolerance
*adv.* intolerably
*adv.* intolerantly
*adj.* intolerant

*adj.* difficult or painful to experience; not able to accept different ways of thought or behavior

*syn.* unbearable

Any opposition to the rules is *intolerable*.

His boss was *intolerant* of his tardiness.

**observe**

n.   observation
n.   observer
adj.   observant
adj.   observable

*v.*   to see and watch carefully; to examine

*syn.*   notice

Human beings like to *observe* the behavior of monkeys.
I made the *observation* that you are not happy.

**ongoing**

*adj.*   continuing

*syn.*   current

The tutoring project is an *ongoing* program of the school.
Maintaining roads is an *ongoing* job.

**propose**

n.   proposal
n.   proposition
adj.   proposed

*v.*   to suggest or plan to do something

*syn.*   suggest

The governor is going to *propose* new taxes.
Her *proposal* was well accepted.

**restore**

n.   restoration
adj.   restored

*v.*   to give back or bring back something; √
to return to the original condition

*syn.*   revitalize

He *restored* my confidence in him.
It is a beautiful *restoration* of the old table.

**vital**

n.   vitality
adv.   vitally

*adj.*   of great importance; full of life

*syn.*   indispensable

Money is *vital* to the success of the program.
His intense *vitality* was easily observable.

## MATCHING

Choose the synonym.

1. indispensable
   (A) abrupt
   (B) abroad
   (C) vital
   (D) frail

2. restore
   (A) appeal
   (B) revitalize
   (C) attract
   (D) disrupt

3. conform
   (A) annoy
   (B) divide
   (C) encourage
   (D) adapt

4. notice
   (A) observe
   (B) refine
   (C) distribute
   (D) analyze

5. current
   (A) energetic
   (B) ideal
   (C) ongoing
   (D) intense

6. observe
   (A) alter
   (B) notice
   (C) anticipate
   (D) modify

7. intense
   (A) strong
   (B) intolerant
   (C) vitally
   (D) allowable

8. enrich
   (A) alter
   (B) dispense
   (C) disrupt
   (D) enhance

9. unbearable
   (A) inspiring
   (B) unfavorable
   (C) intolerable
   (D) ancient

10. proposal
    (A) question
    (B) attention
    (C) benefit
    (D) suggestion

## LESSON 3—MULTIPLE-CHOICE TEST QUESTIONS

1. The point at which pain becomes **intolerable** is known as the pain perception threshold. Studies have found this point to be similar among different social and cultural groups. However, the pain tolerance threshold varies significantly among these groups. A stoical, unemotional response to pain may be seen as a sign of braveness in certain cultural or social environments. However, this behavior can also mask the seriousness of an injury to an examining physician.

   The word **intolerable** in the passage is closest in meaning to

       Ⓐ   elusive
       Ⓑ   altered
       Ⓒ   intensified
       Ⓓ   unbearable

2. Nutritional additives are utilized to restore nutrients lost during production, to **enrich** certain foods in order to correct dietary deficiencies, or to add nutrients to food substitutes. Nowadays, vitamins are commonly added to many foods in order to increase their nutritional value. For example, vitamins A and D are added to dairy and cereal products, and several of the B vitamins are added to cereals.

   The word **enrich** in the passage is closest in meaning to

       Ⓐ   alter
       Ⓑ   enhance
       Ⓒ   produce
       Ⓓ   restore

3. In modern manufacturing production facilities that produce equipment sensitive to environmental contamination, a dust-free working area with strict temperature and humidity controls is of **vital** importance. Seamless plastic walls and ceilings, external lighting, a continuous flow of dust-free air, and daily cleaning are features of this "clean room." Workers wear special clothing, including head coverings. When entering this room, they pass through a "shower" to remove contaminants.

   The word **vital** in the passage is closest in meaning to

       Ⓐ   indispensable
       Ⓑ   lively
       Ⓒ   extreme
       Ⓓ   dubious

4. Human populations are classified in terms of genetically transmitted traits. For groups that have lived for generations in certain locations, research illustrates the long-term genetic effects of environmental factors such as climate and diet. **Ongoing** investigations track the history of evolution and its genetic changes and help to explain the origin of genetically determined diseases and their long-term influence.

The word **ongoing** in the passage is closest in meaning to

    Ⓐ  current
    Ⓑ  thorough
    Ⓒ  proposed
    Ⓓ  temporary

5. In the 1890s, a rising generation of young antiorganization leaders came on the political scene. These leaders transformed the art and practice of politics in the United States, by exercising strong leadership and by bringing about institutional changes that helped **revitalize** political democracy. Most important was their achievement of economic and social objectives, such as legislation to prevent child labor, and accident insurance systems to provide compensation to injured workers.

The word **revitalize** in the passage is closest in meaning to

    Ⓐ  intensify
    Ⓑ  establish
    Ⓒ  reform
    Ⓓ  restore

6. There are more than 100 types or species of chameleon. A member of the lizard family, the chameleon lives in countries as diverse as Madagascar, Spain, and Sri Lanka. It is thought to change color to **conform to** its surroundings, but that is rarely true. While changes do occur with changes in light or temperature, especially when the chameleon is frightened, its new color rarely matches its immediate surroundings.

In stating that the chameleon's color **conforms to** its surroundings, the author means that it

    Ⓐ  differs from the color of its setting.
    Ⓑ  contrasts with its surroundings.
    Ⓒ  clashes with the colors around it.
    Ⓓ  looks the same as its environment.

## LESSON 3—COMPUTER-BASED TEST QUESTIONS

1. Examination of infrared light emissions is particularly helpful to astronomers. The composition and temperature of heavenly bodies can often be determined by **analysis** of photos taken with a film that is sensitive to infrared light emissions. Using infrared detectors, astronomers can observe cooler celestial objects than they can with optical devices, since infrared radiation is less affected by interstellar dust than is light.

   Find the word in the passage closest in meaning to the word **analysis**.

2. As a result of stiff competition from other drink manufacturers, and in order to maintain market share of its products, the Coca-Cola company changed the secret formula of the popular drink. Despite the public's negative reaction to the **altered** beverage, the move was still considered a brilliant promotional strategy, because the changed formula gave the popular drink international publicity.

   Find the word in the passage closest in meaning to the word **altered**.

3. Working environments in which loud noise is frequent can be more than just bothersome to the employee. Aside from simply being **annoying**, the most measurable physical effect of noise pollution is damage to hearing. This may be either temporary or permanent and may cause disruption of normal activities. In work areas where noise is a problem, care should be taken to protect the ears with ear plugs.

   Find the word in the passage closest in meaning to the word **annoying**.

4. The need for adequate shelter is as old as humankind itself. The construction of shelter, found among the first stable human societies about 5,000 years ago, is considered to be among the most important of all **ancient** human activities. The systematic placement of groups of housing marked a momentous cultural transition toward the formation of towns. It generated new needs and resources and was accompanied by a significant increase in technological innovation.

   Find the word in the passage closest in meaning to the word **ancient**.

5. Seeking to take advantage of new economic trends of the late 1800s, Manitoba's leaders made important changes in economic policies. These changes, which predicted new directions in economic development of the region, took advantage of the unique business attributes of the province. Having **anticipated** the business environment, the province was productive during the early 1900s.

Find the word in the passage closest in meaning to the word **anticipate.**

# LESSON 4

- ambiguous ■ apparent ■ arbitrary ■ assert
- astounding ■ astute ■ authorize ■ deceptively
- determined ■ elicit ■ forbid ■ petition ■ relinquish
- resilient ■ tempt

---

**ambiguous**

*adv.* ambiguously
*n.* ambiguity

*adj.* of unclear meaning; something that can be understood in more than one way

*syn.* vague

The men received an *ambiguous* message from their boss.

His letter was full of *ambiguities*.

**apparent**

*adv.* apparently

*adj.* to be clear in meaning or open to view, easily understood

*syn.* visible

It was *apparent* that he needed to rest.

No one *apparently* knew how to solve the problem.

**arbitrary**

*adv.* arbitrarily
*n.* arbitrariness

*adj.* an action or decision made with little thought, order, or reason

*syn.* haphazard

Her choice of clothing seemed *arbitrary*.

The teacher *arbitrarily* decided to give the class a test.

**assert**

*adv.* assertively
*n.* assertiveness
*n.* assertion
*adj.* assertive

*v.* to express or defend oneself strongly; to state positively

*syn.* declare

The government *asserted* its control over the banking system.

The company president is an *assertive* individual.

**astounding**     *adj.*   very surprising

  *v.*    astound       *syn.*   astonishing
  *adv.*   astoundingly

The scientists made an *astounding* discovery.

The fans were *astounded* by their team's success.

**astute**     *adj.*   very intelligent, smart, clever

  *adj.*   astutely       *syn.*   perceptive
    *n.*   astuteness

He was an *astute* worker, finishing in half the time it took the others to finish.

They *astutely* determined that there would be no chance to finish on time.

**authorize**     *v.*   to give permission or power to do something

  *adj.*   authorized       *syn.*   empower
    *n.*   authority

Only *authorized* employees are allowed in the laboratory.

The dean has the *authority* to resolve academic problems of students.

**deceptively**     *adv.*   making something appear true or good
                                      when it is false or bad

  *adj.*   deceptive
    *v.*   deceive       *syn.*   misleadingly
    *n.*   deception

The magician *deceptively* made the rabbit disappear.

Richard *deceived* Joe about the cost of the coat.

**determined**     *adj.*   strong in one's opinion, firm in conviction,
                                   to find out

    *n.*   determination
    *v.*   determine       *syn.*   resolute

They were *determined* to go to graduate school.

The judge *determined* that the man was lying.

**elicit**     *v.*   to get the facts or draw out the truth

    *n.*   elicitation       *syn.*   extract

A lawyer will *elicit* all the facts necessary to prove her case.

*Elicitation* of the truth can be difficult at times.

**forbid**

*adj.* forbidden
*adj.* forbidding*
*adv.* forbiddingly*

*v.* to command not to do something
* to have a dangerous look, a bad feeling
*syn.* ban

His father will *forbid* him to use the car.
The cave looks *forbidding*; let's not go in.

**petition**

*n.* petition

*v.* to make a request
*syn.* appeal

Canada *petitioned* the United Nations to consider its case.
The student's *petition* was denied.

**relinquish**

*n.* relinquishment

*v.* to give up control
*syn.* abdicate

The troubled executive *relinquished* his control of the company.
The *relinquishment* of his claim to the building will allow the building to be sold.

**resilient**

*adv.* resiliently
*n.* resilience

*adj.* strong enough to recover from difficulty or disease
*syn.* tenacious

She has a *resilient* personality and will soon feel better.
The doctor was surprised by his patient's *resilience*.

**tempt**

*adv.* temptingly
*n.* temptation
*adj.* tempting

*v.* to make it attractive to do something, usually something wrong
*syn.* entice

The idea of getting rich quickly *tempted* him to invest his life savings.
Desserts are more *tempting* when one is on a diet.

## MATCHING

Choose the synonym.

1. appeal
   - (A) detect
   - (B) assert
   - (C) petition
   - (D) allow

2. astounding
   - (A) celebrated
   - (B) astonishing
   - (C) visible
   - (D) energetic

3. ban
   - (A) forbid
   - (B) empower
   - (C) intensify
   - (D) restore

4. elicit
   - (A) declare
   - (B) authorize
   - (C) conform
   - (D) extract

5. abdicate
   - (A) relinquish
   - (B) alter
   - (C) encourage
   - (D) heighten

6. misleadingly
   - (A) abruptly
   - (B) deceptively
   - (C) progressively
   - (D) truly

7. resolute
   - (A) determined
   - (B) perfect
   - (C) renown
   - (D) perceptive

8. resilient
   - (A) bothersome
   - (B) vital
   - (C) unbearable
   - (D) tenacious

9. tempt
   - (A) entice
   - (B) divide
   - (C) discourage
   - (D) notice

10. vague
    - (A) intolerable
    - (B) adverse
    - (C) beautiful
    - (D) ambiguous

## LESSON 4—MULTIPLE-CHOICE TEST QUESTIONS

1. The creation and analysis of optical illusions involve mathematical and geometric principles, such as the proportionality between the areas of similar figures. Optical illusions and their effects are often created through careful physical attributes, such as a nonstandard use of perspective, distorted angles, **deceptive** shading, unusual juxtaposition, and color effects.

   The word **deceptive** in the passage is closest in meaning to

       Ⓐ  elusive
       Ⓑ  misleading
       Ⓒ  altered
       Ⓓ  ambiguous

2. The Seneca Falls Convention, held in 1848, started the woman's suffrage movement in the United States. A "Declaration of Sentiments," which called upon women to organize and to **petition** for their rights, was passed. However, one controversial resolution, calling for the right of women to vote, narrowly passed. The ridicule of that provision of the Declaration caused many backers of women's rights to withdraw their support later on.

   The word **petition** in the passage is closest in meaning to

       Ⓐ  vote
       Ⓑ  demand
       Ⓒ  appeal
       Ⓓ  persist

3. Space law is concerned with the proper uses of outer space. The most important treaty of space law was the 1967 Outer Space Treaty. It stated that the moon and all other celestial bodies were to be free for exploration and use by all states and their signatories. It also recognized that weapons of mass destruction, including nuclear weapons, were to be **forbidden** in space.

   The word **forbidden** in the passage is closest in meaning to

       Ⓐ  advanced
       Ⓑ  banned
       Ⓒ  destroyed
       Ⓓ  avoided

4. It is a common misconception that the U.S. Congress has the constitutional power to legislate nearly anything for the general welfare. The Constitution gives Congress many powers, but it does not give Congress the power to legislate freely for the general welfare. In many instances, the Congress cannot force the states to abide, although it has the power to **tempt** states by the offer of money. Congress may try to cause the states to do something by means of offers of subsidies or grants, but it cannot compel them to accept the incentives.

The word **tempt** in the passage is closest in meaning to

    Ⓐ   coerce
    Ⓑ   entice
    Ⓒ   solicit
    Ⓓ   persuade

5. Due to the **astounding** progress of integrated-circuit technology, an enormous number of transistors can be placed onto a single integrated-circuit chip. The first commercially successful microprocessor chip had only 4,800 transistors, but the newest chips now have 3,200,000 transistors.

The word **astounding** in the passage is closest in meaning to

    Ⓐ   astonishing
    Ⓑ   rapid
    Ⓒ   solid
    Ⓓ   resilient

6. Deer populations have grown dramatically in the northeast United States in the last 20 years. Many residents are happy to have deer in their communities, but many others see them as a menace. Deer often host insects that carry disease, wander into traffic, cause automobile accidents, trample lawns, and eat flowers. Therefore, many residents are **determined to** restrict their movements, fence them out, or even eliminate them altogether.

In stating that many people are **determined to** eliminate the deer, the author means that they

    Ⓐ   want to decide what to do.
    Ⓑ   support their increase.
    Ⓒ   insist on reducing them.
    Ⓓ   favor enlarging the herd.

## LESSON 4—COMPUTER-BASED TEST QUESTIONS

1. The game of chess was not well organized until 1946, when the world chess governing body, FIDE, **asserted** its control over international play. At that time, national chess groups immediately welcomed the chance to join the new federation and declared their support of the action. However, FIDE's authority has not been universally recognized and even today there is no general agreement as to the status of the world championship.

   Find the word in the passage closest in meaning to the word **asserted.**

2. Social anthropologists attempt to illustrate the social emergence and evolution of the human race and to determine differences between human social organization and that of other primates. Despite the fact that all classifications of human societies and cultures are **arbitrary,** they also attempt to note differences between various human societies. In spite of these haphazard systems of classification, anthropologists have made great advances in the identification and grouping of human civilizations.

   Find the word in the passage closest in meaning to the word **arbitrary.**

3. Paul Newman, one of the most charming and witty film personalities of the 1960s and 1970s, was visibly one of the most handsome actors to grace the wide screen. Yet, he is most famous for his **apparently** effortless acting skill. Because of this talent, he was able to play a variety of characters in a number of stage and screen genres.

   Find the word in the passage closest in meaning to the word **apparently.**

4. The Monroe Doctrine **authorized** the United States to intervene in the affairs of Latin American countries in case of foreign invasion. After the United States empowered itself to act on behalf of its neighbors to the south, incidents of foreign intervention decreased until the 1960s, when Cuba sought the support and economic aid of the former Soviet Union.

   Find the word in the passage closest in meaning to the word **authorized.**

5. J. Edgar Hoover was an **astute** professional who served as Director of the FBI for 48 years. A resilient, perceptive, and determined government official, Hoover's tenure spanned one of the most important eras of modern U.S. history. His policies helped to shape and create what has now become a highly respected modern investigative organization.

Find the word in the passage closest in meaning to the word **astute.**

# LESSON 5

■ amaze ■ baffle ■ bear ■ block ■ blur ■ brilliant
■ caution ■ challenge ■ delicate ■ enhance ■ intrigue
■ persuade ■ replace ■ shed ■ unique

**amaze**                    *v.*  to fill with great surprise

*adv.*  amazingly       *syn.*  astonish
  *n.*  amazement
*adj.*  amazing

I was *amazed* that I received an A on the calculus test.
The actor gave an *amazing* performance.

**baffle**                    *v.*  to confuse to a point at which no progress
*adj.*  baffling                can be made
  *n.*  bafflement
                         *syn.*  puzzle

The causes of many harmful diseases have *baffled* doctors for centuries.
That was a *baffling* question.

**bear**                    *v.*  to produce, to carry; to show; to endure

*adv.*  bearably        *syn.*  yield
*adj.*  bearable

This orchard *bears* many fine harvests of apples.
Although stock prices declined, losses have been *bearable* for most investors.

**block**                    *v.*  to prevent movement, progress, or success

  *n.*  blockage       *syn.*  obstruct
*adj.*  blocked

The government *blocked* the sale of the airline.
The streets were flooded due to a *blockage* in the pipes.

**blur**                    *v.*  to make something difficult to see

*adj.*  blurred        *syn.*  cloud
  *n.*  blur

The rain *blurred* everyone's view of the valley.
The whole accident is just a *blur* in my mind.

**brilliant**

*adv.* brilliantly
*n.* brilliance

*adj.* intensely bright or colorful; intelligent

*syn.* radiant

Einstein was a *brilliant* thinker.
She *brilliantly* produced a solution to the problem.

**caution**

*adj.* cautious
*adj.* cautionary
*adv.* cautiously
*n.* caution

*v.* to alert someone of danger, warn someone to take care or pay attention to something

*syn.* warn

The officer *cautioned* the motorist to slow down.
They entered into the negotiations *cautiously*.

**challenge**

*adj.* challenging
*v.* challenge

*n.* an invitation to compete; something that demands competitive action or much thought

*syn.* dare

Finishing the 26-mile race was a *challenge* for most of the participants.
It was a *challenging* math problem.

**delicate**

*adv.* delicately

*adj.* needing careful treatment; sensitive, easily broken

*syn.* fragile

Because of its controversial nature, it was a challenge to discuss such a *delicate* issue in public.
You must handle the antique *delicately*.

**enhance**

*n.* enhancement
*adj.* enhanced

*v.* to increase in a positive way, such as in value, power, or beauty

*syn.* strengthen

Passing the exam should *enhance* your chances of being admitted to college.
The computer *enhanced* our productivity.

**intrigue**

*v.* to interest greatly  ✓

*adj.* intriguing
*adv.* intriguingly
*n.* intrigue

*syn.* fascinate

He was *intrigued* by the acclaim that he received.

The *intriguing* question baffled historians.

**persuade**

*v.* to change a belief or behavior by argument or reason

*adv.* persuasively
*adj.* persuasive
*n.* persuasion

*syn.* convince

They couldn't *persuade* their critics to see their point of view.

John presented a *persuasive* argument for his salary increase.

**replace**

*v.* to change for another thing; to take the place of

*adj.* replaceable
*n.* replacement

*syn.* substitute

They have *replaced* all of the old office equipment.

The new employee was the *replacement* for Mr. Topper, who retired last month.

**shed**

*v.* to throw off naturally; to give out

*syn.* discard

In order to grow, crabs must *shed* their shells.

The experiments *shed* no new information on the cause of the disease.

**unique**

*adj.* to be the only one of a kind; special

*adv.* uniquely
*n.* uniqueness

*syn.* rare

He was presented with a *unique* opportunity to attend the conference.

His style of writing is *uniquely* his own.

## MATCHING

Choose the synonym.

1. confront
   - (A) astonish
   - (B) challenge
   - (C) petition
   - (D) forbid

2. obstruct
   - (A) warn
   - (B) tempt
   - (C) enhance
   - (D) block

3. intrigue
   - (A) fascinate
   - (B) elicit
   - (C) intensify
   - (D) enrich

4. substitute
   - (A) advantage
   - (B) replacement
   - (C) blockage
   - (D) frail

5. delicate
   - (A) ambiguous
   - (B) vital
   - (C) fragile
   - (D) resilient

6. convince
   - (A) assert
   - (B) persuade
   - (C) restore
   - (D) yield

7. rare
   - (A) determined
   - (B) ideal
   - (C) vague
   - (D) unique

8. shed
   - (A) discard
   - (B) refine
   - (C) alter
   - (D) cloud

9. enhance
   - (A) entice
   - (B) strengthen
   - (C) relinquish
   - (D) encourage

10. puzzled
    - (A) advanced
    - (B) assertive
    - (C) baffled
    - (D) astute

## LESSON 5—MULTIPLE-CHOICE TEST QUESTIONS

1. A newborn chick uses its egg tooth to break the shell of its egg and escape from it at hatching. This toothlike structure is then **shed** since its only use is to help the bird to break the eggshell. Some animals, such as lizards and snakes, develop a true tooth that projects outside the row of other teeth. This tooth helps adults to hatch their young.

   The word **shed** in the passage is closest in meaning to

   Ⓐ guarded
   Ⓑ preserved
   Ⓒ discarded
   Ⓓ replaced

2. Imitation gems are usually made of glass or plastics. In recent years, an enormous array of plastics has become available for imitations, but these materials are soft and lack the clarity present in real gemstones. Therefore, they are less satisfactory for the purpose than glass. Flint glasses, containing lead oxide, have higher refractive indices and therefore possess a **brilliance** not found in plastics. This makes flint glasses more suitable than plastic for imitation gems.

   The word **brilliance** in the passage is closest in meaning to

   Ⓐ radiance
   Ⓑ lightness
   Ⓒ enhancement
   Ⓓ appeal

3. During a shower, meteors appear to spread from a point in the sky, called the radiant. These radiant points give each shower its name. For example, the Perseids shower appears to radiate from the constellation Perseus. During the heaviest showers, 30 to 70 meteors may be seen every hour, but on **unique** occasions in a spectacular display, that number may be visible every second.

   The word **unique** in the passage is closest in meaning to

   Ⓐ intriguing
   Ⓑ amazing
   Ⓒ ideal
   Ⓓ rare

4. Sometimes, advertisers impact society by the use of advocacy ads, whose purpose is not to **persuade** the public to buy a product, but to change the public's view about a specific issue. Companies use this advertising to influence public opinion. Critics say that such ads are unfairly one-sided; advertisers say that the mass media have been equally one-sided in failing to report company views.

The word **persuade** in the passage is closest in meaning to

    Ⓐ   convince
    Ⓑ   dissuade
    Ⓒ   solicit
    Ⓓ   encourage

5. In the mid-1800s, gold and silver were common components of dentures. As a result, they were very expensive. In 1851 a process to harden the juices of certain tropical plants into vulcanized rubber was discovered. This new material could be molded against a model of the patient's mouth and artificial porcelain teeth could be attached. It allowed for the manufacture of less expensive dentures. Later, acrylic plastic became a **replacement** for the use of rubber and porcelain in denture construction.

The word **replacement** in the passage is closest in meaning to

    Ⓐ   a substitute
    Ⓑ   a market
    Ⓒ   an application
    Ⓓ   a material

6. The issue of where human life first arose has always been an **intriguing question** for science. Many guesses, or hypotheses, have been advanced, ranging from Asia to Europe. However, the oldest known human bones, or fossils, were discovered in East Africa in 1972. They are nearly 2 million years old. Their age was determined by measuring the age of the rocks surrounding them and comparing them to other fossils.

In stating that the origin of human life is an **intriguing question**, the author means that it

    Ⓐ   interests a lot of scientists.
    Ⓑ   can never be answered.
    Ⓒ   receives too much attention.
    Ⓓ   will always be a mystery.

## LESSON 5—COMPUTER-BASED TEST QUESTIONS

1. The Sioux and Cheyenne peoples warned outsiders not to look for gold on Indian land. Eventually, the Sioux and Cheyenne had to defend their land against a U.S. army force in the Battle of the Little Bighorn. This battle, also known as "Custer's Last Stand," was led by General George Custer. Custer was **cautioned** by his advisors not to underestimate the strength of his opponent, but ignored their advice, resulting in the defeat of the U.S. force.

   Find the word in the passage closest in meaning to the word **cautioned**.

2. Woven cotton cloth was the dominant material used for clothing among southwest native American populations. Brilliant costumes often reflected the social status of an individual. Body painting and tattooing; lip, ear, and nose plugs or rings; and bracelets, arm bands, necklaces, and head ornaments made of **bright** feathers were traditionally used by many groups to enhance beauty or to indicate status.

   Find the word in the passage closest in meaning to the word **bright**.

3. Image enhancement improves the clarity of images, perhaps for human viewing or as a step in an algorithm for machine vision. Removing clouded parts of the image, increasing contrast, and revealing details are examples of enhancement operations. For example, the image of the shipwreck under water might be of low contrast and somewhat **blurred**, but could be improved by reducing the blurring and increasing the contrast range.

   Find the word in the passage closest in meaning to the word **blurred**.

4. Species of alyssum are particularly suitable as edging plants for flower gardens. Alyssum is generally grayish and the plant produces yellow or white flowers. One popular species is sweet alyssum, a perennial that grows up to nine inches tall. The narrow, green-gray leaf of the sweet alyssum usually **bears** many silvery hairs.

   Find the word in the passage closest in meaning to the word **bears**.

5. In ancient times, the labyrinth was a structure composed of a complex series of passageways and chambers, probably at first designed to **baffle** enemies. A labyrinth either had branched paths with misleading ends designed to puzzle anyone inside, or it contained one long meandering path that led to a central end.

Find the word in the passage closest in meaning to the word **baffle**.

# LESSON 6

- chiefly - coarse - commonplace - comparatively
- complex - conventional - curious - exceedingly
- exclusively - immense - indeed - rigid - routinely
- sufficiently - visibly

---

**chiefly**
*adj.* chief

*adv.* the most important or most common
*syn.* mostly

Houses are made *chiefly* of wood products.
Corn is the *chief* crop of the Midwest.

**coarse**
*adv.* coarsely
*n.* coarseness

*adj.* not fine or smooth; not delicate
*syn.* rough

Sandpaper is an extremely *coarse* material.
Wool clothing has a certain *coarseness* in texture.

**commonplace**
*adj.* ordinary
*syn.* frequent

Soon it will be *commonplace* to see the person to whom you are talking on the phone.
Female lawyers are *commonplace* in the United States.

**comparatively**
*adj.* comparative
*v.* compare
*n.* comparison

*adv.* being measured or judged by comparison
*syn.* relatively

It was *comparatively* easy for him to learn baseball because he had been a cricket player.
If you *compare* algebra and trigonometry, you'll discover that algebra is less complex.

**complex**

*n.* complexity

*adj.* difficult to understand or explain; having many parts

*syn.* complicated

The businessmen astutely approached the *complex* production problem.

The universe has a *complexity* beyond comprehension.

**conventional**

*adv.* conventionally
*n.* convention

*adj.* following accepted rules or standards

*syn.* traditional

Professor Canfield agreed with the *conventional* theory about the origin of the Basque language.

To become integrated into a society, you must learn the *conventions* of that society.

✓**curious**

*adv.* curiously
*n.* curiosity

*adj.* odd or strange; eager to learn

*syn.* peculiar

A *curious* object was discovered in the remains.

Sally was *curiously* interested in the history of Alaska.

**exceedingly**

*v.* exceed
*n.* excess
*adj.* excessive
*adv.* excessively

*adv.* very; to an unusual degree

*syn.* extremely

In tropical zones, it is *exceedingly* hot and humid.

It is not safe to *exceed* the speed limit.

**exclusively**

*adj.* exclusive
*n.* exclusion
*v.* exclude

*adv.* no one else; nothing else; not shared with others

*syn.* restrictively

This room is used *exclusively* by the faculty.

They *excluded* everyone under 21 from the contest.

| **immense** | *adj.* extremely large |
| *adv.* immensely | *syn.* massive |
| *n.* immensity | |

From the mountaintop you can see the *immense* valley.

She was *immensely* interested in the idea of teaching a foreign language.

| **indeed** | *adv.* certainly; really; used to make a statement stronger |
| | *syn.* truly |

Did he *indeed* go to the infirmary?

It is very hot *indeed*.

| **rigid** | *adj.* not easy to bend; firm; inflexible |
| *adv.* rigidly | *syn.* stiff |

The teacher was very *rigid* in his ideas about class attendance.

He adhered *rigidly* to his opinions about marriage.

| **routinely** | *adv.* regularly; usually done |
| *adj.* routine | *syn.* ordinarily |
| *n.* routine | |

She *routinely* gets a physical examination.

It is *routine* for students to become homesick at times.

| **sufficiently** | *adv.* enough; in a satisfying manner |
| *n.* sufficiency | *syn.* adequately |
| *adj.* sufficient | |
| *v.* suffice | |

Jenny is *sufficiently* mature to make her own decisions.

Her income is *sufficient* for her needs.

| **visibly** | *adv.* can be seen |
| *adj.* visible | * power of imagination or wisdom, especially with regard to the future |
| *n.* vision* | |
| *v.* view | |
| *adj.* visionary* | *syn.* noticeably |

Ken was *visibly* upset about his performance evaluation.

Stars are more clearly *visible* on a clear fall evening.

85

## MATCHING

Choose the synonym.

1. stiff
   (A) delicate
   (B) agile
   (C) rigid
   (D) astute

2. traditional
   (A) arbitrary
   (B) astounding
   (C) conventional
   (D) frequent

3. indeed
   (A) truly
   (B) albeit
   (C) abroad
   (D) only

4. curious
   (A) apparent
   (B) brilliant
   (C) peculiar
   (D) enhanced

5. adequately
   (A) sufficiently
   (B) deceptively
   (C) intensely
   (D) amazingly

6. immense
   (A) abrupt
   (B) massive
   (C) ongoing
   (D) complicated

7. exceedingly
   (A) resiliently
   (B) extremely
   (C) assertively
   (D) resolutely

8. visibly
   (A) noticeably
   (B) frequently
   (C) persuasively
   (D) encouragingly

9. ordinarily
   (A) restrictively
   (B) coarsely
   (C) cautiously
   (D) routinely

10. restrictively
    (A) exclusively
    (B) adversely
    (C) roughly
    (D) relatively

## LESSON 6—MULTIPLE-CHOICE TEST QUESTIONS

1. North American trade patterns offer remarkable contrasts. Canada has a small population but with vast resources and high productivity. It has a low home consumption and depends on foreign trade more than any other developed country on the North American continent. The United States, on the other hand, has an **immense** domestic market and the highest per capita consumption of goods in the world. It depends mainly on trade within its national borders.

   The word **immense** in the passage is closest in meaning to

     Ⓐ   massive
     Ⓑ   successful
     Ⓒ   prominent
     Ⓓ   significant

2. Letters, reports, and documents can be easily prepared on personal computers, because the user can see on the monitor what the text will look like when printed. The task of writing is made even easier by programs that check spelling and grammar before printing. In addition, a wide range of fonts is now available, and their number is far greater than that of **conventional** printing processes. Because of progress in laser printer technology, text printed by a laser printer often rivals that of commercially typeset material.

   The word **conventional** in the passage is closest in meaning to

     Ⓐ   restricted
     Ⓑ   available
     Ⓒ   traditional
     Ⓓ   competing

3. Contour mapping is the process by which a map is formed by constructing lines of equal values of that property from available data points. For example, a topographic map reveals the relief of an area by means of contour lines that represent elevation. In addition to topography, there are examples of geophysical, geochemical, meteorological, sociological, and other variables that are **routinely** mapped by the method. The availability of plotting devices in recent years has permitted mapping by computer, which reduces the effect of human bias on the final product.

The word **routinely** in the passage is closest in meaning to

&#9398; ordinarily
&#9399; effectively
&#9400; sluggishly
&#9401; efficiently

4. Motion-picture technology is a **curious** blend of the old and the new. In much of the equipment, state-of-the-art digital electronics may be working with a mechanical system invented in 1895. Moreover, the technology of motion pictures is based not only on the invention of still photography but also on a combination of several more or less independent technologies: camera and projector design, film manufacture and processing, sound recording and reproduction, and lighting and light measurement.

The word **curious** in the passage is closest in meaning to

&#9398; productive
&#9399; peculiar
&#9400; coveted
&#9401; appealing

5. The durable surfacing of a road, airstrip, or similar area, is known as a pavement. Its primary function is to transmit loads to the sub-base and underlying soil. Modern flexible pavements contain sand and gravel or crushed stone. These are compacted with a binder of bituminous material, such as asphalt or tar. Such a pavement demonstrates enough plasticity to absorb shocks. **Rigid** pavements are made of concrete, composed of coarse and fine aggregate and portland cement, and usually reinforced with steel rod or mesh.

The word **rigid** in the passage is closest in meaning to

    (A) strong
    (B) stiff
    (C) pliable
    (D) complex

6. Research indicates that Internet use may cause a person's attention span to shorten. Some experts estimate that the habitual user's span can drop to as little as that of a goldfish, roughly nine seconds. Of course, attention depends as much on content as delivery. It is **comparatively easy** to switch off some images, but comparatively hard to abandon others. For example, computer games usually hold a user's attention longer than advertising.

In stating that it is **comparatively easy** to switch off some images, the author means that

    (A) all images or games are equally engaging.
    (B) some have less of a hold on a user's attention.
    (C) some even lengthen a user's attention span.
    (D) users never vary in their Internet preferences.

## LESSON 6—COMPUTER-BASED TEST QUESTIONS

1. Water is a powerful, intricate solvent that acts as a catalyst for many reactions. It also stores heat and cold well. In terms of its composition, water has an unusually high boiling and freezing point. It also shows unusual volume changes with temperature. Water is easily the most **complex** of all common substances that are single chemical compounds.

   Find the word in the passage closest in meaning to the word **complex**.

2. Contrary to popular opinion, the origin of the circus is **comparatively** recent, having little in common with ancient Roman circuses. It originated in 1768, when Philip Astley brought acts, including trick riding, juggling, tumbling, and even the exhibiting of wild animals together, and displayed them in a ring near London. This exhibition created this relatively new form of entertainment.

   Find the word in the passage closest in meaning to the word **comparatively**.

3. The cotton gin, invented by Eli Whitney, was **commonplace** on many nineteenth-century farms. Although patented in 1794, the ingenious design was imitated so much by others that Whitney gained only a modest financial reward from his simple invention. The cotton gin became a standard implement on most farms in the South.

   Find the word in the passage closest in meaning to the word **commonplace**.

4. The delicate look and feel of silk are deceptive. It is a strong, rough natural fiber, ranked in strength with synthetic nylon. To the naked eye, it appears to be smooth, but under the microscope, cultivated silk fiber looks **coarse**. It is the coolest of hot-weather fabrics, and it can absorb up to 30 percent of its weight in moisture without feeling wet.

   Find the word in the passage closest in meaning to the word **coarse**.

5.  Because up to five months of warm weather are required for adequate yields of the sweet potato, it is **chiefly** grown in the southern regions of the United States. The yam, frequently confused with the sweet potato, is mostly used as an ornamental vine in northern regions during the summer months.

    Find the word in the passage closest in meaning to the word **chiefly**.

# LESSON 7

■ appropriate ■ clarify ■ conceal ■ confirm ■ constantly
■ convenient ■ core ■ critical ■ distort ■ diverse
■ prosperous ■ purposefully ■ reveal ■ scarcely
■ theoretically

---

**appropriate**

*n.* appropriateness
*adv.* appropriately

*adj.* correct or good for the purpose

*syn.* proper

It is not *appropriate* to cheat on tests.

For the job interview she was dressed *appropriately* in a suit.

---

**clarify**

*n.* clarification

*v.* to make more easily understood; to make clear

*syn.* explain

Chapter 2 in the textbook *clarifies* the process of osmosis.

A *clarification* of the government's position on this matter is necessary.

---

**conceal**

*n.* concealment

*v.* to prevent from being seen or discovered

*syn.* hide

The students *concealed* their feelings about the course.

His *concealment* of the evidence made his case more difficult to prove.

---

**confirm**

*adj.* confirmed
*n.* confirmation

*v.* to make certain; give support

*syn.* prove

The director *confirmed* that the meeting would be on the tenth.

We have just received *confirmation* of your reservation on the flight to Los Angeles.

---

**constantly**

*adj.* constant

*adv.* in an unchanging manner; happening all the time

*syn.* continually

Philosophy *constantly* questions the nature of human existence.

The speed of light is *constant* at 186,000 miles a second.

**convenient**       *adj.*   easy to reach; near; suitable to one's needs

*adv.*   conveniently       *syn.*   practical
*n.*    convenience

The student union is *convenient* to the physical sciences building.

For the *convenience* of the student body, the library is located in a central location.

**core**       *adj.*   the central or most important part

*n.*    core       *syn.*   chief

The *core* of curriculum consists of courses that are required of all students.

They are loyal to the *core*.

**critical** ✓       *adj.*   very serious or unsafe; finding fault

*v.*    critique       *syn.*   dangerous
*n.*    criticism
*n.*    critic
*adv.*  critically

It is *critical* to follow the directions for the experiment exactly as the instructor indicates.

The runner accepted *criticism* from his coach very well.

**distort**       *v.*   to change from the original shape or

*adj.*   distorted           condition, usually in an unnatural way
*n.*    distortion
       *syn.*   deform

Time and space are *distorted* when traveling at the speed of light.

*Distortion* of the image from a microscope can be caused by low light.

**diverse**       *adj.*   various; distinct from others

*adv.*   diversely       *syn.*   different
*n.*    diversity
*v.*    diversify

Freud had many *diverse* interests in psychology.

The *diversity* of life forms on the earth makes zoology an interesting area of study.

**prosperous**

*adj.* successful, wealthy

*adv.* prosperously
*v.* prosper
*n.* prosperity

*syn.* thriving

In the early 1900s, San Francisco was a *prosperous* city.

Bacteria *prosper* under the proper conditions.

**purposefully**

*adv.* done for a special reason

*adj.* purposeful
*adv.* purposely
*n.* purpose

*syn.* deliberately

The course syllabus was designed *purposefully* to be easy to follow.

He was authorized to spend the money for business *purposes*.

**reveal**

*v.* to uncover; to expose

*adv.* revealingly
*adj.* revealing
*n.* revelation

*syn.* disclose

The president *revealed* some of his ideas before he gave his speech.

The report made some *revelations* about the nature of the conflict.

**scarcely**

*adv.* almost not

*adj.* scarce
*n.* scarcity

*syn.* hardly

The woman *scarcely* spoke a word of English.

Due to a *scarcity* of water, a rationing plan was established.

**theoretically**

*adv.* according to a reasoned, but not proven, point of view

*adj.* theoretical
*n.* theory
*v.* theorize

*syn.* hypothetically

His argument was *theoretically* appealing, but not realistic.

Leonardo da Vinci *theorized* that the earth was not the center of the universe.

## MATCHING

Choose the synonym.

1. deform
   - (A) hide
   - (B) distort
   - (C) amaze
   - (D) block

2. scarcely
   - (A) delicately
   - (B) visibly
   - (C) continually
   - (D) hardly

3. proper
   - (A) appropriate
   - (B) practical
   - (C) rigid
   - (D) complex

4. clarify
   - (A) shed
   - (B) enhance
   - (C) explain
   - (D) elicit

5. dangerous
   - (A) chief
   - (B) deceptive
   - (C) critical
   - (D) routine

6. thriving
   - (A) prosperous
   - (B) resilient
   - (C) convenient
   - (D) tolerable

7. purposefully
   - (A) comparatively
   - (B) deliberately
   - (C) constantly
   - (D) sufficiently

8. different
   - (A) noticeable
   - (B) diverse
   - (C) conventional
   - (D) curious

9. hypothetically
   - (A) exceedingly
   - (B) haphazardly
   - (C) theoretically
   - (D) routinely

10. reveal
    - (A) disclose
    - (B) baffle
    - (C) conceal
    - (D) confirm

## LESSON 7—MULTIPLE-CHOICE TEST QUESTIONS

1. The geologic history of the Earth **reveals** much information about the evolution of the continents, oceans, atmosphere, and biosphere. The layers of rock at Earth's surface contain evidence of the evolutionary processes these components underwent when each layer was formed. By studying this rock record from the beginning, it is possible to track their development through time.

   The word **reveals** in the passage is closest in meaning to

   - Ⓐ teaches
   - Ⓑ discloses
   - Ⓒ traces
   - Ⓓ donates

2. Day-to-day weather constitutes a major element of the environment and an important factor in human well-being and activity. Agriculture, animal husbandry, transportation, and public health and safety are all greatly influenced by weather. It is not surprising that one of humanity's oldest environment-related interests has been to manage the weather **purposefully**.

   The word **purposefully** in the passage is closest in meaning to

   - Ⓐ prosperously
   - Ⓑ constantly
   - Ⓒ exceedingly
   - Ⓓ deliberately

3. Illumination plays a great role in our psychological and physical well-being. Light can model objects or flatten them, reveal colors or **distort** them, provide a cheerful environment or a gloomy one. Glare and reflected glare can cause discomfort and reduce visibility. In addition to calculating illumination, a lighting engineer must deal with all of these problems through the choice of light sources and fixtures.

   The word **distort** in the passage is closest in meaning to

   - Ⓐ hide
   - Ⓑ accentuate
   - Ⓒ deform
   - Ⓓ highlight

4. The different appearance of animals is chiefly superficial; the **diverse** variety of known forms can be assorted among only a half-dozen basic body plans. These plans are established during the embryonic stages of development and limit the size and complexity of the animals. Symmetry, number, and development of tissue, presence, and nature of body cavities, and several aspects of early development define these fundamental plans of organization.

The word **diverse** in the passage is closest in meaning to

      Ⓐ  recognized
      Ⓑ  acknowledged
      Ⓒ  different
      Ⓓ  critical

5. When the settlers of the western United States abandoned their original log cabins, sod houses, and dugouts, they built small, wood-framed dwellings of one or two rooms without a basement. Rooms were usually added as **prosperous** families grew larger. This usually resulted in a series of large, open rooms laid end to end so that each would have an equal amount of sunlight.

The word **prosperous** in the passage is closest in meaning to

      Ⓐ  numerous
      Ⓑ  thriving
      Ⓒ  prominent
      Ⓓ  courageous

6. The medical profession is sometimes accused of being more interested in itself than the quality of care it delivers. Many patients feel they don't get the attention they deserve; many see the profession as selfish **to its core**. Doctors rarely agree, as a recent survey comparing their attitudes and that of the public shows. Seventy percent of the public were disappointed in the quality of care; only 35 percent of the doctors agreed.

In stating that the medical profession is selfish **to its core**, the author means that it

      Ⓐ  is entirely interested only in itself.
      Ⓑ  contains a group of bad doctors.
      Ⓒ  has wide support among patients.
      Ⓓ  includes good and bad physicians.

## LESSON 7—COMPUTER-BASED TEST QUESTIONS

1. Industrial cities appeared after the full development of industrial capitalism in the **core** nation-states of the eighteenth century. One of the central features of this industrial revolution was a dramatic increase in per capita production. This increase was made possible by the improved methods of manufacturing that were adopted by factories.

   Find the word in the passage closest in meaning to the word **core**.

2. The earliest complete calendars were probably based on lunar observations. But lunar years were not **convenient** for agricultural purposes. Therefore, to keep in step with the sun, lunar-solar calendars were formed by adding an additional "leap" month when the observation of crops made it seem necessary. Eventually the Gregorian civil calendar, a solar calendar that is calculated without reference to the moon, became the most popular and practical method of measuring years.

   Find the word in the passage closest in meaning to the word **convenient**.

3. All things consist of molecules, which are in continuous motion. Molecules are groups of atoms held together by chemical bonds. Each molecule of a given substance contains fixed numbers and kinds of atoms. In a chemical reaction, the formerly **constant** bonds are severed, and a rearrangement of atoms takes place to form new substances.

   Find the word in the passage closest in meaning to the word **constant**.

4. Mollusks have existed for some 500 million years, and about 10,000 extinct species are known. There are 350 or more living species of cephalopods from the Mollusk family. One of these is the cuttlefish. Fossil evidence **confirms** that the ancient cuttlefish has existed in its present form for more than 20 million years. When we compare the modern-day cuttlefish to the ancient fossils, we see evidence that proves that the well-developed head, the many arms, two gills, two kidneys, and three hearts of the contemporary cuttlefish were also present in the cuttlefish of long ago.

   Find the word in the passage closest in meaning to the word **confirms**.

5.  The first swimsuits **concealed** the shape of the human body. Over the decades, attitudes relaxed regarding the public display of one's body shape. Designers could move away from styles that hid the body and promote styles that revealed a body's physical attributes.

    Find the word in the passage closest in meaning to the word **concealed**.

# LESSON 8

■ accelerate ■ crack ■ create ■ creep ■ crush
■ cultivate ■ dictate ■ distinguish ■ flaw ■ harvest
■ mirror ■ obtain ■ particle ■ settle ■ transport

---

**accelerate**                    *v.* to go faster

*n.* acceleration          *syn.* hasten
*n.* accelerator

The action of molecules *accelerates* when they are heated.

The poor condition of the motor made *acceleration* difficult.

**crack**                          *n.* a thin opening caused by breaking; a flaw

*v.* crack                 *syn.* fracture

*Cracks* in the ice allowed for fishing.

The wall *cracked* due to poor construction.

**create**                         *v.* to cause something new to exist;  to make

*adj.* creative            *syn.* produce
*adv.* creatively
*n.* creation
*n.* creator
*n.* creativity
*n.* creativeness

Thomas Edison *created* numerous inventions.

Jonas Salk was an extremely *creative* scientist.

**creep**                          *v.* to move slowly and quietly close to the
*adj.* creeping                ground; to begin to happen

                           *syn.* crawl

Some mistakes are beginning to *creep* into his work.

Ivy is a *creeping* variety of plant.

**crush**

*adj.* crushing
*n.* crush

*v.* to press together so as to completely distort the shape or nature of the object

*syn.* grind

The machine *crushes* corn to produce cornmeal.

Passage of the legislation was a *crushing* blow to the president's program.

**cultivate**

*adj.* cultivated
*n.* cultivation

*v.* to plant and raise a crop; to encourage growth of a relationship or friendship

*syn.* grow

The professionals had common interests that allowed them to *cultivate* a working relationship with each other.

The *cultivation* of diverse crops in preColumbian America is well documented.

**dictate**

*adj.* dictatorial
*n.* dictator

*v.* to state demands with the power to enforce

*syn.* impose

The workers were not in a position to *dictate* demands to management.

His boss resembled a *dictator*.

**distinguish**

*adj.* distinguishable
*adj.* distinguished
*adj.* distinguishing

*v.* to hear, see, or recognize differences

*syn.* discriminate

Some people cannot *distinguish* colors well.

Anteaters are *distinguished* by their long noses.

**flaw**

*adj.* flawed

*n.* a small sign of damage that makes an item imperfect

*syn.* defect

There is a *flaw* in his theory.

They noticed that the contract was *flawed*.

**harvest**
adj.  harvested
v.  harvest

*n.*  the act of collecting a crop; the crops gathered

*syn.*  gather

The United States had a comparatively good grain *harvest* this year.

They were able to *harvest* the crop before the rain.

**mirror**
n.  mirror

*v.*  to show, as in a mirror

*syn.*  reflect

The results of the study *mirror* public opinion.

The strength of the economy is *mirrored* in the standard of living of the people.

**obtain**
adj.  obtainable

*v.*  to gain or secure something

*syn.*  gain

The university *obtained* a new particle accelerator.

The painting by Whistler was not *obtainable*.

**particle**

*n.*  a very small piece of something

*syn.*  fragment

*Particles* of dust can destroy electronic instruments.

Small *particles* of matter hold the keys to understanding the origin of life.

**settle**
adj.  settled
n.  settlement

*v.*  to establish a home; to resolve a disagreement

*syn.*  colonize

People arriving from the south *settled* in California.

The lawyers *settled* their differences and came to an agreement.

**transport**
adj.  transportable
adj.  transported
n.  transportation

*v.*  to move from one place to another

*syn.*  carry

Flying is not always the fastest way to *transport* passengers to their destination.

The *transportation* expenses of products increase the final cost of the item.

## MATCHING

Choose the synonym.

1. flaw
   (A) particle
   (B) agile
   (C) defect
   (D) creation

2. dictate
   (A) transport
   (B) create
   (C) grow
   (D) impose

3. hasten
   (A) crawl
   (B) crush
   (C) conceal
   (D) accelerate

4. crop
   (A) harvest
   (B) advice
   (C) mirror
   (D) settlement

5. fragment
   (A) authorization
   (B) particle
   (C) cultivation
   (D) advantage

6. transport
   (A) reveal
   (B) carry
   (C) clarify
   (D) restore

7. obtain
   (A) gain
   (B) allow
   (C) baffle
   (D) assert

8. discriminate
   (A) enhance
   (B) persuade
   (C) distinguish
   (D) distort

9. reflect
   (A) mirror
   (B) confirm
   (C) produce
   (D) grind

10. colonize
    (A) crawl
    (B) cultivate
    (C) replace
    (D) settle

## LESSON 8—MULTIPLE-CHOICE TEST QUESTIONS

1. Testing metals for quality assurance can be accomplished by several methods. One common nondestructive technique, used to locate surface cracks and **flaws** in metals, employs a penetrating liquid. Normally this fluid is brightly dyed or fluorescent. After being spread over the surface of the material, it soaks into any tiny cracks. The liquid is cleaned off, allowing cracks and blemishes to be easily seen.

   The word **flaws** in the passage is closest in meaning to

   Ⓐ bends
   Ⓑ defects
   Ⓒ cavities
   Ⓓ dents

2. An important task of management is to motivate individual workers to coordinate their collective efforts to achieve an organization's goals. The concepts and methods used to structure work and to design organizations have changed considerably. An organization's age can often be predicted by the way work is structured. Work practices tend to **reflect** the organization's design theory present at the time the organization was founded.

   The word **reflect** in the passage is closest in meaning to

   Ⓐ influence
   Ⓑ mirror
   Ⓒ cultivate
   Ⓓ accelerate

3. The Mayflower Compact was a document signed by 41 of the male passengers on the Mayflower before their landing at Plymouth, Massachusetts. The passengers, concerned that some members of the company might leave the group and **settle** on their own, created the document. The Mayflower Compact created a political body whose purpose was to form a government. Those who signed pledged to abide by any future laws and regulations.

   The word **settle** in the passage is closest in meaning to

   Ⓐ enlist
   Ⓑ move
   Ⓒ linger
   Ⓓ colonize

4. Before the invention of electroacoustic equipment that generates and measures sound, the available hearing tests gave approximate results in the best cases. A person's hearing could be explained in terms of the ability to **distinguish** between the ticking of a watch and the clicking of coins or to determine the distance at which conversational speech or a whispered voice could no longer be understood.

The word **distinguish** in the passage is closest in meaning to

- Ⓐ discriminate
- Ⓑ listen
- Ⓒ clarify
- Ⓓ conceal

5. When DNA is subjected to restriction-enzyme activity, **fragments** of various sizes are formed. This process reveals a unique pattern of restriction-enzyme DNA. This specific DNA pattern found in each human genetic lineage is unique, because each person, except for identical twins, is formed from different combinations of the genetic material from two family lines. The pattern of sizes of the DNA from an individual is unique and can serve as a "DNA fingerprint" of that person.

The word **fragments** in the passage is closest in meaning to

- Ⓐ growths
- Ⓑ modifications
- Ⓒ flaws
- Ⓓ particles

6. The invention of the airplane was a **crushing blow** for proponents of hot air ballooning. Early advocates of ballooning such as Jean-Pierre Blanchard and John Jeffries thought it would transform international travel. Instead, the cost of launching a balloon, the problem of controlling a balloon in high winds, and the instant attractiveness of more stable airplane travel have kept ballooning from becoming more than a hobby for a limited number of wealthy adventurers.

In stating that the airplane's invention was a **crushing blow** for proponents of ballooning, the author means that it

- Ⓐ led directly to the invention of the airplane.
- Ⓑ caught on immediately among the public.
- Ⓒ promoted hot air ballooning internationally.
- Ⓓ kept ballooning from becoming more popular.

## LESSON 8—COMPUTER-BASED TEST QUESTIONS

1. Farming continues to be an important activity on the eastern shore of Maryland. The eastern shore specializes in chickens for urban markets along the East Coast. Although market vegetables are also grown for the same urban markets, corn and soybeans continue to be the two most important crops **cultivated** on Maryland's eastern shore.

   Find the word in the passage closest in meaning to the word **cultivated**.

2. The earliest mills were hand-powered devices used to grind grain. Querns, which have been used for centuries to **crush** grains, are examples of such milling devices. A quern has an upper grinding stone with a handle. This handle rotates inside another stone that contains the grain.

   Find the word in the passage closest in meaning to the word **crush**.

3. From the core mouth on the underside of the starfish, channels with two or four rows of tube feet radiate outward along the arms. A hydraulic system that allows the starfish to crawl is connected to the tube feet. These rows of suctionlike feet enable the starfish to feed on mollusks and to **creep** along the ocean floor.

   Find the word in the passage closest in meaning to the word **creep**.

4. The economic depression that plagued the United States in the 1930s was unique in its size and its consequences. During the worst period of the depression, in 1933, one in every four American workers was out of a job. The poor business environment **created** an unprecedented lack of confidence in the economy. The great industrial slump produced extreme hardship throughout the world that persisted throughout the 1930s.

   Find the word in the passage closest in meaning to the word **created**.

5. Opals are popular, porous gemstones that lose their color and may develop **cracks** if allowed to dry out. The vivid colors of the opal are produced by slight impurities or small fractures in the stone. A popular example of the opal is the water opal. This opal is clear and iridescent. The most valuable of all opals is the black opal, which is widely recognized as the finest example of this class of gemstone.

Find the word in the passage closest in meaning to the word **cracks**.

# LESSON 9

■ accurate ■ classify ■ currency ■ deep ■ dense
■ depend on ■ dim ■ display ■ exports ■ gigantic
■ impressive ■ lasting ■ treasury ■ uniform ■ vibrant

---

**accurate**

*adv.* accurately
*n.* accuracy

*adj.* careful and exact

*syn.* precise

She was able to make *accurate* observations with the new telescope.
Experiments must be conducted with *accuracy*.

**classify**

*adj.* classified
*n.* classification

*v.* to place into groups according to type

*syn.* arrange

Biologists *classify* life forms into many phylla.
The library's catalog is a *classification* of books in the library.

**currency**

*n.* monetary unit

*syn.* money

The purchase must be paid for in the national *currency*.
The French *currency* is gaining strength.

**deep**

*adv.* deeply
*n.* depth
*v.* deepen

*adj.* far below the surface; complete understanding

*syn.* thorough

Lake Baikal is the *deepest* lake in the world.
The *depth* of his understanding of math is remarkable.

**dense**

*adv.* densely
*n.* density

*adj.* closely packed or crowded; difficult to see through

*syn.* thick

The boating accident was caused by the *dense* fog.
Hong Kong is one of the most *densely* populated cities in the world.

**depend on**          *v.*  to count on; to be supported by

*adv.*  dependably      *syn.*  trust
*adj.*  dependable
  *n.*  dependance
  *n.*  dependency
  *n.*  dependent

The farmers *depend on* rain to produce a good harvest.

His *dependency* on alcohol destroyed his marriage.

**dim**          *adj.*  not bright or clear

*adv.*  dimly      *syn.*  faint
  *v.*  dim
  *n.*  dimness

The light was too *dim* for studying.

The stars *dimly* lit the evening sky.

**display**          *v.*  to show; reveal

  *n.*  display      *syn.*  exhibit

The model *displayed* the details of the human hand.

The candidate's *display* of anger was unfortunate.

**exports**          *n.*  products sold abroad

*adj.*  exported      *syn.*  foreign sales
  *v.*  export

Until recently the United States' *exports* exceeded its imports.

*Exported* goods are usually high in quality.

**gigantic**          *adj.*  very large

*adv.*  gigantically      *syn.*  enormous

Reaching the moon was a *gigantic* step in space exploration for mankind.

New methods of farming offer *gigantic* advantages over the old methods.

**impressive**          *adj.*  causing admiration because of an object's importance, size, or quality

*adv.*  impressively
  *v.*  impress      *syn.*  imposing
  *n.*  impression

Lincoln's power of persuasion was *impressive*.

Everyone left with a good *impression* of the play.

**lasting**

*v.* last

*adj.* forever; without end

*syn.* enduring

Kennedy left a *lasting* impression on the people who heard his inaugural address.

The introduction of robots will have a *lasting* effect on industry.

**treasury**

*adj.* treasured
*v.* treasure

*n.* the agency that controls and spends money; a collection of valued things

*syn.* bank

The *treasury* was under pressure to lower interest rates.

Encyclopedias are a *treasury* of information.

**uniform**

*adv.* uniformly
*n.* uniformity

*adj.* every part being the same

*syn.* consistent

Bread has a *uniform* texture.

The grades on the test were *uniformly* poor.

**vibrant**

*adv.* vibrantly
*n.* vibrance

*adj.* lively; powerful; full of action; bright

*syn.* brilliant

His *vibrant* personality made him well liked by everyone.

The *vibrance* of the city is attractive to many individuals.

**MATCHING**

Choose the synonym.

1. enormous
   - (A) prosperous
   - (B) appropriate
   - (C) gigantic
   - (D) classified

2. foreign sales
   - (A) flaws
   - (B) money
   - (C) treasury
   - (D) exports

3. vibrant
   - (A) brilliant
   - (B) critical
   - (C) paint
   - (D) deep

4. depend on
   - (A) distort
   - (B) trust
   - (C) settle
   - (D) conceal

5. imposing
   - (A) impressive
   - (B) creative
   - (C) intriguing
   - (D) ambiguous

6. uniform
   - (A) rigid
   - (B) diverse
   - (C) complex
   - (D) consistent

7. bank
   - (A) fragment
   - (B) treasury
   - (C) export
   - (D) advent

8. lasting
   - (A) enduring
   - (B) enriching
   - (C) energetic
   - (D) enhancing

9. precise
   - (A) accurate
   - (B) gigantic
   - (C) thick
   - (D) prosperous

10. classify
   - (A) trust
   - (B) learn
   - (C) create
   - (D) arrange

## LESSON 9—MULTIPLE-CHOICE TEST QUESTIONS

1. Written by Adam Smith in 1776, *The Wealth of Nations* is a **vibrant** attack against mercantilism and one of the most influential books ever written on economics. One of its main ideas is that when people pursue their own selfish interests, society as a whole benefits. Competition, rather than private or government monopoly, should regulate prices and wages. He also postulated that competition produces socially beneficial consequences and that government should not interfere with market forces.

   The word **vibrant** in the passage is closest in meaning to

   Ⓐ critical
   Ⓑ brilliant
   Ⓒ intriguing
   Ⓓ gigantic

2. Despite its weaknesses and inner conflicts, the humanistic movement was heroic in its scope and energy, and exceptional in its aspirations. For human development in all fields, it created a context of seldom-equaled fertility. Its characteristic modalities of thought, speech, and vision lent themselves to induce the genius of humankind and became the media for **enduring** achievement.

   The word **enduring** in the passage is closest in meaning to

   Ⓐ trivial
   Ⓑ spectacular
   Ⓒ significant
   Ⓓ lasting

3. The **gigantic**, intricately formed chasm of the Grand Canyon contains a great many impressive peaks, canyons, and ravines between its outer walls. The canyon includes a number of side canyons and surrounding plateaus. The deepest and most impressively beautiful section is within Grand Canyon National Park, which encompasses the Colorado River's length from Lake Powell to Lake Mead.

   The word **gigantic** in the passage is closest in meaning to

   Ⓐ deep
   Ⓑ wide
   Ⓒ enormous
   Ⓓ thrilling

4. The unified classical architectural style of the 1893 World's Columbian Exposition buildings proved to be the most **impressive** and influential style of its time. A committee of East Coast architects and firms gathered in December 1890 to plan the fair buildings. The collective result was the construction of a group of 150 buildings known as the White City. Their design established white, columnar architecture as the only acceptable public style in the United States for 40 years thereafter.

The word **impressive** in the passage is closest in meaning to

        (A) imposing
        (B) influential
        (C) massive
        (D) enduring

5. *Maclean's,* a semimonthly news magazine published in Toronto, has earned a reputation for its **depth** of coverage of Canada's national affairs and of North American and world news from a Canadian perspective. This coverage, along with its reputation for outstanding photography, has made it Canada's leading magazine. Founded in 1905, it has consistently featured articles and fiction reflecting a conservative view of Canadian life and values.

The word **depth** in the passage is closest in meaning to

        (A) breadth
        (B) techniques
        (C) consistency
        (D) thoroughness

6. The Netherlands is the most **densely populated** country in the European Union. It has 460 inhabitants per square kilometer. By comparison, the United Kingdom has 240 inhabitants and Italy, 195. However, many European countries are agricultural, and their populations are unevenly distributed. For example, Paris has 20,000 inhabitants per square kilometer, while many parts of the rest of the country contain fewer than 20 people per square kilometer.

In stating that the Netherlands is **densely populated**, the author means that its

        (A) people are very unevenly distributed.
        (B) population is the largest in Europe.
        (C) population is the largest per square kilometer.
        (D) cities are the largest cities in Europe.

## LESSON 9—COMPUTER-BASED TEST QUESTIONS

1. In the field of artificial intelligence, scientists are studying methods for developing computer programs that **display** aspects of intelligent behavior. Research into all aspects of artificial intelligence is vigorous. However, some researchers doubt that artificial intelligence can truly exhibit forms of intelligent behavior like that observed in intelligent living organisms. Indeed, artificial intelligence programs are simple when compared to the intuitive reasoning and induction capabilities of the human brain.

   Find the word in the passage closest in meaning to the word **display.**

2. Early astronomers noted many faint patches of light. They called these nebulae. These objects baffled early astronomers, and their true nature was a subject of great controversy. Later, in 1924, it was discovered that the **dim** nebulae consisted of at least four different kinds of objects: distant clusters of stars, planetary nebulae, glowing, asymmetric-shaped gas clouds, and expansive galaxies.

   Find the word in the passage closest in meaning to the word **dim.**

3. Canadian thistle is a bothersome North American weed that grows in thick clusters. However, some species such as the Scotch, or cotton thistle, which have **dense** heads of small pink or purple flowers, can make attractive garden plants and are widely cultivated for ornamental purposes throughout the Northeast.

   Find the word in the passage closest in meaning to the word **dense.**

4. The Sun is the only star known to be accompanied by an extensive planetary system. However, a few nearby stars are now known to be encircled by particles of undetermined size; this opens the strong, unproven, hypothesis that the universe is filled with many solar systems. No **deep** understanding of the Solar System can be achieved without a thorough appreciation of the basic properties of the Sun.

   Find the word in the passage closest in meaning to the word **deep.**

5. An exchange rate is the rate at which one country's money may be exchanged for that of another. Exchange rates have been governed in recent years primarily by the forces of supply and demand. The value of a nation's **currency** normally changes, depending upon the strength of its economy and its trade balance.

   Find the word in the passage closest in meaning to the word **currency.**

# LESSON 10

■ distinct ■ dominant ■ dormant ■ drab ■ dramatic
■ elaborate ■ exceptional ■ hazardous ■ minuscule
■ prime ■ rudimentary ■ sensitive ■ superficial
■ terrifying ■ vigorous

---

**distinct**

*adv.* distinctly
*adj.* distinctive
*n.* distinction

*adj.* clearly noticed; different

*syn.* definite

There was a *distinct* aroma of coffee in the restaurant.

The two theories are *distinctly* different from each other.

**dominant**

*adv.* dominantly
*v.* dominate
*n.* domination

*adj.* primary or principal; having or exercising control over something

*syn.* major

The *dominant* life forms of the Paleozoic era lived in the water.

The skyscraper *dominated* the skyline.

**dormant**

*n.* dormitory

*adj.* not growing or producing; asleep

*syn.* inactive

The volcano had been *dormant* for hundreds of years before the eruption last month.

The seniors live in the new *dormitory*.

**drab**

*adv.* drably
*n.* drabness

*adj.* lacking color; uninteresting, boring

*syn.* colorless

Their clothing was quite *drab*.

The *drabness* of the desert made driving less interesting.

**dramatic**

*adv.* dramatically
*v.* dramatize
*n.* drama

*adj.* something that captures the imagination; exciting

*syn.* emotional

The *dramatic* finish to the game left us speechless.
The hurricane *dramatically* changed the coastline.

**elaborate**

*adv.* elaborately
*v.* elaborate
*n.* elaboration

*adj.* something with a large number of parts; full of details

*syn.* complex

An *elaborate* head dress indicated rank within the Aztec community.
His *elaboration* of the issue was quite thorough.

**exceptional**

*adv.* exceptionally

*adj.* unusual in a positive way

*syn.* phenomenal

The orchestra's performance was *exceptional*.
The North Star is *exceptionally* bright.

**hazardous**

*adv.* hazardously
*n.* hazard

*adj.* very risky, unsafe

*syn.* dangerous

Handling flammable liquids is *hazardous*.
There are many *hazards* involved with starting a business.

**minuscule**

*adj.* minute
*n.* minutia

*adj.* of little consequence; very small

*syn.* tiny

The sale of the building had a *minuscule* effect on the profits of the corporation.
Some leaves are covered with *minute* hairs.

**prime**

*adj.* primed
*adj.* prime*
*n.* prime

*v.* to make ready;
* first in importance or in time

*syn.* prepare

The directors *primed* the actors before the performance.
Mozart passed away in the *prime* of his life.

**rudimentary**      *adj.*   simple; not complex

  *n.*   rudiment        *syn.*   basic

He has a *rudimentary* knowledge of computers.

The *rudiments* of grammar are taught in all English classes.


**sensitive**      *adj.*   fast to show the effect of something

  *adv.*   sensitively        *syn.*   delicate
    *n.*   sensitivity

Film varies according to its *sensitivity* to light.

This equipment is very *sensitive* to changes in temperature.


**superficial**      *adj.*   simple; not deep; near the surface

  *adv.*   superficially        *syn.*   shallow

The inspector determined that the crack in the bridge was only *superficial.*

You should not try to answer the question *superficially.*


**terrifying**      *adj.*   filled with fear

  *adv.*   terrifyingly        *syn.*   frightening
    *v.*   terrify

To be in a violent storm is a *terrifying* experience.

They are *terrified* by dogs.


**vigorous**      *adj.*   powerful, full of action

  *adv.*   vigorously        *syn.*   strong
    *n.*   vigor

His *vigorous* defense of the issues impressed everyone.

He approached his work with *vigor.*

**MATCHING**

Choose the synonym.

1. exceptional
   - (A) dominant
   - (B) dense
   - (C) phenomenal
   - (D) acceptable

2. terrify
   - (A) distort
   - (B) frighten
   - (C) challenge
   - (D) settle

3. prepare
   - (A) create
   - (B) display
   - (C) depend
   - (D) prime

4. delicate
   - (A) vibrant
   - (B) distinct
   - (C) diverse
   - (D) sensitive

5. dangerous
   - (A) hazardous
   - (B) rigid
   - (C) commonplace
   - (D) intolerable

6. elaborate
   - (A) gigantic
   - (B) impressive
   - (C) complex
   - (D) dramatic

7. minuscule
   - (A) tiny
   - (B) dim
   - (C) drab
   - (D) major

8. superficial
   - (A) emotional
   - (B) lasting
   - (C) shallow
   - (D) curious

9. rudimentary
   - (A) dormant
   - (B) ideal
   - (C) basic
   - (D) arbitrary

10. vigorous
   - (A) dominant
   - (B) convenient
   - (C) uniform
   - (D) strong

**LESSON 10—MULTIPLE-CHOICE TEST QUESTIONS**

1. The development of centralized governments was not accompanied by centralized responsibility for road maintenance. One important development in the construction and maintenance of public transportation systems was the establishment of turnpike trusts. Entrepreneurs would join together to obtain government permission to take over a length of road for 21 years or build a new one and pay for its maintenance by collecting tolls. However, in its early years, road engineering was **rudimentary**, and many trusts did not know how to preserve the roads.

   The word **rudimentary** in the passage is closest in meaning to

           Ⓐ   elaborate
           Ⓑ   advanced
           Ⓒ   flawed
           Ⓓ   basic

2. Language is a system of communication specific to the human race. It is primarily oral-aural, since all naturally evolved large-scale linguistic systems have orderly patterns of sound produced by the human voice and perceived and processed by the ear. Despite the great variety of languages spoken throughout the world and the **superficial** differences among them, most linguists agree that all languages are essentially similar in structure and function.

   The word **superficial** in the passage is closest in meaning to

           Ⓐ   certain
           Ⓑ   frightening
           Ⓒ   exceptional
           Ⓓ   shallow

3. The layers of volatile gases and liquids near and above the surface of the Earth are of **prime** importance, along with solar energy, to the maintaining of life on Earth. They are distributed and recycled throughout the relatively thin atmosphere of the Earth. This atmosphere is a mixture of gases, primarily nitrogen and oxygen. However, the atmosphere also contains much smaller amounts of gases such as argon, carbon dioxide, methane, and water vapor along with minute solid and liquid particles in suspension.

The word **prime** in the passage is closest in meaning to

     Ⓐ  chief
     Ⓑ  dubious
     Ⓒ  superficial
     Ⓓ  dramatic


4. Avoidance is the most common form of defense in reptiles. At the first sign of danger, most snakes and lizards slither or dart away under cover; turtles and crocodiles plunge out of sight into water. But, in cases where danger presents itself abruptly and flight may be **hazardous**, reptiles may attack.

The word **hazardous** in the passage is closest in meaning to

     Ⓐ  futile
     Ⓑ  dangerous
     Ⓒ  arbitrary
     Ⓓ  unacceptable


5. As the Industrial Revolution developed in the nineteenth century, the era of wooden-hulled sailing ships gave way to that of steam-powered iron ships. **Phenomenal** changes took place in nearly every facet of ship design and operation. By the mid-1800s, these changes caused the end of the majestic wooden-hulled ship line. Despite its demise, another half century would elapse before it was clear what form its replacement would take.

The word **phenomenal** in the passage is closest in meaning to

     Ⓐ  vigorous
     Ⓑ  definite
     Ⓒ  exceptional
     Ⓓ  debilitating

6.  Research suggests that musical ability is genetic. Twins have the same genetic makeup. Therefore, researchers asked more than 500 children to sing along with recorded popular songs and discovered that 80 percent were equally able or unable to duplicate the melody. These results support the claim that musical talent is inherited—many children have some talent, but few are **exceptionally talented**, and only they have any hope of becoming concert pianists.

In stating that few children are **exceptionally talented**, the author means that

        Ⓐ   musical ability is evenly distributed.
        Ⓑ   almost everyone should study music.
        Ⓒ   the most talented are few in number.
        Ⓓ   twins cannot sing along with a song.

## LESSON 10—COMPUTER-BASED TEST QUESTIONS

1.  In the social sciences, conflict theory refers to the theoretical approach that views social phenomena as the result of emotional conflict between individuals or groups. Conflict theory has developed at both micro and macro levels. Since much of the documented behavior is **dramatic** and unpredictable, theories of such behavior are more evaluative than analytic.

    Find the word in the passage closest in meaning to the word **dramatic.**

2.  Feathers, whether brilliant or colorless, serve as an adaptable cover for the body of a bird. They form a smooth surface that reduces friction with the air, and they furnish flexible strong wings for flight and tails for steering. Feathers also act as superb insulation to conserve body heat and are relatively waterproof. Many songbirds in temperate zones reveal a **drab** plumage during the winter, in contrast to their brilliant springtime mating plumage.

    Find the word in the passage closest in meaning to the word **drab.**

3.  Most seeds remain inactive during a cold or dry season and grow into a plant when growing conditions are favorable. Seeds are also the primary dispersal agent of plants. Depending on the structure of the plant, angiosperms may be dispersed as seeds or as part of a fruit. They are often **dormant** at the time that they are shed by their parents.

    Find the word in the passage closest in meaning to the word **dormant.**

4.  Comic books began as collections of newspaper comic strips and took on a life of their own in the 1930s. The favorite reading matter of several generations of children, the major comic books dealt with heroic characters who fought crime or terror. The newspaper strip and the comic book represent the **dominant** graphic mythology of the twentieth century.

    Find the word in the passage closest in meaning to the word **dominant.**

5. The vast majority of animals exhibit a **distinct** symmetrical form, therefore making form a fundamental, representative characteristic for most animals. All animals with a bilateral symmetry, those that have a definite right and left side and a front and rear end, are classified together as Bilateria, a division of multicellular animals. Bilateria contrast with multicellular animals, which have a radial symmetry. An example is the jellyfish, which has no definite right or left sides.

Find the word in the passage closest in meaning to the word **distinct.**

# LESSON 11

■ amenity ■ destroy ■ disperse ■ dwelling ■ element
■ elementary ■ eliminate ■ emphasize ■ encircle
■ erratic ■ exaggerate ■ mention ■ pier ■ prevalent
■ release

| | |
|---|---|
| **amenity** | *n.* something that makes life easier or more enjoyable |
| | *syn.* convenience |

She had all the *amenities* of home when she went camping.

One expects many *amenities* at a five-star hotel.

| | |
|---|---|
| **destroy** | *v.* to put an end to the existence of something |
| *adj.* destructive | |
| *adv.* destructively | *syn.* ruin |
| *n.* destructiveness | |
| *n.* destruction | |
| *n.* destroyer | |

The factory was *destroyed* by the fire.

The *destruction* of the old landmark was opposed by a concerned group of citizens.

| | |
|---|---|
| **disperse** | *v.* to cause to move in many different directions |
| *adj.* dispersed | |
| | *syn.* circulate |

The high winds and rain *dispersed* the crowd.

After the hurricane, *dispersed* belongings cluttered the street.

| | |
|---|---|
| **dwelling** | *n.* where people live |
| *n.* dweller | *syn.* house |
| *v.* dwell | |

Cavelike *dwellings* have been discovered throughout the world.

City *dwellers* often have trouble adjusting to life in the country.

**element**
*adj.* elemental
*n.* element*

*n.* a part of the whole
   * environment
*syn.* component

City dwellers are out of their *element* in the country.

Hard work and perseverance are the basic *elements* of success.

**elementary**

*adj.* simple in structure, easy to do
*syn.* primary

The solution to the problem was actually quite *elementary*.

You must take *Elementary* Physics before you can enroll in the advanced course.

**eliminate**
*adj.* eliminated
*n.* elimination

*v.* to remove, free oneself of something
*syn.* delete

Mistakes must be *eliminated* before you hand in a term paper.

The *elimination* of the runner from the race was decided by the judge.

**emphasize**
*adv.* emphatically
*adj.* emphatic
*n.* emphasis

*v.* to show that something is especially important or exceptional
*syn.* highlight

The professor *emphasized* certain aspects of the historical period.

When asked if they would like to leave class early, the students answered with an *emphatic* "yes."

**encircle**
*adj.* encircled

*v.* to make a circle around
*syn.* surround

The players *encircled* their coach after winning the big game.

The *encircled* celebrity actually became afraid of her fans.

**erratic**
*adv.* erratically

*adj.* no regular pattern in thinking or movement; changeable without reason
*syn.* inconsistent

The artist's paintings have an *erratic* quality, some being excellent, and others mediocre.

The unstable chemical reacted *erratically*.

**exaggerate**      *v.*  to make something more than what it is

*adj.*  exaggerated      *syn.*  overstate
  *n.*   exaggeration

The federal government *exaggerated* the success of its programs.

To say that his business is successful would be a slight *exaggeration.*

**mention**      *v.*  to say;  relate in written form

*adj.*  mentioned      *syn.*  remark
  *n.*   mention

Theatergoers often *mention* that they enjoy watching movies on a large screen.

The book *mentioned* above was included in the bibliography that was handed out in class last  week.

**pier**      *n.*  a place where boats arrive to take on or land cargo and passengers

      *syn.*  dock

The submarine arrived at the *pier* on time.

The goods were unload onto the *pier.*

**prevalent**      *adj.*  existing widely or commonly

  *n.*   prevalence      *syn.*  commonplace

Comfortable Trade Winds are *prevalent* in the Caribbean islands.

There is a *prevalence* of disease where poor sanitation conditions exist.

**release**      *v.*  to allow to come out; to give freedom

  *n.*   release      *syn.*  free

A new movie was just *released.*

The *release* of the records was expected today.

## MATCHING

Choose the synonym.

1. amenity
   (A) advice
   (B) convenience
   (C) element
   (D) emphasis

2. ruin
   (A) destroy
   (B) conform
   (C) forbid
   (D) baffle

3. mention
   (A) surround
   (B) remark
   (C) assert
   (D) clarify

4. emphasize
   (A) frighten
   (B) highlight
   (C) delete
   (D) persuade

5. exaggerate
   (A) impress
   (B) dominate
   (C) elaborate
   (D) overstate

6. disperse
   (A) circulate
   (B) classify
   (C) distort
   (D) encircle

7. release
   (A) free
   (B) replace
   (C) settle
   (D) block

8. inconsistent
   (A) destructive
   (B) emphatic
   (C) circulated
   (D) erratic

9. commonplace
   (A) elementary
   (B) rudimentary
   (C) prevalent
   (D) uniform

10. pier
    (A) depth
    (B) crack
    (C) dock
    (D) prime

## LESSON 11—MULTIPLE-CHOICE TEST QUESTIONS

1. Kapok is made from the silky fiber that **encircles** the seeds of the tropical silk-cotton tree. This dense mat of cottony fibers surrounds each seed within the fruit. However, unlike cotton fibers, kapok fibers do not lend themselves to spinning. Since they are water resistant and buoyant, kapok fibers were extensively used for padding and insulation until the development of synthetic fibers.

   The word **encircles** in the passage is closest in meaning to

   - Ⓐ  releases
   - Ⓑ  circulates
   - Ⓒ  surrounds
   - Ⓓ  disperses

2. Lewis and Clark's expedition's central objective, the discovery of the "water communication," was not realized. However, a huge blank space on the map of North America had been filled as a result of the expedition. The rumor and myth related to the American West had been **eliminated** and new knowledge about the Wild West was made known to the American people.

   The word **eliminated** in the passage is closest in meaning to

   - Ⓐ  released
   - Ⓑ  circulated
   - Ⓒ  deleted
   - Ⓓ  exaggerated

3. The most **elementary** type of convection can be explained by the fact that heat rises. Convection currents permit buildings to be heated without the use of circulatory devices. The heated air moves solely by gravity. In the atmosphere, convection causes the wind to blow. Most severe weather conditions, such as tornadoes, result from particularly sharp convection currents.

   The word **elementary** in the passage is closest in meaning to

   - Ⓐ  dispersed
   - Ⓑ  erratic
   - Ⓒ  prevalent
   - Ⓓ  primary

4. The key **element** of the air conditioner is a fluorocarbon refrigerant that flows constantly through the conditioner's mechanisms. It becomes a liquid and gives off heat when it is compressed, and becomes a gas and absorbs heat when the pressure is removed. The mechanisms that evaporate and compress the refrigerant are divided into two areas, one on the interior, which includes an air filter, fan, and cooling coil, and one on the exterior, which includes a compressor, condenser coil, and fan.

The word **element** in the passage is closest in meaning to

        Ⓐ   amenity
        Ⓑ   component
        Ⓒ   purpose
        Ⓓ   advantage

5. A common inhabitant of the southwest United States, the prairie dog lives in groups called coteries. A breeding coterie contains one male, one to four females, and the young of the past two years. Several coteries form large groups called wards, which are determined by the structure of the terrain. The wards in turn are united into towns—complex **dwellings** of interconnecting burrows and many entrances. The towns may cover as many as 65 to 160 acres, which contain thousands of individuals.

The word **dwellings** in the passage is closest in meaning to

        Ⓐ   abodes
        Ⓑ   systems
        Ⓒ   tunnels
        Ⓓ   shifts

6. The sport utility vehicle, or SUV, is the most popular type of automobile in the United States today. SUVs are spacious, powerful, and rugged; they have more room for passengers, equipment, groceries, and boxes than ordinary cars. Therefore, they are more commonly found in the country than in the city, and in some suburban neighborhoods they are **more prevalent than** compact cars or vans. Even their high consumption of gas has little effect on their popularity.

In stating that SUVs are **more prevalent than** compact cars, the author means that they

    Ⓐ   cost more than compact cars.
    Ⓑ   are more numerous than compacts.
    Ⓒ   take up more parking space.
    Ⓓ   use more gas than other vehicles.

## LESSON 11—COMPUTER-BASED TEST QUESTIONS

1. Water whirlwinds, commonly called waterspouts, are whirling columns of air and watery mist. Brief whirlwinds are **erratic** in motion, but the longer-lasting ones move slowly with the prevailing winds and are less inconsistent in their movement. Storms generate most waterspouts, but tornado spouts, generated in thunderstorms, in association with tropical cyclones, are the most dangerous.

   Find the word in the passage closest in meaning to the word **erratic.**

2. The shipworm can grow to almost a meter. The shell of the shipworm is small, and covers only a part of the animal. Shipworms digest the cellulose of wood and cause great damage to submerged wood structures such as docks. They are a particular menace to wooden ships and **piers,** boring into all wood below the waterline.

   Find the word in the passage closest in meaning to the word **piers.**

3. Partly because it has promoted U.S. interests, the Monroe Doctrine has had considerable effect and enjoyed strong support in the United States. It has been used to justify intervention in the internal affairs of other American nations. However, U.S. diplomatic relations are strained due to growing anxiety over the **prevalent** instability of Latin American politics and commonplace controversial interventions.

   Find the word in the passage closest in meaning to the word **prevalent.**

4. A caricature is a picture or other representation that **exaggerates** a particular physical trait, facial appearance, or dress, or embellishes the manners of an individual to produce a distinct comical effect. It is also used to ridicule political, social, or religious situations and institutions, or actions by individuals, groups, or classes of a society. The latter types of caricature are usually done with satirical rather than humorous intent, in order to encourage political or social change.

   Find the word in the passage closest in meaning to the word **exaggerates.**

5. Geologic changes provide a convincing explanation for the puzzling way that plant species are scattered around the world. The conifers of the genus *Araucaria*, for example, have large seeds that do not float in seawater and are **dispersed** only short distances. However, they have been found either as fossils or as actively growing plants on all continents and on some islands that appear to be fragments of continents.

Find the word in the passage closest in meaning to the word **dispersed.**

# LESSON 12

- benefit ▪ blind ▪ broaden ▪ burgeon ▪ conspicuously
- demand ▪ endorse ▪ enormous ▪ entirely ▪ erode
- evaporate ▪ recover ▪ reportedly ▪ shift ▪ suffer

---

**benefit**

*adv.* beneficially
*adj.* beneficial
*n.* benefit
*n.* beneficiary

*v.* to be useful or helpful

*syn.* assist

Use of solar power will *benefit* all mankind.

It is extremely *beneficial* to prepare for a test.

**blind**

*adv.* blindly
*n.* blindness

*adj.* unable to see or understand; to conceal; showing poor judgment or understanding

*syn.* unaware

They were *blind* to the fact that they had little chance to succeed.

He went into the job *blindly*, with no previous experience.

**broaden**

*adv.* broadly
*adj.* broad
*n.* breadth

*v.* to make larger or greater

*syn.* enlarge

Education will *broaden* your opportunities to land a good job.

The *breadth* of his knowledge is impressive.

**burgeon**

*adj.* burgeoning

*v.* growing at a fast pace

*syn.* thrive

The *burgeoning* population of major cities is creating a demand for more services.

His talent as a pianist *burgeoned* at the age of 14.

**conspicuously**      *adv.* attracting attention

*adj.* conspicuous      *syn.* noticeably

His name was *conspicuously* absent from the list of winners.

The attorneys were *conspicuous* for their aggressive manner in the courtroom.

**demand**      *v.* to ask for something in a strong way

*adv.* demandingly      *syn.* insist
*adj.* demanding
  *n.* demand

She *demanded* to know the truth.

The employees' *demands* for better working conditions caused the work stoppage.

**endorse**      *v.* to express approval

  *n.* endorsement      *syn.* support

The union *endorsed* the new contract.

The president's *endorsement* of the project guaranteed its funding.

**enormous**      *adj.* very large

*adv.* enormously      *syn.* tremendous
  *n.* enormity

His *enormous* wealth allows him to contribute to many charities.

A diet with many fruits and vegetables is *enormously* beneficial to the body.

**entirely**      *adv.* completely

*adj.* entire      *syn.* thoroughly
  *n.* entirety

They are *entirely* right about the economy.

The president released the speech in its *entirety* before the news conference.

**erode**      *v.* to wear away; disappear slowly

  *n.* erosion      *syn.* deteriorate

The senator's support is *eroding* because of his unpopular positions on the major issues.

It took millions of years of *erosion* for nature to form the Grand Canyon.

**evaporate**           *v.* to vanish

*n.* evaporation      *syn.* disappear

The chances of the two sides reaching an agreement have *evaporated*.

The *evaporation* of the funds was unexplainable.


**recover**            *v.* to get back; to have something returned;
*adj.* recovered               to regain strength or health
*adj.* recoverable     *syn.* retrieve
*n.* recovery

The NASA team was unable to *recover* the space capsule.

The *recovered* objects had not been damaged.


**reportedly**         *adv.* to know by report; unconfirmed; supposedly

*adj.* reported        *syn.* rumored
*v.* report
*n.* report

The students *reportedly* sent a representative, but she has not arrived yet.

The *reported* tornado has not been confirmed.


**shift**              *n.* a change in position or direction

*adj.* shifting        *syn.* switch
*v.* shift
*adj.* shifty

The *shift* in the wind was helpful to the sailors.

Earthquakes are caused by *shifting* layers of earth along faults.


**suffer**             *v.* to experience difficulty; to worsen in
*adj.* suffering               quality; to experience pain
*n.* suffering         *syn.* endure
*n.* sufferer

The old man *suffers* from loss of memory.

Many families experience the *suffering* of difficult economic times.

## MATCHING

Choose the synonym.

1. benefit
   (A) prosper
   (B) demand
   (C) assist
   (D) distinguish

2. noticeably
   (A) constantly
   (B) enormously
   (C) conspicuously
   (D) broadly

3. rumored
   (A) routinely
   (B) purposefully
   (C) comparatively
   (D) reportedly

4. blind
   (A) oblivious
   (B) visible
   (C) sensitive
   (D) shifting

5. thrive
   (A) exaggerate
   (B) burgeon
   (C) dominate
   (D) endorse

6. endure
   (A) suffer
   (B) erode
   (C) release
   (D) disappear

7. broaden
   (A) impress
   (B) elicit
   (C) reveal
   (D) enlarge

8. switch
   (A) enrich
   (B) shift
   (C) propose
   (D) support

9. retrieve
   (A) recover
   (B) deteriorate
   (C) disperse
   (D) relinquish

10. insist
    (A) demand
    (B) mention
    (C) disperse
    (D) intrigue

## LESSON 12—MULTIPLE-CHOICE TEST QUESTIONS

1. Politics are an integral aspect of modern sports. In many places, political decisions determine which sports will be encouraged, how much public support will be available to promote recreational sports, and whether or not athletes will be free to compete in certain international competitions. Bitter controversies have arisen as some political support for popular sporting events has **evaporated** in various parts of the world.

   The word **evaporated** in the passage is closest in meaning to

   - Ⓐ  burgeoned
   - Ⓑ  suffered
   - Ⓒ  broadened
   - Ⓓ  disappeared

2. Rolltop desks are named after their sliding roll tops, or tambours, that cover the working surface of the upper part and can be locked. First introduced into England from France in the late eighteenth century, the rolltop desk had become a standard piece of office equipment by the end of the nineteenth century. It was mass-produced in large quantities. Shortly after this period of mass production, its popularity **eroded.**

   The word **eroded** in the passage is closest in meaning to

   - Ⓐ  recovered
   - Ⓑ  shifted
   - Ⓒ  intensified
   - Ⓓ  deteriorated

3. The American architect Frank Lloyd Wright designed furniture, but its distinctive appearance defies categorization. The furniture design was **entirely** dependent on the design of the building; the same motifs appear in both. He consistently favored built-in furniture because then the furniture was part of the architecture.

   The word **entirely** in the passage is closest in meaning to

   - Ⓐ  slowly
   - Ⓑ  reportedly
   - Ⓒ  completely
   - Ⓓ  conspicuously

4. While the potential **benefit** of genetic engineering is substantial, the potential dangers may be equivalent. Improper handling could pose a health hazard to the public. For example, the introduction of cancer-causing genes into common infectious organisms like the influenza virus could be one of these dangers.

The word **benefit** in the passage is closest in meaning to

        Ⓐ  danger
        Ⓑ  assistance
        Ⓒ  endorsement
        Ⓓ  recovery

5. Jogging has been **endorsed** by many medical authorities as valuable exercise for the heart and for general physical conditioning. It should be conducted every other day. Other medical authorities, however, warn that fallen arches and other ailments can result from jogging. Warm-up exercises before jogging, properly designed shoes, proper jogging technique, loose clothing, and general good health are vital for safe participation in this activity.

The word **endorsed** in the passage is closest in meaning to

        Ⓐ  reported
        Ⓑ  supported
        Ⓒ  criticized
        Ⓓ  exaggerated

6. In 1900, when countries like Russia, Italy, and Japan claimed an exclusive right to trade with China, the secret society of "Boxers" was formed to oppose this intrusion into Chinese affairs. Members of the group were reported to have magical powers that protected them in attacks from invading foreigners. Nevertheless, more than 20,000 foreign troops eventually landed in China, successfully attacked Beijing, established their right to remain, and disbanded the Boxers.

In stating that the Boxers were **reported to** have magical powers, the author means that their magical powers

        Ⓐ  were an established fact.
        Ⓑ  were alleged to exist.
        Ⓒ  had been reported as false.
        Ⓓ  had been verified as true.

## LESSON 12—COMPUTER-BASED TEST QUESTIONS

1. From 1890 to 1940, Los Angeles was the core of a thriving orange-growing area. The city was inland from any potential port, but city leaders persuaded the U.S. Congress to finance a breakwater at the city of San Pedro. The territory between the two cities was annexed, and a great harbor was constructed between 1899 and 1914. As a result, Los Angeles experienced **burgeoning** economic growth.

   Find the word in the passage closest in meaning to the word **burgeoning.**

2. Normal schools were established chiefly to train elementary-school teachers. They were commonly state-supported and offered a two-year course beyond high school. In the twentieth century, schools **broadened** their teacher-training requirements to at least four years. Therefore, after World War II, teacher training institutions enlarged their programs. By the 1960s, most former normal schools had been absorbed into colleges or universities as departments or schools of education.

   Find the word in the passage closest in meaning to the word **broadened.**

3. Economic development policy must consider both businesses and workers. A rapidly evolving technological environment generates frequent **shifts** in market demands. Skilled workers must switch to and develop new skills and those unskilled workers must learn some marketable skills. Job training is an essential part of any successful economic development strategy.

   Find the word in the passage closest in meaning to the word **shifts.**

4. Experiments are under way to prove the usefulness of new oil discovery technology. They will enable vast accumulations of crude oil to be **recovered** along both the Athabasca River in north central Alberta, Canada, and along the Orinoco River in eastern Venezuela. If these experiments are successful and a significant volume of crude oil can be retrieved, the world's petroleum supply may be extended by several decades.

   Find the word in the passage closest in meaning to the word **recovered.**

5. The telephone network offers **enormous** flexibility because many kinds of terminals and telephones can be connected to it. Examples of such terminal devices are modems, which transmit tremendous amounts of computer data over the telephone network; facsimile machines, which send data in the form of electrically coded visual images; and codecs, which digitally encode images from television cameras and carry them over the telephone network.

Find the word in the passage closest in meaning to the word **enormous**.

# LESSON 13

- dignitary ■ crucial ■ elude ■ evident ■ exhaust
- extensive ■ extremely ■ face ■ facet ■ hero
- inaccessible ■ obviously ■ predictably ■ solve
- suitable

---

**dignitary**

*n.* a very important or famous person, usually associated with a high position in government

*syn.* notable

Every *dignitary* in Washington was invited to the wedding.

All of the high-ranking *dignitaries* attended the economic summit.

**crucial**

*adv.* crucially

*adj.* of great importance; extremely necessary

*syn.* critical

Favorable weather is *crucial* to a good harvest.

Having all the information necessary to make a good decision is *crucially* important.

**elude**

*adj.* elusive
*n.* elusiveness

*v.* to escape in a tricky way

*syn.* evade

The criminal has *eluded* the police for months.

Success has been *elusive* for the team.

**evident**

*adv.* evidently
*n.* evidence

*adj.* easy to see, usually because of some proof

*syn.* apparent

It is *evident* that you are not feeling well.

All the *evidence* points to the presence of hydrogen.

**exhaust**

*adv.*  exhaustively
*adj.*  exhaustive
*adj.*  exhausting
*adj.*  exhausted
*n.*  exhaustion

*v.*  to use completely; to expend all energy; very thorough

*syn.*  deplete

They *exhausted* their energy in ten minutes.
The *exhaustive* report was acclaimed by everyone.

**extensive**

*adv.*  extensively
*v.*  extend*
*n.*  extension*

*adj.*  large in area or number
*  to offer; to make longer
*syn.*  comprehensive

The *extensive* snowfall caused problems throughout the city.
The professor *extended* a warm welcome to the new student.

**extremely**

*adj.*  extreme
*adj.*  extremist
*n.*  extreme
*n.*  extremist

*adv.*  very; to the very end, the highest extent
*syn.*  highly

When the concert was canceled, some customers became *extremely* upset.
He will go to any *extreme* to get what he wants.

**face**

*v.*  to be in the presence of and oppose
*syn.*  confront

The mountain climbers *faced* grave danger on the cliff.
He finds it difficult to *face* his problems.

**facet**

*adj.*  faceted

*n.*  element or component
*syn.*  aspect

The proposal had many beneficial *facets*.
It was a *multifaceted* problem that challenged the entire student body.

**hero**

*adv.* heroically
*adj.* heroic
*n.* heroine
*n.* heroics

*n.* a person remembered for an act of goodness or bravery

*syn.* idol

She is a *hero* in the eyes of her admirers.

They gave a *heroic* effort to no avail.

**inaccessible**

*n.* inaccessibility
*adv.* inaccessibly

*adj.* unable to be reached or communicated with

*syn.* remote

The summit of the mountain was *inaccessible*.

The dignitary's *inaccessibility* frustrated the reporter.

**obviously**

*adj.* obvious

*adv.* in a clear, easy to understand way

*syn.* evidently

It had *obviously* rained.

It was *obvious* that he had not practiced his oral report.

**predictably**

*adj.* predictable
*v.* predict
*n.* prediction

*adv.* in a way that foretells future events

*syn.* expectedly

She *predictably* forgot to do her assignment.

The government's *predictions* were accurate.

**solve**

*n.* solution

*v.* to find the answer

*syn.* resolve

They *solved* the problem in a way that benefitted the entire neighborhood.

The *solution* to the problem was elusive.

**suitable**

*adv.* suitably
*v.* suit

*adj.* appropriate; correct; convenient

*syn.* appropriate

Her dress was not *suitable* for the occasion.

The agreement *suits* all the members of the negotiating team.

## MATCHING

Choose the synonym.

1. solve
   (A) restore
   (B) resolve
   (C) confront
   (D) exhaust

2. critical
   (A) prevalent
   (B) elusive
   (C) prime
   (D) crucial

3. predictably
   (A) extremely
   (B) expectedly
   (C) conspicuously
   (D) extensively

4. hero
   (A) idol
   (B) amenity
   (C) benefit
   (D) mention

5. inaccessible
   (A) depleted
   (B) apparent
   (C) remote
   (D) enormous

6. elude
   (A) erode
   (B) evade
   (C) endorse
   (D) enrich

7. extensive
   (A) sensitive
   (B) impressive
   (C) comprehensive
   (D) disruptive

8. celebrity
   (A) treasury
   (B) dignitary
   (C) element
   (D) dweller

9. evidently
   (A) routinely
   (B) entirely
   (C) exceptionally
   (D) obviously

10. suitable
   (A) appropriate
   (B) annoying
   (C) ambiguous
   (D) astute

## LESSON 13—MULTIPLE-CHOICE TEST QUESTIONS

1. Engineering geologists survey the geology of an area, and then prepare a geological map. One of their main responsibilities is to determine whether the geological structure of a location is **suitable** for the building of huge structures such as dams.

   The word **suitable** in the passage is closest in meaning to

   - Ⓐ appropriate
   - Ⓑ extensive
   - Ⓒ recoverable
   - Ⓓ perfect


2. Experts believe that a child's family experiences are **crucial** for personality development. The ways that basic needs are met in infancy, along with later techniques of child rearing, can leave a permanent mark on personality. Children learn behavior appropriate to their sex by identifying with the parent of the same sex. A warm, caring relationship with that parent helps such learning.

   The word **crucial** in the passage is closest in meaning to

   - Ⓐ evident
   - Ⓑ extensive
   - Ⓒ critical
   - Ⓓ obvious


3. The Everglades comprises one of the wildest and most **inaccessible** areas in the United States. Its wildlife is plentiful and is largely protected within the Everglades National Park. The only inhabitants of the Everglades are several hundred Seminole Indians.

   The word **inaccessible** in the passage is closest in meaning to

   - Ⓐ remote
   - Ⓑ indiscriminate
   - Ⓒ inactive
   - Ⓓ immense

4. Bank credit cards, now also used in Europe, are examples of a general purpose card. Establishments offering almost every product or service are honoring such cards. It is **predicted** that credit cards may someday eliminate the need for carrying cash.

The word **predicted** in the passage is closest in meaning to

- Ⓐ  inconceivable
- Ⓑ  evident
- Ⓒ  contradicted
- Ⓓ  anticipated

5. In Western culture, until about the middle of the seventeenth century, biography was generally commemorative. Its purpose was to enlighten and motivate. It dealt with the foolish lives of doers of bad deeds and tyrants and with the exemplary lives of **heroes** and heroines.

The word **heroes** in the passage is closest in meaning to

- Ⓐ  dignitaries
- Ⓑ  idols
- Ⓒ  benefactors
- Ⓓ  philanthropists

6. Kinesics is the name given to the study of nonverbal interactions such as facial expressions, gestures, and eye contact. In many cultures, direct eye contact is seen as a sign of disrespect in **face-to-face encounters**. Students, for example, are expected to lower their eyes while addressing a teacher. In other cultures, lowered eyes are construed as an indication of shame, embarrassment, or dishonesty. Kinesics focuses on many such cultural differences.

In discussing **face-to-face encounters**, the author is referring to social interactions in which two people are

- Ⓐ  sitting back to back.
- Ⓑ  in front of each other.
- Ⓒ  keeping their eyes down.
- Ⓓ  staring into space.

## LESSON 13—COMPUTER-BASED TEST QUESTIONS

1. High standards and rigorous early training are **evident** where dance is an art performed before an audience. In early cultures, dance was something in which everyone participated; dancers were not singled out and trained because of their apparent skill or charm. Once religious worship developed into ritual, it became important for dancers to be as skilled as possible.

   Find the word in the passage closest in meaning to the word **evident.**

2. Mineral deposits form because there is a transporting agent for the ore minerals. The transporting agent removes the minerals it carries from one area and deposits them in another. Groundwater and seawater are examples of transporting agents. The transporting agent process is involved in the creation of deposits of both abundant and depleted metals. The latter deposits, as learned from past experience, can be **exhausted.**

   Find the word in the passage closest in meaning to the word **exhausted.**

3. A preference for certain colors is an **extremely** personal matter. Factors that affect color perception include age, mood, and mental health. People who share specific personal traits often share color preferences. Analysis of an individual's responses to color can be highly effective in providing information about an individual's mental condition.

   Find the word in the passage closest in meaning to the word **extremely.**

4. The independent African states **face** numerous problems in implementing an educational policy that will encourage economic and social development. The difficulties most governments confront are basically political. There is also concern about the financial problems of the different states. The lack of communication between educational policy makers and economic and social planners may also create hardships.

   Find the word in the passage closest in meaning to the word **face.**

5. Pop artists seek to portray all **facets** of modern culture. Their art emphasizes modern social values, the sprawl of urban life, and the transitory, offensive, frivolous, and flashy aspects of modern life. These values are the very opposites of the values cherished by artists of the past.

Find the word in the passage closest in meaning to the word **facets.**

# LESSON 14

- ample - arid - avoid - defy - enact - even
- feign - fertile - freshly - function - fundamental
- indiscriminate - selective - spacious - withstand

---

**ample**

*adv.* amply

*adj.* more than enough

*syn.* sufficient

There is *ample* evidence that the young man was speeding when the accident occurred.

She was *amply* paid for the work she completed.

---

**arid**

*adj.* having little rain or water.

*syn.* dry

The area known as the Sahara Desert is one of the most *arid* places in the world.

The valley on the leeward side of the mountain was extremely *arid*.

---

**avoid**

*adj.* avoidable
*n.* avoidance

*v.* to miss or keep away from

*syn.* avert

She could not *avoid* letting her feelings show.

The incident would have been *avoidable* if he had told the truth.

---

**defy**

*adv.* defyingly
*adj.* defying

*v.* to show little fear or regard for rules or established norms; to challenge

*syn.* resist

I *defy* you to find that book in the library's collection.

The circus performer demonstrated her death-*defying* routine.

**enact**

adj.   enacted
n.    enactment

*v.*  to pass a law

*syn.*  legislate

Congress *enacted* the legislation during its last session.

The *enactment* of the laws was in the hands of the Senate.

**even**

adv.   evenly
n.    evenness

*adj.*  regular, smooth; in equal parts

*syn.*  equitable

The sound isn't *even*; turn up the left speaker.

The profits were divided *evenly* among the investors.

**feign**

adj.   feigned

*v.*  to pretend; make believe

*syn.*  simulate

She *feigned* illness when it was time to visit the dentist.

Her unhappiness was *feigned.*

**fertile**

v.   fertilize
n.   fertility
n.   fertilizer

*adj.*  able to produce abundantly

*syn.*  rich

The delta areas of rivers are known for their *fertile* soil.

*Fertilizers* are used on crops to increase yields.

**freshly**

adj.   fresh
v.    freshen
n.    freshness

*adv.*  caught or produced not long ago

*syn.*  recently

*Freshly* harvested produce is hard to find in the winter months.

The product's *freshness* depends on an efficient transportation system to bring it to market.

**function**

adv.   functionally
adj.   functional
v.    function

*n.*  the normal purpose of something

*syn.*  role

It is the *function* of the director to organize and lead the department.

Most appliances cannot *function* without electricity.

**fundamental**        *adj.*  a primary or basic element

*adv.*  fundamentally    *syn.*  essential

The student government promised *fundamental* changes in the registration process.

He is *fundamentally* strong in his area of expertise.

**indiscriminate**    *adj.*  not chosen carefully; unplanned

*adv.*  indiscriminately    *syn.*  arbitrary

The *indiscriminate* arrangement of the products made the store confusing.

The book's chapters seem to be organized *indiscriminately*.

**selective**        *adj.*  carefully chosen

*adv.*  selectively    *syn.*  discriminating
*adv.*  select
  *v.*  select
  *n.*  selection
  *n.*  selectivity

They were very *selective* when they chose the members of the academic team.

He *selected* Spanish as his language class.

**spacious**        *adj.*  having a lot of room

*adv.*  spaciously    *syn.*  expansive
  *n.*  space
  *n.*  spaciousness

The *spacious* plains of the Midwest make up the nation's breadbasket.

A vacuum is an empty *space*.

**withstand**      *v.*  to fight without surrender; to persist

              *syn.*  survive

She cannot *withstand* the pressures of her job.

The old building *withstood* the terrible storm.

**MATCHING**

Choose the synonym.

1. sufficient
   (A) crucial
   (B) essential
   (C) ample
   (D) extensive

2. survive
   (A) erode
   (B) weaken
   (C) elude
   (D) withstand

3. defy
   (A) resist
   (B) demand
   (C) simulate
   (D) discriminate

4. indiscriminate
   (A) predictable
   (B) arbitrary
   (C) functional
   (D) constant

5. arid
   (A) dry
   (B) fertile
   (C) fresh
   (D) drab

6. avoid
   (A) avert
   (B) amaze
   (C) assert
   (D) allow

7. selective
   (A) inaccessible
   (B) rich
   (C) recent
   (D) discriminating

8. even
   (A) fundamental
   (B) erratic
   (C) evident
   (D) equitable

9. spacious
   (A) sensitive
   (B) superficial
   (C) minuscule
   (D) expansive

10. legislate
    (A) enact
    (B) feign
    (C) solve
    (D) exhaust

## LESSON 14—MULTIPLE-CHOICE TEST QUESTIONS

1. Naturally formed caves evolve mainly as a result of the solvent action of water and the chemical compounds it contains. Known as caves of solution, they are most common in regions that have **ample** rainfall.

   The word **ample** in the passage is closest in meaning to

   - Ⓐ infrequent
   - Ⓑ abundant
   - Ⓒ exemplary
   - Ⓓ erratic

2. In the early days of gliding, gliders were towed by cars. Today, gliders are towed in the sky by airplanes to a height between 600 and 900 meters above the ground. Flight duration depends on finding updrafts of air along mountain slopes, near cumulus clouds, or over **arid** terrain where rising thermal currents occur.

   The word **arid** in the passage is closest in meaning to

   - Ⓐ rocky
   - Ⓑ hot
   - Ⓒ dry
   - Ⓓ high

3. The Conestoga Indians were a powerful people, **defying** the invading Iroquois, until the Iroquois defeated them about 1675. Part of the tribe fled to the Roanoke River. Others subsequently settled at Conestoga, near what is now Lancaster, Pennsylvania.

   The word **defying** in the passage is closest in meaning to

   - Ⓐ ridiculing
   - Ⓑ honoring
   - Ⓒ resisting
   - Ⓓ overthrowing

4. Fasting has been practiced for centuries for many diverse purposes. Some fasts were to induce fertility. Others were intended to **avert** catastrophe or to serve as penance for sin. American Indians held tribal fasts to escape threatening disasters. The Aztecs of Mexico and the Incas of Peru observed penitential fasts to pacify their gods.

   The word **avert** in the passage is closest in meaning to

   Ⓐ overcome
   Ⓑ assert
   Ⓒ confirm
   Ⓓ avoid

5. Monte Albán, near Oaxaca, Mexico, was the center of the Zapotec culture that flourished around the year 100 A.D. Its gigantic stone structures were set around a **spacious** plaza created by leveling the top of a mountain.

   The word **spacious** in the passage is closest in meaning to

   Ⓐ exhaustive
   Ⓑ expansive
   Ⓒ circular
   Ⓓ fertile

6. Space exploration has had its share of problems throughout the years. A flaw in the *Challenger*'s design led to a fatal accident in 1986, the Mir station was often in trouble, and the *Columbia* shuttle crashed on reentry in 2003. Despite these tragedies, the program has profited from its mistakes, and from new engineering and new materials. Today, NASA is confident that spacecraft are **fundamentally sound** and perfectly safe.

   In saying that spacecraft are **fundamentally sound**, the author means that they are

   Ⓐ basically well designed and built.
   Ⓑ equipped with electronic music.
   Ⓒ dangerously old and worn.
   Ⓓ entirely new and experimental.

## LESSON 14—COMPUTER-BASED TEST QUESTIONS

1.  The idea of human rights as **fundamental** rights is not without
    its detractors, even at this otherwise receptive time. Frequently
    associated with orthodox religion, natural rights are perceived as
    "inalienable" and "unalterable." Thus, their basic character is
    often unattractive or unacceptable to those on the left.

    Find the word in the passage closest in meaning to the
    word **fundamental.**

2.  Food serves three **functions** in most living organisms. First, it
    provides material that is used to sustain the activities of the
    organism. Second, food supplies the electron donors required for
    the formative processes that occur within the cell. Third, food
    provides the materials from which all of the structural
    components of the living cell can be assembled. The roles of food
    are not limited to one of these; it may function in all three ways.

    Find the word in the passage closest in meaning to the
    word **functions.**

3.  Recently harvested wood is dried and preserved as a treatment
    against insect infestation and rot. These processes ensure that
    it will last. Some wood products, such as posts and poles,
    are **freshly** cut. Most other wood products are made up of
    intermediate materials, which require further processing before
    they are manufactured into final products.

    Find the word in the passage closest in meaning to the
    word **freshly.**

4.  Loess is a rich topsoil left by glaciers. Vast deposits of loess make
    the midwestern plain of the United States extremely **fertile**
    and one of the most important farming areas in the world. In
    addition, the soils in the land along the many rivers and streams
    of the region also add to its farming potential.

    Find the word in the passage closest in meaning to the
    word **fertile.**

5.  Since opossums are largely arboreal, their homes are often found
    in hollow trees or under stumps and roots. **Feigning** death is one
    of the opossum's principal defense mechanisms. By pretending to
    be dead and confusing its predators, the opossum is able to
    escape from danger.

    Find the word in the passage closest in meaning to the
    word **feigning.**

# LESSON 15

■ durable ■ favor ■ gain ■ generate ■ halt ■ handle
■ harbor ■ harmful ■ insignificant ■ mysterious ■ perilous
■ postpone ■ promote ■ reject ■ substantial

---

**durable**

*n.* durability
*n.* duration*

*adj.* something that lasts a long time
\* time during which something lasts
*syn.* sturdy

It was a *durable* refrigerator, but it finally broke.

The *durability* of tires is a key factor in determining their quality.

**favor**

*adv.* favorably
*adj.* favorable*
*adj.* favorite
*n.* favor

*v.* to treat unfairly in a positive way to the disadvantage of others; to believe in
\* advantageous
*syn.* support

The supervisor *favored* the first of the two plans.

The weather was *favorable* for the contest.

**gain**

*adj.* gainful
*n.* gain

*v.* to obtain something needed or useful; to increase to the amount of something
*syn.* attain

He *gained* a lot of experience working as a volunteer.

His *gain* in knowledge was impressive.

**generate**

*adj.* generated
*n.* generation
*n.* generator

*v.* to produce
*syn.* create

The appearance of the dance troupe *generated* a lot of excitement.

The *generator* provides power to the building during a blackout.

**halt**                     *v.*  to stop or discontinue

*adv.*  haltingly          *syn.*  stop
*adj.*  halting
*n.*  halt

Bus service to the city was *halted* due to poor road conditions.

The supervisor put a *halt* to the tardiness of the employees.

**handle**                   *v.*  to deal with or control

*n.*  handling            *syn.*  manage

They *handled* themselves very well given the circumstances.

The president's *handling* of the crisis was widely applauded.

**harbor**                   *v.*  to give protection; to not express a
                                   desire or opinion, usually bad

                             *syn.*  shelter

He *harbors* ill feelings for her.

They *harbored* the political refugee in their home.

**harmful**                  *adj.*  something that causes pain or damage

*adv.*  harmfully          *syn.*  unhealthy
*v.*  harm
*n.*  harm

Excessive radiation is *harmful* to the body.

Bleach *harms* certain fabrics.

**insignificant**            *adj.*  not important; of little value

*adv.*  insignificantly    *syn.*  meaningless
*n.*  insignificance

The amount of rainfall this summer has been *insignificant.*

The *insignificance* of his comment became apparent with the passing of time.

**mysterious**               *adj.*  not easily understood or figured out

*adv.*  mysteriously       *syn.*  baffling
*n.*  mystery
*n.*  mysteriousness

He had a *mysterious* effect on everyone who heard him speak.

The man's disappearance was a *mystery.*

**perilous**
*adv.* perilously
*n.* peril

*adj.* threatening or risky; harmful
*syn.* dangerous

It is *perilous* to exceed the speed limit.

There are ample *perils* in the sport of mountain climbing.

**postpone**
*n.* postponement

*v.* to reschedule at a later time
*syn.* delay

The teacher *postponed* the lab experiment.

The *postponement* of the flight for three hours was unavoidable.

**promote**
*n.* promoter
*n.* promotion

*v.* to encourage or advertise; to elevate in rank or grade
*syn.* boost

Many nations *promote* tourism to lure foreign currency.

The customers responded favorably to the half-price *promotion*.

**reject**
*n.* rejection

*v.* to refuse
*syn.* refuse

The insurance company *rejected* the claim.

The *rejection* of his work was difficult for him to understand.

**substantial**
*adv.* substantially
*adj.* substantive

*adj.* important; strongly made; of value
*syn.* significant

The discovery of a vaccine for smallpox was a *substantial* medical achievement.

This *substantive* article will change your opinion of rock music.

## MATCHING

Choose the synonym.

1. favor
   (A) manage
   (B) support
   (C) feign
   (D) conform

2. halt
   (A) evaporate
   (B) avoid
   (C) defy
   (D) stop

3. postpone
   (A) attain
   (B) delay
   (C) harbor
   (D) elude

4. durable
   (A) ample
   (B) crucial
   (C) dominant
   (D) sturdy

5. create
   (A) generate
   (B) gain
   (C) release
   (D) solve

6. substantial
   (A) haphazard
   (B) diverse
   (C) significant
   (D) perilous

7. promote
   (A) shelter
   (B) boost
   (C) harm
   (D) face

8. mysterious
   (A) unhealthy
   (B) dangerous
   (C) dramatic
   (D) baffling

9. insignificant
   (A) meaningless
   (B) rudimentary
   (C) vigorous
   (D) spacious

10. refuse
    (A) recover
    (B) exhaust
    (C) reject
    (D) withstand

**LESSON 15—MULTIPLE-CHOICE TEST QUESTIONS**

1.  Scientists can only speculate on the possible fate of the Cosmos.
    If the universe is unbound, there is little possibility that its
    expansion will **halt**. Thus, eventually the galaxies and stars will
    all die. The Cosmos then would be a cold, dark, and virtually
    empty place. If the universe *is* bound, the mass and energy
    content will come together again in a big fiery squeeze.

    The word **halt** in the passage is closest in meaning to

    Ⓐ  continue
    Ⓑ  stop
    Ⓒ  expand
    Ⓓ  intensify

2.  The perception of depth and distance depends on information
    transmitted through various sense organs. Sensory cues indicate
    the distance at which objects are located from the individual and
    from each other. The senses of sight and hearing transmit depth
    and distance cues that are **substantially** independent of one
    another.

    The word **substantially** in the passage is closest in meaning to

    Ⓐ  significantly
    Ⓑ  absurdly
    Ⓒ  critically
    Ⓓ  vigorously

3.  Because the needs of human communication are so various, the
    study of meaning is probably the most difficult and **mysterious**
    aspect of serious language study. Traditionally, language has
    been defined as the expression of thought. But this idea is far too
    narrow an interpretation of language and far too broad a view of
    thought to be worthwhile. The expression of thought is just one
    of the many roles of language.

    The word **mysterious** in the passage is closest in meaning to

    Ⓐ  substantial
    Ⓑ  meaningful
    Ⓒ  promising
    Ⓓ  baffling

4. The theory of environmental determinism says that the physical surroundings of a people, including natural resources, climate, and geography, are the major determining factors in the development of their culture. Therefore, determinism **rejects** the idea that history and tradition, social and economic factors, and other elements of culture explain social development.

The word **rejects** in the passage is closest in meaning to

    Ⓐ  refuses
    Ⓑ  ignores
    Ⓒ  promotes
    Ⓓ  withstands

5. The greatest benefit of a regular exercise program is an improvement in overall fitness. Appropriate exercise **boosts** muscular strength and endurance, flexibility, and cardiorespiratory endurance. The level of maximum oxygen intake or cardiorespiratory endurance is usually not of great importance to most individuals. The most important thing is to attain their maximum level of performance.

The word **boosts** in the passage is closest in meaning to

    Ⓐ  harms
    Ⓑ  manages
    Ⓒ  promotes
    Ⓓ  alters

6. The number of giant pandas in the world is dwindling. The chief reason is that their natural habitat in China has been reduced as bamboo forests have been cleared to increase available land for China's vast human population. In fact, the world came **perilously close** to losing the panda altogether in the 1980s as a result. Today, the panda's future is brighter. The Chinese government now protects most of the panda's natural habitat.

In saying that the world came **perilously close** to losing the panda, the author means that the giant panda

    Ⓐ  has been set free from zoos.
    Ⓑ  endangered human beings.
    Ⓒ  threatened the extinction of bamboo.
    Ⓓ  was nearly entirely eliminated.

## LESSON 15—COMPUTER-BASED TEST QUESTIONS

1. Several pilots were killed during the dangerous competition for the Orteig prize, which was promised to the first pilot to fly nonstop from New York to Paris. Charles Lindbergh believed he could win it if he had the right airplane, and he was right. He received the $25,000 prize in 1927 for being the first to make the **perilous** flight across the Atlantic.

   Find the word in the passage closest in meaning to the word **perilous.**

2. In parts of the world that lack modern sewage treatment plants, water carrying human waste can flow into drinking water supplies. Disease-carrying bacteria in the waste can make the drinking water unhealthy. Even in certain U.S. cities, such contaminants have been found in **harmful** amounts in urban water supplies.

   Find the word in the passage closest in meaning to the word **harmful.**

3. Desert areas that seem to be uninhabited actually **harbor** many forms of life. Most desert animals are not seen because they avoid the extreme midday heat of the desert. Many small animals burrow themselves underground while larger desert animals shelter themselves in shady areas during the day.

   Find the word in the passage closest in meaning to the word **harbor.**

4. Commercial arbitration has been practiced in European countries for many years. In the United States, commercial arbitration to **handle** disputes is gaining in popularity. The American Arbitration Association hires panels of arbitrators who manage disagreements and propose solutions. The decisions of these panels have been enforced by the courts of many states.

   Find the word in the passage closest in meaning to the word **handle.**

5. Martin Luther King had a magnificent speaking ability. This quality enabled him to effectively express African-Americans' need for social justice. He **gained** the support of millions of people, both black and white, through his eloquent pleas for nonviolent social action. He attained international recognition when he received the 1964 Nobel Peace Prize, after many years of struggle to assure basic civil rights for all citizens.

Find the word in the passage closest in meaning to the word **gained**.

# LESSON 16

- conscientious ■ convey ■ encompass ■ expansion
- heighten ■ highlight ■ inadvertently ■ inevitable
- infancy ■ miraculously ■ retrieve ■ systematically
- unlikely ■ unwarranted ■ zenith

**conscientious**
*adv.* conscientiously

*adj.* showing serious purpose; one who works carefully and with enthusiasm

*syn.* meticulous

She is a *conscientious* representative of the student body.
They approached the task *conscientiously.*

**convey**

*v.* to make something known to others; to communicate

*syn.* communicate

The manager of the store *conveyed* his displeasure directly to the workers.
He was able to *convey* his message to the audience with ease.

**encompass**

*v.* to surround completely; to envelop

*syn.* include

Her plan of study *encompasses* every aspect of computer science.
The course *encompasses* all the literature of the nineteenth century.

**expansion**
*adj.* expandable
*v.* expand
*n.* expansion

*n.* the act of making larger

*syn.* growth

*Expansion* occurs when matter is heated.
The laboratory is *expanding* its capacity to produce computer chips.

**heighten**

*adj.* heightened
*n.* height

*v.* to cause to become greater

*syn.* intensify

A very successful interview can *heighten* a candidate's chances to get a job.

The public was in a *heightened* state of nervousness as the hurricane approached.

**highlight**

*n.* highlight

*v.* to emphasize the part of a greater whole

*syn.* emphasize

The manual *highlights* basic operation of the videotape player.

The final goal was the *highlight* of the game.

**inadvertently**

*adj.* inadvertent

*adv.* by accident; without paying attention; unexpectedly

*syn.* carelessly

The reporters had *inadvertently* failed to include the name of one of the dignitaries.

His *inadvertent* calculation caused him to derive the wrong answer.

**inevitable**

*adv.* inevitably
*n.* inevitability

*adj.* something that cannot be prevented from happening

*syn.* unavoidable

When two weather systems meet, unsettled weather conditions are *inevitable*.

The *inevitability* of the outcome made the challenge less exciting.

**infancy**

*adj.* infantile
*n.* infant

*n.* in the beginning stages of development

*syn.* beginning

The new theory is in its *infancy* and will be thoroughly tested by its critics.

Certain head injuries can cause *infantile* behavior.

**miraculously**

*adj.* miraculous
*n.* miracle

*adv.* caused by something that cannot be explained by the laws of nature

*syn.* astonishingly

*Miraculously*, he was unharmed after being hit by lightning.

Given the extent of her injuries, it is almost a *miracle* that she is still alive.

**retrieve**

*adj.* retrieved
*n.* retrieval

*v.* to find and bring back

*syn.* recover

Will Detroit *retrieve* its status as the car manufacturing center of the world?

This computerized information *retrieval* system is the most up-to-date system available.

**systematically**

*adj.* systematic
*n.* system

*adv.* done according to a plan

*syn.* methodically

The plan was developed *systematically* by a team of experts.

*Systematic* changes in foreign policy have been proposed.

**unlikely**

*adj.* not probable

*syn.* doubtful

Rain is *unlikely* during the summer.

It is *unlikely* that he will want to attend the conference.

**unwarranted**

*adj.* without good reason or cause; inappropriate

*syn.* unjustified

His negative reaction was *unwarranted*.

The motorist felt that the ticket for the infraction was *unwarranted*.

**zenith**

*n.* the highest point

*syn.* apex

He reached the *zenith* of his profession at a very young age.

The publication of the book represented the *zenith* of his career.

## MATCHING

Choose the synonym.

1. convey
   - (A) intensify
   - (B) promote
   - (C) communicate
   - (D) solve

2. unlikely
   - (A) suitable
   - (B) persistent
   - (C) doubtful
   - (D) inevitable

3. growth
   - (A) expansion
   - (B) function
   - (C) highlight
   - (D) recover

4. meticulously
   - (A) haphazardly
   - (B) conscientiously
   - (C) inadvertently
   - (D) conspicuously

5. retrieve
   - (A) generate
   - (B) recover
   - (C) accelerate
   - (D) broaden

6. encompass
   - (A) emphasize
   - (B) gain
   - (C) heighten
   - (D) include

7. apex
   - (A) facet
   - (B) zenith
   - (C) pier
   - (D) flaw

8. systematically
   - (A) unexpectedly
   - (B) persuasively
   - (C) astoundingly
   - (D) methodically

9. unwarranted
   - (A) insignificant
   - (B) unjustified
   - (C) unacceptable
   - (D) unappealing

10. miraculously
    - (A) exceedingly
    - (B) astonishingly
    - (C) theoretically
    - (D) appropriately

## LESSON 16—MULTIPLE-CHOICE TEST QUESTIONS

1. The first elevated rail system was successfully operated in New York City in 1871, using steam power. Because steam power had many disadvantages, the lines were later electrified. An extensive network of elevated lines was built in New York City. It was in service for many years, but was **systematically** eliminated because of its antiquated appearance and because it contributed to traffic congestion.

   The word **systematically** in the passage is closest in meaning to

   - Ⓐ inadvertently
   - Ⓑ miraculously
   - Ⓒ meticulously
   - Ⓓ methodically

2. Municipal solid waste must be collected and treated in order to reduce the total volume and weight of the material that requires final disposal. Treatment changes the form of the waste and makes it easier to handle. It can also be used to **recover** certain materials, as well as heat energy, for recycling or reuse.

   The word **recover** in the passage is closest in meaning to

   - Ⓐ retrieve
   - Ⓑ convey
   - Ⓒ generate
   - Ⓓ develop

3. American biographer and historian Samuel Eliot Morrison colorfully recreated notable stories of modern history. Combining a gift for storytelling with **meticulous** scholarship, he took the reader back into history to relive the adventures of such characters as Ferdinand Magellan, Christopher Columbus, and Sir Francis Drake. He also recorded the accomplishments of the U.S. Navy during World War II.

   The word **meticulous** in the passage is closest in meaning to

   - Ⓐ unwarranted
   - Ⓑ infantile
   - Ⓒ miraculous
   - Ⓓ conscientious

4. Space medicine protects human beings from the environment of space and studies their reactions to that environment. The foundations of space medicine can be traced to aviation medicine. The term aerospace medicine has evolved to **encompass** practice in both areas. Aerospace medicine has been a certified subspecialty of the American Board of Preventive Medicine since 1953.

The word **encompass** in the passage is closest in meaning to

&#9400; favor
&#9401; promote
&#9402; emphasize
&#9403; include

5. If some motion is possible according to physical laws, then a motion in which events appear in reverse order is also possible. For example, it would be unusual to observe a real process in which a vase broken on the floor collects itself and flies up whole into a person's hand. Nevertheless, according to known physical laws, such a process is not impossible, although it is too **unlikely** to expect it to actually happen.

The word **unlikely** in the passage is closest in meaning to

&#9400; difficult
&#9401; doubtful
&#9402; astonishing
&#9403; superficial

6. In 1896 a Swedish chemist first assessed the effects of greenhouse gases. He showed that activities such as burning coal, destroying forests, and even raising cattle dangerously increase atmospheric concentrations of such gases as carbon dioxide, methane, and nitrous oxide. Since then, **heightened awareness** of the effects cars and factories have on the environment has led to more concern about these gas concentrations. Recently they have been blamed for an apparent warming trend in the earth's atmosphere.

In referring to **heightened awareness**, the author means that people are

&#9400; less conscious of the situation.
&#9401; more conscious of the situation.
&#9402; unconcerned about the problem.
&#9403; ashamed that the problem exists.

## LESSON 16—COMPUTER-BASED TEST QUESTIONS

1. Great technological advances were made during the **infancy** of the United States' industrial growth. But the modern trends of the 1920s brought about problems as well as benefits. Many Americans had trouble adjusting to the impersonal, fast-paced life of cities. This disorientation led to the beginnings of juvenile delinquency, crime, and other antisocial behavior. The complex life in cities also tended to weaken the strong family ties that had always been part of American society.

   Find the word in the passage closest in meaning to the word **infancy**.

2. Careful testing is one of a pharmaceutical company's most important responsibilities. Pharmaceutical companies and the Food and Drug Administration constantly guard against the possibility of a harmful drug being sold to the public. But even the most careful testing cannot always reveal the possibility that a drug may produce an **inadvertent** harmful effect. Unfortunately there are several tragic examples of unexpected side effects that resulted in serious harm or death to the patient.

   Find the word in the passage closest in meaning to the word **inadvertent**.

3. Some people believe that the Western idea of property is an **inevitable** development of the forces of progress or civilization. Therefore, the tendency for property to gather rights, which is characteristic of property law in the West, is unavoidable.

   Find the word in the passage closest in meaning to the word **inevitable**.

4. Basketball was invented in the United States in 1891. Today, it is the world's most popular indoor sport. Basketball **emphasizes** teamwork. It highlights the athletic qualities of endurance, agility, and skill. Tall players have an advantage because they can reach closer to the basket or above other players to shoot and rebound the ball. But smaller players also make contributions to their teams as shooters and ball handlers.

   Find the word in the passage closest in meaning to the word **emphasizes**.

5. Daniel Webster was a well-known American speaker, and one of the most capable lawyers and statesmen of his time. He used his speaking ability to intensify his efforts to establish a strong national government in the Senate. He also applied the speaking skills he had mastered as a lawyer to **heighten** his appeal for the end to slavery.

Find the word in the passage closest in meaning to the word **heighten**.

# LESSON 17

- agitate ■ confidential ■ delighted ■ discreetly
- documented ■ gradually ■ influence ■ inordinate
- instantly ■ intentionally ■ intrinsic ■ inundate
- involve ■ nominal ■ presumably

| | | |
|---|---|---|
| **agitate** | *v.* | to shake or move; to cause worry |
| *n.* agitation | *syn.* | disturb |
| *n.* agitator | | |

The fact that she had not arrived by midnight *agitated* her parents.
He was known as a political *agitator*.

| | | |
|---|---|---|
| **confidential** | *adj.* | to be said or written in secret |
| *v.* confide | *syn.* | secret |
| *adj.* confidential | | |
| *adv.* confidentially | | |
| *n.* confidant | | |

We were told that the information is strictly *confidential*.
She *confided* to me that she had always wanted to be a movie star.

| | | |
|---|---|---|
| **delighted** | *adj.* | to be satisfied; very happy |
| *adj.* delightfully | *syn.* | elated |
| *adj.* delightful | | |
| *n.* delight | | |

He was *delighted* with the results of the experiment.
It was a *delightful* afternoon.

| | | |
|---|---|---|
| **discreetly** | *adv.* | in a careful, polite manner |
| *adj.* discreet | *syn.* | cautiously |

The teacher *discreetly* told the parents about her problems.
You can count on me to be *discreet*.

**documented**  *adj.* proven with written evidence

*adj.* documentary  *syn.* proven
*v.* document
*n.* documentation

He had *documented* proof that the bank had made an error.

The car's *documentation* was in order.

**gradually**  *adv.* slowly, but surely

*adj.* gradual  *syn.* steadily

The bay has *gradually* deteriorated over the years.

There has been a *gradual* change in the climate over the past decade.

**influence**  *v.* to have an effect on a person's point of view or behavior; to change the course of events

*adj.* influential
*n.* influence

*syn.* affect

He was unable to *influence* his friend's decision.

The drought was due to the *influence* of a warm water current called "el niño."

**inordinate**  *adj.* a large amount or quantity; more than reasonable

*adv.* inordinately

*syn.* excessive

The airlines had to cancel an *inordinate* number of flights due to the fog.

There was an *inordinately* large number of whales off the coast.

**instantly**  *adv.* happening immediately; in a short period of time

*adj.* instantaneous
*adj.* instant  *syn.* immediately
*n.* instant

The computer finished the job *instantly*.

It happened in an *instant*.

**intentionally**

*adj.* intentional
*n.* intention
*n.* intent

*adv.* with definite purpose and planning
*syn.* deliberately

The machine was left on *intentionally.*

Her action was an indication of her good *intentions.*

**intrinsic**

*adv.* intrinsically

*adj.* being a primary part of something
*syn.* inherent

A penny has little *intrinsic* value.

The forests of the Northwest are *intrinsically* rich in natural resources.

**inundate**

*n.* inundation

*v.* to flood
*syn.* overwhelm

The radio stations were *inundated* with reports of a severe traffic accident.

The foundation experienced an *inundation* of requests for money.

**involve**

*adj.* involved
*n.* involvement

*v.* to become concerned with or connected to
*syn.* include

She *involved* herself in many activities to help her make new friends.

His *involvement* in right-wing politics is well documented.

**nominal**

*adv.* nominally

*adj.* very small; in form, but not in substance
*syn.* moderate

The office building was sold at a *nominal* price.

She was *nominally* successful as an actress.

**presumably**

*adj.* presumable
*v.* presume
*n.* presumption

*adv.* reported, but not confirmed
*syn.* supposedly

The old wreck was *presumably* located to the southwest of Florida.

I *presume* that you have been camping before.

**MATCHING**

Choose the synonym.

1. influence
   (A) affect
   (B) include
   (C) gain
   (D) overwhelm

2. secretly
   (A) conscientiously
   (B) confidentially
   (C) comparatively
   (D) constantly

3. documented
   (A) proven
   (B) intrinsic
   (C) substantial
   (D) durable

4. nominal
   (A) moderate
   (B) inherent
   (C) inevitable
   (D) harmful

5. excessive
   (A) impressive
   (B) lasting
   (C) deliberate
   (D) inordinate

6. discreetly
   (A) obviously
   (B) cautiously
   (C) unlikely
   (D) deceptively

7. agitate
   (A) heighten
   (B) reject
   (C) inundate
   (D) disturb

8. steadily
   (A) evenly
   (B) uniquely
   (C) intentionally
   (D) immediately

9. presumably
   (A) supposedly
   (B) actually
   (C) obviously
   (D) instantly

10. delighted
   (A) involved
   (B) elated
   (C) overwhelm
   (D) highlight

## LESSON 17—MULTIPLE-CHOICE TEST QUESTIONS

1. Modes of suggestion, while usually verbal, may be visual or may **involve** any other sense. The suggestion may be symbolic. For instance, a person who is allergic to roses may develop an attack of asthma from looking through a seed catalog. Suggestion also plays a significant role in group behavior and hypnosis.

   The word **involve** in the passage is closest in meaning to

   Ⓐ include
   Ⓑ influence
   Ⓒ agitate
   Ⓓ overwhelm

2. The American actor-director Orson Welles worked on the stage and in films for nearly 50 years. Yet his fame rests principally on two projects. The first, his 1938 radio adaptation of H. G. Wells's *The War of the Worlds*, was a fictitious eyewitness report of a Martian attack. The radio broadcast created a panic among listeners who, believing the attack to be real, **inundated** law enforcement agencies with numerous inquiries.

   The word **inundated** in the passage is closest in meaning to

   Ⓐ agitated
   Ⓑ overwhelmed
   Ⓒ astonished
   Ⓓ delighted

3. The use of cast-metal pieces as a medium of exchange is an ancient tradition. It probably developed out of the use in commerce of ordinary ingots of bronze and other metals that had an **intrinsic** value. Until the development of bills of exchange in medieval Europe and paper currency in medieval China, metal coins were the only means of exchange for goods and services.

   The word **intrinsic** in the passage is closest in meaning to

   Ⓐ inherent
   Ⓑ nominal
   Ⓒ documented
   Ⓓ inordinate

4.  The stimuli in a projective test are **intentionally** ambiguous and open to diverse interpretations so that each person will project his unique reactions in his answers. Techniques for evaluating such responses range from the intuitive impressions of the rater to complex schemes for scoring and interpretation that require extensive calculations and interpretation.

    The word **intentionally** in the passage is closest in meaning to

    - Ⓐ  confidentially
    - Ⓑ  constantly
    - Ⓒ  arbitrarily
    - Ⓓ  deliberately

5.  Anaximander argued that human beings are so helpless at birth that they would **instantly** die if left on their own. He also argued that known elements are continuously opposing and changing into one another and that as a result something different from these elements must underlie and cause changes.

    The word **instantly** in the passage is closest in meaning to

    - Ⓐ  gradually
    - Ⓑ  presumably
    - Ⓒ  immediately
    - Ⓓ  discreetly

6.  Some economists resist the notion that cutting taxes is beneficial. Theoretically, decreasing taxes returns money to citizens, therefore increasing jobs and improving conditions for everyone. Some economists say that will happen only with a large, sudden tax reduction. A gradual decrease, they say, will not stimulate spending or result in more jobs or a stronger economy. Still others oppose tax reduction altogether.

    In referring to a **gradual decrease** in taxes, the author means one that

    - Ⓐ  is imposed all at once.
    - Ⓑ  occurs slowly over time.
    - Ⓒ  stimulates a lot of jobs.
    - Ⓓ  affects everyone equally.

**LESSON 17—COMPUTER-BASED TEST QUESTIONS**

1. Without exception, a child of most Southwest Indians tribes was treated with warmth and permissiveness during the period of infancy. Peaceful growth and development during this time was not to be disturbed. Weaning was gradual, and training in cleanliness was delayed until a child could walk. Care was taken so that the child was not unduly **agitated**, and that he or she was protected from harm.

    Find the word in the passage closest in meaning to the word **agitated**.

2. Most Latin-American countries achieved **nominal** independence in the nineteenth century. Yet they remained politically, economically, and culturally dependent on U.S. and European powers throughout the first half of the twentieth century. By 1960 people cited this dependency as the reason for Latin America's moderate development and believed that the circumstances could best be alleviated through educational reform.

    Find the word in the passage closest in meaning to the word **nominal**.

3. Opinion polls have been developed since the 1930s. Polls are a scientific way of learning what large numbers of people think about various topics. They are used extensively in politics and business. In both fields many polling companies provide political candidates and businesses with **confidential** information about their public image. This information is often used in developing advertising programs and planning the secret strategies of political campaigns.

    Find the word in the passage closest in meaning to the word **confidential**.

4. *Homo Erectus*, the first human species, most likely originated in Africa. Eventually, the species migrated into Asia and probably into parts of Europe. This history can be **documented** directly from the many sites that have yielded fossil remains of *Homo Erectus*. Other sites from which animal bones and stone tools have been recovered have proven that this species was present, but there is no evidence of the people themselves.

    Find the word in the passage closest in meaning to the word **documented**.

5.  At a meeting to discuss the Federal Constitution, John Hancock
    was persuaded to support ratification. To get his support, he was
    promised a nomination for the presidency if George Washington
    declined. Though appearing to be among the leaders of the
    revolutionaries, he was not considered an independent figure.
    Rather, he was a tool of Samuel Adams, who took advantage of
    Hancock's excessive ambition, vanity, and **inordinate** love of
    popularity.

    Find the word in the passage closest in meaning to the
    word **inordinate**.

# LESSON 18

- absurd ■ abuse ■ allocation ■ balanced
- conservation ■ fallacious ■ feasible ■ lack ■ limber
- means ■ narrow ■ preconception ■ robust
- steady ■ swift

---

**absurd**

*adv.* absurdly
*n.* absurdity

*adj.* clearly false; without reason

*syn.* ridiculous

Confidentially, I think his suggestion is *absurd*.

They are *absurdly* irrational about the issue.

**abuse**

*adv.* abusively
*adj.* abusive
*v.* abuse

*n.* the act of using or treating things in an incorrect way

*syn.* misuse

The constant *abuse* of the environment will have grave consequences in the future.

He received an *abusive* letter from an irate citizen.

**allocation**

*adj.* allocated
*v.* allocate

*n.* a share; a part set aside for a special purpose; an assignment of portions

*syn.* distribution

His *allocation* of materials was gradually used up.

*Allocating* office space in the building was a difficult task.

**balanced**

*v.* balance
*n.* balance

*adj.* a state where everything is of the same size or weight; an element on one side that counters an equal element on the other

*syn.* equalized

He made a *balanced* presentation of both points of view.

The museum contains a pleasant balance of paintings from the eighteenth and nineteenth centuries.

**conservation**

*v.* conserve
*n.* conservative*
*n.* conservationist
*n.* conservatism*

*n.* the act of using carefully; setting aside for future use

\* favoring traditional values

*syn.* preservation

*Conservation* of forest land is the primary objective of the National Forest Service.

The Republican Party is generally known to be more *conservative* than the Democratic Party.

**fallacious**

*adv.* fallaciously
*n.* fallacy

*adj.* having errors

*syn.* incorrect

Her *fallacious* argument could not be defended.

It is a *fallacy* to think that money will bring you happiness.

**feasible**

*adv.* feasibly
*n.* feasibility

*adj.* able to be done

*syn.* possible

It is a *feasible* design for the high-rise building.

Before they begin the project, a study must be done of its *feasibility*.

**lack**

*adj.* lacking
*v.* lack

*n.* a need for; an insufficient amount

*syn.* shortage

There was a inordinate *lack* of rain last fall.

The mathematician was *lacking* in communication skills.

**limber**

*adj.* to be stretched; easily shaped

*syn.* flexible

The dancer has a *limber* body.

She was able to make the *limber* movements that are required of gymnasts.

**means**

*n.* ways

*syn.* methods

He was told to finish the job by any *means* available to him.

The most convenient *means* of communicating with someone is by phone.

**narrow**        *adj.*   small from one side to the other; limited

*adv.*   narrowly        *syn.*   thin
*n.*    narrowness

The canal was extremely *narrow*.

The driver *narrowly* escaped injury when his car ran off the road.

**preconception**      *n.*   an opinion formed in advance without experience or knowledge of something

*adj.*   preconceived
*v.*    preconceive      *syn.*   bias

It is difficult to overcome *preconceptions* if we are not open to new ideas.

His *preconceived* notions about Los Angeles disappeared after he visited the city.

**robust**        *adj.*   showing good health; in good shape

*adv.*   robustly        *syn.*   energetic
*n.*    robustness

The *robust* economy is expected to continue growing quickly.

The new product is selling *robustly*.

**steady**        *adj.*   firm; in a fixed position; without change; reliable; dependable

*adv.*   steadily
*v.*    steady        *syn.*   constant
*n.*    steadiness

*Steady* growth is projected for companies involved in genetic engineering.

The secretary has *steadily* earned respect for her work.

**swift**        *adj.*   quick

*adv.*   swiftly        *syn.*   fast
*n.*    swiftness

The contestants were *swift* thinkers.

They *swiftly* agreed with the conclusion of the report.

## MATCHING

Choose the synonym.

1. preconception
   (A) expansion
   (B) bias
   (C) function
   (D) disapproval

2. steady
   (A) constant
   (B) ample
   (C) arid
   (D) nominal

3. robust
   (A) energetic
   (B) flexible
   (C) narrow
   (D) ridiculous

4. fast
   (A) swift
   (B) spacious
   (C) intrinsic
   (D) vital

5. balanced
   (A) rigid
   (B) documented
   (C) fundamental
   (D) equalized

6. distribution
   (A) shortage
   (B) allocation
   (C) methods
   (D) disapproval

7. fallacious
   (A) inordinate
   (B) incorrect
   (C) unwarranted
   (D) inevitable

8. conservation
   (A) preservation
   (B) exportation
   (C) agitation
   (D) documentation

9. feasible
   (A) absurd
   (B) possible
   (C) limber
   (D) selective

10. abuse
    (A) involve
    (B) agitate
    (C) misuse
    (D) disperse

**LESSON 18—MULTIPLE-CHOICE TEST QUESTIONS**

1. Carrier waves picked up by a receiving TV antenna are carried to the television receiver. Inside the receiver the video and audio signals are separated and amplified. They then pass into the picture tube, which reproduces a picture of the original image from the video signals using a **narrow** beam of electrons that bombard, in a scanning motion, the back of a screen coated with a fluorescent compound.

   The word **narrow** in the passage is closest in meaning to

   - Ⓐ steady
   - Ⓑ balanced
   - Ⓒ thin
   - Ⓓ negative

2. A simple example of a **means** by which energy is converted from one form to another is demonstrated in the tossing of a ball into the air. When the ball is thrown vertically from the ground, its speed and its kinetic energy decreases steadily until it comes to rest momentarily at its highest point.

   The word **means** in the passage is closest in meaning to

   - Ⓐ description
   - Ⓑ method
   - Ⓒ theory
   - Ⓓ benefit

3. The First Continental Congress was formed to protest the British Parliament's intrusion into certain colony affairs. This congress urged the colonies to arm themselves for defense of their rights. It believed that it would be **absurd** not to give a forceful response to England's closing of the port of Boston. By the time the Second Congress convened, the American Revolution had begun.

   The word **absurd** in the passage is closest in meaning to

   - Ⓐ ridiculous
   - Ⓑ difficult
   - Ⓒ feasible
   - Ⓓ fallacious

4. The modern sport of gymnastics was essentially the result of the work of the German Friedrich Jahn, in the early nineteenth century. He invented many of the exercises and some of the apparatus of later gymnastics, such as the parallel bars, the rings, and the horizontal bar. Jahn's work was aimed mainly at strengthening the body. The result of gymnastics training is a well-toned, **limber** body.

The word **limber** in the passage is closest in meaning to

    Ⓐ   flexible
    Ⓑ   slender
    Ⓒ   tiny
    Ⓓ   disciplined


5. Many experts believe that in the early years of the twenty-first century the **lack** of water, rather than the availability of fertile land, will be the major obstacle to increased worldwide food production. As with land, the amount of water available for agricultural use cannot easily be increased. Research is now being conducted to improve water availability and thereby increase the amount of land available for farming.

The word **lack** in the passage is closest in meaning to

    Ⓐ   misuse
    Ⓑ   abuse
    Ⓒ   shortage
    Ⓓ   distribution

6. The aim of TV advertising is to motivate viewers to spend money on products; the aim of TV news is to give a **balanced view** of people, products, and events. These aims sometimes conflict with each other. While advertisers stress product features that contribute to a feeling of well-being or enhanced status, reporters have an obligation to describe products more objectively. Reporters have a responsibility to describe both positive and negative product features.

In referring to a **balanced view**, the author is referring to

    Ⓐ   a clearly biased summary.
    Ⓑ   information for and against.
    Ⓒ   an advocate's point of view.
    Ⓓ   factual support for TV ads.

## LESSON 18—COMPUTER-BASED TEST QUESTIONS

1. A typical cellar may be located beneath a house. It may also be located outdoors, partly underground, with the upper part mounded over with earth. This would protect items from freezing and maintain a fairly uniform temperature and humidity level. Unheated basements or heated and insulated ground-level buildings make it possible to store fruits and vegetables for short periods. Outdoor pits or mounds covered with straw, stalks, and earth are also used, making a storage time of a few months **feasible**.

   Find the word in the passage closest in meaning to the word **feasible**.

2. The operating system of a computer network protects computers from access by illegal users. It also prevents data corruption introduced by unintentional mistakes made by legitimate users. A strong security scheme is particularly important for computers that are connected to a communications network, since it has many potential users. Authorized users are allowed access by using a **robust** individual password, and then a computer usage fee is charged to the account of each user.

   Find the word in the passage closest in meaning to the word **robust**.

3. Knowledge of how early wheels were constructed is derived from "chariot burials" found in the city-states of Kish and Ur. Wheels were formed from three planks of wood that were clamped by wooden struts and bound with leather tires that were held in place by copper nails. The simplicity of their design allowed for **swift** repairs. The sturdy construction of the early wheel is thought to have made fast travel possible under good road conditions and to have served admirably on rough roads.

   Find the word in the passage closest in meaning to the word **swift**.

4. The law of large numbers, popularly known as "the law of averages," is often thought to require that future outcomes balance past outcomes. This is a misconception. A three-digit lottery number has the same probability of being selected every day. The fact that it has not been selected for a given number of days does not increase this probability. It is a gambler's **fallacy** to think that the probability increases. The odds remain the same for each repetition, regardless of the past outcomes.

Find the word in the passage closest in meaning to the word **fallacy**.

5. Despite the **preconception** to the contrary, the family is quite influential for adolescents. Indeed, no social institution has as great an influence throughout development as the family. Most investigations indicate that most adolescents have relatively few serious disagreements with parents. In fact, when choosing their friends, adolescents typically demonstrate a bias toward those who exhibit attitudes and values consistent with those of their parents.

Find the word in the passage closest in meaning to the word **preconception**.

# LESSON 19

- antiquated ∎ coherent ∎ develop ∎ fabricate
- investigation ∎ normally ∎ notice ∎ notion ∎ novel
- opposition ∎ record ∎ relate ∎ suspect ∎ unbiased
- varied

---

**antiquated**

*n.* antique

*adj.* too old to be presently useful; outmoded

*syn.* old-fashioned

This *antiquated* machinery breaks down too frequently.

Their home is filled with *antique* furniture.

**coherent**

*adv.* coherently
*v.* cohere
*n.* coherence
*adj.* cohesive*
*n.* cohesion*

*adj.* well reasoned; ideas that are clearly presented

\* sticking together as a group

*syn.* logical

It was a well-balanced, *coherent* presentation.

There was a *cohesive* feeling among the new workers.

**develop**

*adj.* developing
*n.* development
*n.* developer

*v.* to grow; to increase; to become more complete

*syn.* evolve

The management team *developed* the idea over a period of years.

The country's prospects for rapid *development* depend on approval of the free trade agreement.

**fabricate**

*adj.* fabricated
*n.* fabrication

*v.* to make up, usually with an intent to fool or trick; to lie

*syn.* invent

The executive *fabricated* the story about the merger.

His alibi is the weakest *fabrication* I have ever heard.

**investigation**

adj.  investigative
v.  investigate
n.  investigator

n.  a careful examination in order to determine facts

syn.  probe

The comprehensive *investigation* of the bank revealed no illegal activity.

Some members of the Senate wanted to appoint a special *investigator*.

**normally**

adj.  normal
v.  normalize
n.  normalization
n.  norm

adv.  commonly; usually

syn.  typically

It is *normally* quite cold this time of the year.

The new treaty lead to a *normalization* of relations between the two countries.

**notice**

adv.  noticeably
adj.  noticeable
n.  notice

v.  to sense; to be aware

syn.  observe

The doctor *noticed* a small fracture in the patient's finger.

The weather was *noticeably* cooler.

**notion**

n.  an idea, belief, or opinion

syn.  concept

She has the *notion* that she wants to become an architect.

Some outlandish *notions* about the origin of the solar system have been disproved.

**novel**

adj.  something unusual, uncommon; new

syn.  original

The physicist had some *novel* ideas about traveling at the speed of light.

The *novel* suggestions were implemented.

**opposition**

adj.  opposed
v.  oppose

n.  the state of acting against; not being in agreement

syn.  resistance

The students voiced their *opposition* to the rise in tuition.

The government *opposed* price controls.

**record**

adj.   recorded
n.   record
n.   recording
n.   recorder

v.  to make a written or oral notation; to copy

syn.  register

The coldest temperatures in the United States have been *recorded* at International Falls, Minnesota.

Many businesses are using *recordings* to answer consumer questions.

**relate**

adj.   related
n.   relation
n.   relationship

v.  to tell; to show a connection between two things

syn.  communicate

Although they did not agree with the plan, they did not *relate* their opposition to it.

What is the *relationship* between supply and demand?

**suspect**

adj.   suspected
n.   suspicion
n.   suspect

v.  to think that something is true, but having proof

syn.  speculate

He *suspected* that the substance was not present in the compound.

I have a *suspicion* that he will want to participate in the investigation.

**unbiased**

adj.  with no preconceptions

syn.  objective

Her *unbiased* analysis of the problem allowed her to find the solution more rapidly.

Here is *unbiased* proof that nitrogen exists in this compound.

**varied**

adv.   variably
adj.   variable
adj.   various
v.   vary
n.   variant
n.   variety
n.   variation
n.   variability

adj.  being of many different types

syn.  diverse

The class expressed *varied* opinions about the movie.

There are *various* ways to solve the problem.

## MATCHING

Choose the synonym.

1. fabricate
   - (A) observe
   - (B) invent
   - (C) agitate
   - (D) convey

2. coherent
   - (A) novel
   - (B) original
   - (C) logical
   - (D) robust

3. resistance
   - (A) opposition
   - (B) preservation
   - (C) preconception
   - (D) allocation

4. evolve
   - (A) develop
   - (B) elude
   - (C) involve
   - (D) influence

5. varied
   - (A) diverse
   - (B) feasible
   - (C) hazardous
   - (D) nominal

6. register
   - (A) harbor
   - (B) notice
   - (C) encompass
   - (D) record

7. probe
   - (A) expansion
   - (B) means
   - (C) investigation
   - (D) abuse

8. communicate
   - (A) inundate
   - (B) allocate
   - (C) relate
   - (D) oppose

9. suspect
   - (A) select
   - (B) confide
   - (C) speculate
   - (D) bias

10. unbiased
    - (A) antiquated
    - (B) postponed
    - (C) exhausted
    - (D) objective

## LESSON 19—MULTIPLE-CHOICE TEST QUESTIONS

1. The capacity among animals to reconstruct body appendages is not as common as the ability to compensate for lost tissues. This is due to the complex anatomy of appendages, which requires more elaborate regeneration control mechanisms. Among the vertebrates, salamanders are the best regenerators of appendages. Because of this characteristic, they are the subject of much folklore. For example, the fire salamander is so called because of an **antiquated** belief that it could withstand fire.

   The word **antiquated** in the passage is closest in meaning to

   - Ⓐ  outmoded
   - Ⓑ  old-fashioned
   - Ⓒ  illogical
   - Ⓓ  original

2. Throughout history, most technological progress has been a result of relatively minor improvements and refinements rather than through major inventions. Organized research is well suited for this kind of development. However, organized research may discourage **novel** approaches and inhibit creativity, so seminal discoveries are still likely to be made by inventors in the classic individualistic tradition.

   The word **novel** in the passage is closest in meaning to

   - Ⓐ  original
   - Ⓑ  varied
   - Ⓒ  coherent
   - Ⓓ  unbiased

3. Economist Alfred Marshall received acclaim for his economic ideas that integrated modern and classical economic theory. Classicists believed that price was determined by the cost of producing goods, but the modern school believed that price was dependent on the **notion** of marginal utility, or usefulness of the goods. Marshall's theory that price is determined by both cost and utility gained wide acceptance.

   The word **notion** in the passage is closest in meaning to

   - Ⓐ  investigation
   - Ⓑ  concept
   - Ⓒ  effectiveness
   - Ⓓ  opposition

4. Tidal waves are generated by tectonic displacements. Volcanoes, landslides, or earthquakes on the sea floor can cause a sudden displacement of the water above. This forms a small group of water waves having wavelength equal to the water depth at the point of origin. In deep water, tidal waves are so long and so slight that ships seldom **notice** their presence. But as they reach shallow water they increase in amplitude, making them potentially the most catastrophic of all ocean waves.

The word **notice** in the passage is closest in meaning to

- (A) suspect
- (B) relate
- (C) record
- (D) observe

5. The role of the heart was long considered a mystery and was considered very important. Some thought it was the source of the soul. Others thought it was the center of love, courage, happiness, and sadness. Primitive man was doubtlessly aware of the heartbeat and probably recognized that the tiny heart, **normally** the size of a clenched fist, was an organ whose malfunction could cause sudden death.

The word **normally** in the passage is closest in meaning to

- (A) roughly
- (B) actually
- (C) scarcely
- (D) typically

6. There is a growing sentiment **in opposition to** sea bass fishing. Most sea bass spawn between May and August, which coincides with the height of the fishing season. Fishing affects the reproductive capacity of the species disproportionately since it does not distinguish between males and females. Instead, it captures both indiscriminately. However, it takes six years longer for a female bass to become fertile than a male.

In stating that there is a growing sentiment **in opposition to** sea bass fishing, the author means that people

- (A) favor the fishing of sea bass.
- (B) see it as a positive activity.
- (C) dislike sea bass.
- (D) are against its continuation.

## LESSON 19—COMPUTER-BASED TEST QUESTIONS

1. Gymnastic competitions are judged and scored on both an individual and a team basis. Judges award points to each participant in each event on a 0-to-10 scale, 10 being perfect. The goal of completely objective judging is very difficult to achieve. Although guidelines are provided so that judges can arrive at relatively **unbiased** scores, they seldom agree on the quality of a performance.

   Find the word in the passage closest in meaning to the word **unbiased**.

2. Only now has humankind begun to speculate about some of the intimate chemical mechanisms used for the transmission of hereditary characteristics. As a result, biochemists now **suspect** that the problem of the origin of life is a practical one. The development of living cells from inanimate material is no longer viewed as a fundamentally impossible task.

   Find the word in the passage closest in meaning to the word **suspect**.

3. Sounding rockets are unmanned rockets that are designed to probe atmospheric conditions at heights 50–100 miles beyond the reach of airplanes and balloons. Sounding rockets usually follow a vertical path as they **investigate** upper atmospheric conditions with their scientific instruments.

   Find the word in the passage closest in meaning to the word **investigate**.

4. Reality is perceived through appearances. However, appearances are incompatible with reality. If an oar in water looks broken but feels straight to the touch, this must be acknowledged. Thus, a **coherent** picture of reality requires that we acknowledge that appearances can be deceptive. This is a logical perspective.

   Find the word in the passage closest in meaning to the word **coherent**.

5. "Speedwriting" is a writing system devised and registered in the patent office of the United States by Emma Dearborn in 1924. The system uses words that are **recorded** as they sound, and uses only long vowels. Thus, "you" is written u, and "like" is lik. Some letters are modified for speed; the system also uses abbreviations and flourishes. A flourish is the underlining of a final letter to express "ing."

Find the word in the passage closest in meaning to the word **recorded**.

# LESSON 20

- accentuate ■ disguise ■ finance ■ initiate
- innovative ■ narrate ■ nevertheless ■ occasionally
- omit ■ outlandish ■ overcome ■ partially ■ pass
- portray ■ submit

---

**accentuate**

*adj.* accentuated
*n.* accentuation

*v.* to highlight; to give more importance to

*syn.* emphasize

The colorful dress *accentuated* the joy of the occasion.

The supervisor *accentuated* her preference for hard-working employees during the performance appraisal.

**disguise**

*adj.* disguised
*n.* disguise

*v.* to hide the usual appearance of something

*syn.* conceal

It is hard to *disguise* the fact that business is slow.

Everyone saw through his *disguise*.

**finance**

*adv.* financially
*adj.* financial
*adj.* financed
*n.* finance
*n.* finances

*v.* to provide money

*syn.* fund

The art exhibition was *financed* by a private foundation.

The college was *financially* independent.

**initiate**

*adj.* initiated
*n.* initiation
*n.* initiative

*v.* to begin; to establish; to take decisive action without help

*syn.* launch

The newcomers *initiated* the long citizenship process.

Their work shows a lot of *initiative*.

**innovative**       *adj.* something newly introduced; creative

*n.* innovator      *syn.* creative
*n.* innovation

This *innovative* project is worthy of support.

There have been many *innovations* in the field of genetic engineering.

**narrate**      *v.* to tell a story; relate

*adj.* narrative      *syn.* relate
*n.* narrative
*n.* narration
*n.* narrator

Walter Cronkite *narrated* the documentary film.

Her fabricated *narrative* generated a lot of excitement.

**nevertheless**      *conj.* in spite of that

     *syn.* nonetheless

She was quite sick; *nevertheless*, she attended all of her classes.

His project was flawed; *nevertheless*, it won second prize.

**occasionally**      *adv.* now and then; once in a while

*adj.* occasional      *syn.* sometimes
*n.* occasion

Extreme heat *occasionally* causes health problems.

They were very fine students who, on *occasion*, experienced problems with pop quizzes.

**omit**      *v.* to leave out; not include

*adj.* omitted      *syn.* neglect
*n.* omission

He inadvertently *omitted* some important data from the report.

His paper had several notable *omissions*.

**outlandish**      *adj.* strange and unpleasant; beyond accepted

*adv.* outlandishly      norms

     *syn.* bizarre

His *outlandish* ideas demonstrated his creativity.

Rebellious youth in many countries dress *outlandishly*.

**overcome**    *v.*  to defeat; fight with success; to take control of an individual

*syn.*  conquer

The young woman was *overcome* with emotion when she learned she had won a scholarship.

The family *overcame* many obstacles to purchase the house.

**partially**    *adv.*  a part of the whole; incompletely

*adv.* partly       *syn.*  somewhat
*adj.* partial
*n.* part

The clerk was only *partially* responsible for the error.

The business venture was only a *partial* success.

**pass**    *v.*  to accept formally by vote

*adj.* passable       *syn.*  approve
*n.* passage

The proposed amendment *passed* unanimously.

The *passage* of the resolution is in doubt.

**portray**    *v.*  to represent; to act

*n.* portrayal       *syn.*  depict

The girl *portrayed* an orphan.

The book's *portrayal* of Mozart as a calm, mature individual is absurd.

**submit**    *v.*  to turn in; offer for evaluation

*n.* submission       *syn.*  propose

The architects had to *submit* plans reflecting the new specifications.

The *submission* of the application must be made by February 13.

## MATCHING

Choose the synonym.

1. launch
   - (A) overcome
   - (B) initiate
   - (C) persuade
   - (D) investigate

2. occasionally
   - (A) suitably
   - (B) outlandishly
   - (C) partially
   - (D) sometimes

3. submit
   - (A) approve
   - (B) propose
   - (C) omit
   - (D) develop

4. creative
   - (A) fallacious
   - (B) coherent
   - (C) innovative
   - (D) conspicuous

5. finance
   - (A) fund
   - (B) develop
   - (C) fabricate
   - (D) oppose

6. relate
   - (A) restore
   - (B) record
   - (C) narrate
   - (D) balance

7. nevertheless
   - (A) nonetheless
   - (B) albeit
   - (C) although
   - (D) presumably

8. disguise
   - (A) delight
   - (B) neglect
   - (C) feign
   - (D) conceal

9. emphasize
   - (A) accentuate
   - (B) conquer
   - (C) suspect
   - (D) select

10. portray
    - (A) refine
    - (B) depict
    - (C) pass
    - (D) abuse

## LESSON 20—MULTIPLE-CHOICE TEST QUESTIONS

1. In 1982, after years of debate, the Canadian government agreed to extend a constitutional guarantee to a bill of rights. This Charter of Rights and Freedoms reinforced the Constitution and has a constitutional guarantee. Yet Parliament and the provincial legislatures have limited power to **pass** laws that might conflict with certain charter rights.

   The word **pass** in the passage is closest in meaning to

       Ⓐ   approve
       Ⓑ   submit
       Ⓒ   finance
       Ⓓ   initiate

2. Although the assertion is at least **partially** true, the citizens of Kansas resent the suggestion that they live in a cultural vacuum. Most of the larger cities have amateur theater groups, while Topeka and Wichita support symphony orchestras. The numerous colleges and universities in the state provide a concentration of art and music in many small communities that otherwise would have no similar activities.

   The word **partially** in the passage is closest in meaning to

       Ⓐ   somewhat
       Ⓑ   undeniably
       Ⓒ   nevertheless
       Ⓓ   occasionally

3. Before becoming proficient, sword swallowers must first **overcome** their fear of projecting the sharp sword down their throat. Only after long hours of practice and experience can one swallow the sword comfortably. Beyond their entertainment value, exhibits of sword swallowing have helped to further medicine. By demonstrating to physicians that the pharynx could be accustomed to contact, experimentation and exploration of the involved organs is possible.

   The word **overcome** in the passage is closest in meaning to

       Ⓐ   disguise
       Ⓑ   conquer
       Ⓒ   treat
       Ⓓ   accentuate

4. Sun Ra was an important African-American jazz pianist and bandleader of the 1930s. Having a flare for being creative, he dressed his band in purple blazers, white gloves, and propeller beanies. The band developed into The Arkestra, and over time the costumes and showmanship grew ever more **outlandish**. The musicianship, however, was uniformly excellent, and Sun Ra developed into a serious experimenter, fusing jazz with African music, dance, and acrobatics.

The word **outlandish** in the passage is closest in meaning to

    Ⓐ  prosperous
    Ⓑ  bizarre
    Ⓒ  relaxing
    Ⓓ  melodical

5. Modern descriptions of written languages are in most cases excellent, but they still **omit** an explicit account of a native speaker's competence in his language, by virtue of which one calls him a speaker of English, Japanese, Arabic, or Chinese. Recent studies of language have revealed how more research is needed in order to fully describe linguistic competence.

The word **omit** in the passage is closest in meaning to

    Ⓐ  portray
    Ⓑ  contribute
    Ⓒ  neglect
    Ⓓ  relate

6. All team sports require reactive and proactive players. In soccer, for example, fullbacks, stoppers, sweepers, and midfielders have the job of preventing the opposing team from advancing very far. Goalies are responsible for stopping the ball and keeping their opponents from scoring. By comparison, the center forward has to take the initiative, seize the ball, move it down the field, keep it going, and move it forward into the enemy end zone.

In stating that the center forward has to **take the initiative**, the author means that the center forward's responsibility is to

    Ⓐ  play in an offensive way.
    Ⓑ  assume a supportive role.
    Ⓒ  react to opposing moves.
    Ⓓ  wait for others to score.

## LESSON 20—COMPUTER-BASED TEST QUESTIONS

1. Masks for festive occasions are still commonly used in the twentieth century. These may be outlandish, hideous, or superficially horrible. Festival masks include the Halloween, Mardi Gras, or "masked ball" variety. The **disguise** is assumed to create an interesting or amusing character, often resulting in humorous confusions, or the concealment of a prankster's identity.

   Find the word in the passage closest in meaning to the word **disguise**.

2. Only five years after the launching of music television video programs, the music video craze showed signs of slowing down. The costs of producing promotional videos was very high. This concern led to the **initiation** of serious investigations into the practice of automatically producing a video to accompany each new record album.

   Find the word in the passage closest in meaning to the word **initiation.**

3. The length, content, and form of folktales vary enormously. Both a short joke and an adventure-filled romance requiring several hours to **narrate** can be characterized as folktales. Folktales may be set in a mythical past, in historic times, or in the present. Storytelling is a basic human need. Therefore the necessity to relate folktales, even in technological cultures immersed with electronic media, remains strong.

   Find the word in the passage closest in meaning to the word **narrate**.

4. Jan Swammerdam was a creative and highly systematic worker who studied relatively few organisms, but in great detail. He employed highly **innovative** techniques such as injecting wax into the circulatory system to hold the blood vessels firm. He also dissected fragile structures under water to avoid destroying them.

   Find the word in the passage closest in meaning to the word **innovative**.

5. Contracts between employees and employers emphasize that the worker will do what the employer asks. In return, the employer pays the worker a fee, which the worker can use to purchase goods and services made by other workers who have also entered into a voluntary relationship with another employer. A cooperative spirit and a desire for mutual benefit **accentuate** healthy employer-employee relationships.

   Find the word in the passage closest in meaning to the word **accentuate**.

# LESSON 21

- decline ■ gather ■ motion ■ partisan ■ pattern
- phenomena ■ philanthropic ■ placid ■ plentiful
- reaction ■ rhythm ■ scenic ■ shallow ■ sheltered
- vanishing

---

**decline**      *v.*   to move from good to bad, or from much to
    *n.*   decline           little; to refuse

                *syn.*   decrease

The old man's health has *declined* since he retired.

Serious communicable diseases are on the *decline* in most parts of the world.

**gather**      *v.*   to collect
    *n.*   gathering     *syn.*   collect

He carefully *gathered* his thoughts just before the interview.

A *gathering* of citizens developed outside the courthouse.

**motion**      *n.*   the state of changing one's position
    *v.*   motion*         * to direct by moving

                *syn.*   movement

The *motion* of the flame was hypnotic.

They *motioned* her to leave the area.

**partisan**      *adj.*   strongly supporting a group or point of
                 view

                *syn.*   biased

*Partisan* political infighting caused Congress's influence to decline.

His views reflected his *partisan* bias.

**pattern**      *n.*   a regular, repeated arrangement or action
   *adj.*   patterned     *syn.*   habit
     *v.*   pattern

The bright *pattern* of the monarch butterfly distracts its predators.

The new stadium was *patterned* after the old traditional ballparks.

**phenomena**

 *adv.* phenomenally
 *adj.* phenomenal
  *n.* phenomenon

*n.* natural events or facts; strange or notable happenings

*syn.* events

Rain showers are almost unknown *phenomena* in the Atacama desert of Chile.

The musician's *phenomenal* performance was applauded by the critics.


**philanthropic**

 *n.* philanthropist
 *n.* philanthropy

*adj.* a feeling of love for people, usually resulting in financial aid to worthy causes

*syn.* humanitarian

The *philanthropic* work of the foundation benefits all sectors of society.

His *philanthropy* is recognized around the world.


**placid**

 *adv.* placidly

*adj.* quiet; not easily upset

*syn.* calm

The *placid* nature of her personality made her easy to work with.

The waves moved *placidly* toward shore.


**plentiful**

 *adv.* plentifully
  *n.* plenty

*adj.* more than sufficient

*syn.* abundant

Examples of Miro's art are *plentiful*.

A balanced diet normally provides *plenty* of the necessary vitamins.


**reaction**

 *adv.* reactively
 *adj.* reactive
  *v.* react
 *adj.* reactionary

*n.* a reply; a change that occurs when substances are mixed

*syn.* response

When chlorine and ammonia are mixed, the chemical *reaction* causes chlorine gas.

They *reacted* to the report by making some swift changes in management.

**rhythm**           *n.*  a regular pattern, usually in music

*adv.*  rhythmically      *syn.*  pulse
*adj.*  rhythmic

The *rhythm* of the rain hitting the roof put him to sleep.

She noticed the *rhythmic* beating of her heart as the moment of truth arrived.

**scenic**           *adj.*  concerning pleasant natural surroundings

*adv.*  scenically      *syn.*  picturesque
*n.*  scenery
*n.*  scene

The *scenic* route to the summit is much more interesting than the fastest route.

The *scenery* in rural Japan is impressive.

**shallow**           *adj.*  not far from top to bottom

*adv.*  shallowly      *syn.*  superficial
*n.*  shallowness

Estuaries are typically *shallow* bodies of water.

The results of their research demonstrated the *shallowness* of the hypothesis.

**sheltered**           *adj.*  protected from harmful elements;
*v.*  shelter               isolated from reality
*n.*  shelter      *syn.*  protected

She has led a *sheltered* life, her parents having done everything for her.

Everyone looked for *shelter* from the blazing sun.

**vanishing**           *adj.*  going out of sight.

*v.*  vanish      *syn.*  disappearing

The red squirrel is a *vanishing* species that needs a protected habitat to survive.

No one knows with certainty what caused the dinosaurs to *vanish* from the face of the earth.

## MATCHING

Choose the synonym.

1. picturesque
   (A) scenic
   (B) calm
   (C) outlandish
   (D) fertile

2. partisan
   (A) patterned
   (B) bizarre
   (C) abundant
   (D) biased

3. decrease
   (A) disguise
   (B) decline
   (C) omit
   (D) halt

4. disappear
   (A) vary
   (B) vanish
   (C) reject
   (D) fabricate

5. shallow
   (A) swift
   (B) substantial
   (C) placid
   (D) superficial

6. gather
   (A) broaden
   (B) collect
   (C) distribute
   (D) enhance

7. reaction
   (A) allocation
   (B) investigation
   (C) response
   (D) means

8. motion
   (A) innovation
   (B) narration
   (C) reaction
   (D) movement

9. protected
   (A) plentiful
   (B) phenomenal
   (C) sheltered
   (D) passable

10. rhythm
    (A) pulse
    (B) pattern
    (C) function
    (D) notion

**LESSON 21—MULTIPLE-CHOICE TEST QUESTIONS**

1. Until the latter half of the twentieth century, the Chesapeake Bay's sheltered, nutrient-rich waters supported **plentiful** populations of marine life. Commercial fishing and recreational activities abounded. By the 1970s, however, residential and industrial development of the surrounding land had led to significant pollution of the bay. Various projects have been initiated in an effort to reverse the environmental damage that the bay has suffered.

   The word **plentiful** in the passage is closest in meaning to

   Ⓐ  vanishing
   Ⓑ  abundant
   Ⓒ  fascinating
   Ⓓ  declining

2. The bee family Apidae, which includes honeybees, no longer uses honeypots that could be damaged by exposure to the elements. Instead, honey and pollen are stored in vertical combs with a layer of cells on each surface. Of the four species of honeybees in this family, only three are found in Asia. Their nests have several combs and are **sheltered** in crevices of rocks or hollows of trees.

   The word **sheltered** in the passage is closest in meaning to

   Ⓐ  recovered
   Ⓑ  abundant
   Ⓒ  discovered
   Ⓓ  protected

3. Andrew Carnegie established several independent, **philanthropic** foundations. Among them are funds for the recognition of heroic acts. These include the Carnegie United Kingdom, the Endowment for International Peace, and the Carnegie Foundation for the Advancement of Teaching, which was established in 1905 to provide pensions for college teachers.

   The word **philanthropic** in the passage is closest in meaning to

   Ⓐ  partisan
   Ⓑ  service
   Ⓒ  humanitarian
   Ⓓ  financial

4. The world of magic comprises a wide range of **phenomena**, from the intricate ritual beliefs and practices of religious systems, to acts of conjuring and sleight of hand for entertainment. Magic is a social and cultural phenomenon found in all places and in all periods of history, with varying degrees of importance.

The word **phenomena** in the passage is closest in meaning to

  Ⓐ motions
  Ⓑ patterns
  © expectations
  Ⓓ occurrences

5. A person's need for food is determined by age and by average heights and weights. Individual activity levels are also used to determine the level of ideal calorie consumption. For example, a **decrease** in recommended daily calorie consumption with increasing age is consistent with the known reduction in metabolism that occurs with aging and with a normal decrease in physical activity.

The word **decrease** in the passage is closest in meaning to

  Ⓐ decline
  Ⓑ balance
  © resistance
  Ⓓ development

6. Liquids vary in the amount of acid they contain. For example, water contains relatively little acid, while vinegar contains a large quantity. Acidic content is determined by dipping litmus paper into a liquid. This paper is saturated with a colorant obtained from plants called lichens. The colorant **reacts to** the presence of acid by turning different shades of red—the brightness of the shade can be measured on a scale called a pH scale.

In stating that the colorant **reacts to** the presence of acid in the liquid, the author means that it

  Ⓐ combines chemically with the acid.
  Ⓑ disappears or dissolves in the liquid.
  © causes the liquid to lose its redness.
  Ⓓ neutralizes the acid into a base.

**LESSON 21—COMPUTER-BASED TEST QUESTIONS**

1. Gars are long, slender, predatory fish, with a long, tooth-studded jaw and a tough, armored skin. They are a primitive fish that inhabit **placid** fresh waters of the Western Hemisphere. Because of the highly vascular and cellular nature of the gar's swim bladder, it functions as a lung. This makes the gar able to survive in large numbers in the calm areas of the Everglades of the southern United States.

   Find the word in the passage closest in meaning to the word **placid**.

2. In the human body, different toxins produce different **reactions**. The body can recover from some, while other toxic responses are irreversible. Irritation of the upper respiratory tract by inhaled formaldehyde gas is rapidly reversible because as soon as inhalation ends, the irritation subsides. In contrast, the response produced by silica dust is irreversible, because once the silicotic nodules are formed, they remain in the lung.

   Find the word in the passage closest in meaning to the word **reactions**.

3. Much of the world's unique heritage is endangered by pollution, the advance of human settlements, conflicts over the use of land and resources, and other problems. Thus, many countries are setting aside **scenic** natural areas as rapidly as possible. The tendency of many governments has been to establish as many parks as possible before advancing civilization alters the picturesque character of natural environments.

   Find the word in the passage closest in meaning to the word **scenic**.

4. Studies of European and American folk art over the past century have uncovered certain habits of those involved in folk-art activities. These **patterns** provide a basis on which cultural variations and less widespread occurrences may be considered.

   Find the word in the passage closest in meaning to the word **patterns**.

5. A "must carry" rule is designed to ensure that local TV stations do not disappear from cable TV offerings. It requires cable systems to carry all local broadcast channels within a certain area of their transmitters. The law was struck down in 1985, although many aspects of that case are still being argued. If cable operators prevail, local stations may **vanish** from or pay substantial amounts for the right to be carried on cable TV.

Find the word in the passage closest in meaning to the word **vanish**.

# LESSON 22

■ account ■ archaic ■ hasten ■ hue ■ illustration
■ inactive ■ intricate ■ magnitude ■ oblige ■ overlook
■ poll ■ position ■ practical ■ predominant ■ prompt

---

**account**
*adj.* accountable
*v.* account
*n.* accounting
*n.* accountant

*n.* a report of an event; money kept in a bank; a statement of something used or received, usually a financial report

*syn.* story

His *account* of the incident varied from that of the other witnesses.

We need an *accounting* of all the money that was spent.

**archaic**

*adj.* very old; old-fashioned; no longer used

*syn.* ancient

These *archaic* methods of farming must be brought up to date.

His speech was full of *archaic* expressions.

**hasten**
*adj.* hastily
*adj.* hasty
*n.* hastiness

*v.* to cause to go faster; move forward more quickly

*syn.* accelerate

After notifying his family of the accident, he *hastened* to add that he had not been hurt.

You should not make important decisions *hastily*.

**hue**

*n.* color

*syn.* color

The *hue* of the sunset was beautiful.

The *hue* of the room gave it a warm feeling.

**illustration**                  *n.*   a visual image, typically used to explain

*adj.*   illustrated              *syn.*   picture
*adj.*   illustrative
  *v.*   illustrate
  *n.*   illustrator

The *illustration* makes the process of condensation more understandable.

This experiment *illustrates* how certain chemicals can react violently when combined.

**inactive**                  *adj.*   not moving; not involved

*n.*   inaction              *syn.*   idle
*n.*   inactivity

The virus remains *inactive* for a long period of time.

Her *inaction* has caused her to miss many opportunities to advance her career.

**intricate**                  *adj.*   having many parts; finely detailed

*adv.*   intricately              *syn.*   complex
  *n.*   intricacy

The *intricate* design of the vase made it a valuable piece for her collection.

I cannot begin to understand all of the *intricacies* of modern automobile motors.

**magnitude**                  *n.*   of great size or importance

*adv.*   magnificently              *   to increase
*adj.*   magnificent
  *v.*   magnify*              *syn.*   dimension
  *n.*   magnification*

The *magnitude* of shock waves determines the damage that occurs during an earthquake.

The invention of the telephone was a *magnificent* achievement for mankind.

**oblige**                  *v.*   to have to do something

*adv.*   obligingly              *syn.*   require
*adj.*   obliging
*adj.*   obligatory
  *n.*   obligation

She *obliged* her friend to choose a new lab partner.

Payment of the student activity fee was *obligatory*.

**overlook**

*adj.* overlooked

*v.* to ignore or neglect

*syn.* disregard

Scientists must not *overlook* any aspect of experimental procedure.
The *overlooked* error raised his score on the test.

**poll**

*n.* polling
*n.* pollster

*n.* questionnaire; a vote of public opinion

*syn.* survey

The *poll* indicated that conservation of the environment was the
number one issue with college students.
The *pollster* asked the questions in a nonpartisan manner.

**position**

*n.* place where something can be found; job

*syn.* location

He held a very high *position* in the firm.
The *position* of aircraft wings causes the lift that allows it to leave the
ground.

**practical**

*adv.* practically
*adj.* practicable
*n.* practicality

*adj.* convenient or effective

*syn.* functional

Her ambitious plan was not very *practical.*
Space travel to distant planets is not *practicable* at this time.

**predominant**

*adv.* predominantly
*n.* predominate
*n.* predominance

*adj.* the most noticeable or powerful element

*syn.* principal

The *predominant* export of the Middle East is petroleum.
Many cities in the Southwest are *predominantly* Hispanic.

**prompt**

*adv.* promptly
*n.* promptness

*v.* to cause something to happen; do quickly;
be on time

*syn.* induce

His emotional plea *prompted* the director to give him a second chance.
*Promptness* is an important factor in many societies.

## MATCHING

Choose the synonym.

1. intricate
   (A) functional
   (B) complex
   (C) predominant
   (D) inordinate

2. disregard
   (A) overcome
   (B) disperse
   (C) decline
   (D) overlook

3. idle
   (A) initiated
   (B) inundated
   (C) inactive
   (D) intrinsic

4. archaic
   (A) plentiful
   (B) ancient
   (C) placid
   (D) absurd

5. hasten
   (A) accelerate
   (B) shelter
   (C) heighten
   (D) generate

6. picture
   (A) position
   (B) zenith
   (C) preconception
   (D) illustration

7. size
   (A) allocation
   (B) magnitude
   (C) expand
   (D) advent

8. color
   (A) hue
   (B) illustration
   (C) facet
   (D) scenery

9. require
   (A) survey
   (B) induce
   (C) oblige
   (D) relinquish

10. account
    (A) currency
    (B) poll
    (C) treasury
    (D) story

## LESSON 22—MULTIPLE-CHOICE TEST QUESTIONS

1.  Southeast Asian culture has many themes. The most
    **predominant** of these have been in religion and national history.
    In religion the main interest was not in actual doctrine but in the
    life and personalities of the Buddha and the Hindu gods. In
    national history the interest was in the celebrated heroes of the
    past. This theme appeared only after the great empires had
    vanished and the memories of their glory and power endured.

    The word **predominant** in the passage is closest in meaning to

    Ⓐ   principal
    Ⓑ   inactive
    Ⓒ   archaic
    Ⓓ   overlooked

2.  The experience of the American frontier fostered raucous politics
    and rude manners. Conventions were **disregarded** and contempt
    for intellectual and cultural pursuits flourished. Brazen waste
    and the exploitation of natural resources abounded. The
    predominant spirit was to take while the taking was good.
    Frontier history includes many accounts of men who created
    empires and acquired great wealth within a short time.

    The word **disregarded** in the passage is closest in meaning to

    Ⓐ   hastened
    Ⓑ   defied
    Ⓒ   overlooked
    Ⓓ   induced

3.  For religious reasons, the Egyptians considered Canis Major the
    most important constellation in the sky. Many Egyptian temples
    were aligned so that at the rising or setting of Sirius, the starlight
    reached the interior altar. In the Egyptian calendar, the first
    **practical** calendar created, the advent of Sirius in the morning
    sky before sunrise marked the beginning of the annual flooding of
    the Nile.

    The word **practical** in the passage is closest in meaning to

    Ⓐ   functional
    Ⓑ   accurate
    Ⓒ   standard
    Ⓓ   celestial

4. Airplanes have extensive agricultural value. They are used to distribute fertilizer, to reseed forest land, and to control forest fires. Many rice growers use planes to seed, fertilize, spray pesticides, and even to **hasten** crop ripening by spraying hormones from the air.

The word **hasten** in the passage is closest in meaning to

Ⓐ heighten
Ⓑ enable
Ⓒ curtail
Ⓓ accelerate

5. The CD is an improvement over the conventional record and tape recording because of its complete absence of background noise and wider dynamic range. The CD is also more durable since nothing mechanical touches the surface of the disc when it is played. In addition to its audio recording applications, recent computer trade magazine **polls** confirm that the compact disc is the preferred medium of recording data.

The word **polls** in the passage is closest in meaning to

Ⓐ surveys
Ⓑ accounts
Ⓒ articles
Ⓓ advertisements

6. Scientists are still seeking to **account for** the sudden appearance of precisely patterned circles in grain fields in the north of England. Known as crop circles, they range in size from two to eighty meters in diameter. Their circular geometric pattern is not explained by the way the grain was planted; nor is their flattened appearance easily explained by weather conditions. The farmers who work the land are as mystified as everyone else by these strange phenomena.

In stating that scientists are seeking to **account for** crop circles, the author means that they are trying to

Ⓐ measure them in meters.
Ⓑ describe their geometry.
Ⓒ explain what causes them.
Ⓓ grow them in grain fields.

## LESSON 22—COMPUTER-BASED TEST QUESTIONS

1. Tree buds may be vegetative or reproductive. Vegetative buds produce height growth until the growth process **induces** the formation of flowers. Exactly what is responsible for the formation of a reproductive bud varies, but changes in the number of daylight hours is a common signal in many plants. A change in the levels of hormones and carbohydrates is one factor that prompts the development of buds.

   Find the word in the passage closest in meaning to the word **induces**.

2. The record of courses steered and distances sailed on each trip forms the ship's "reckoning." The **positions** obtained from such a record are "dead reckoning" positions. Because of the difficulty of determining actual courses and distances traveled, and because of the effects of wind and current, these locations are usually inexact. This was not a serious handicap when navigation was confined to the enclosed or coastal waters. However, dead reckoning techniques were inadequate for ocean navigation.

   Find the word in the passage closest in meaning to the word **positions**.

3. Some leaders of the Han period of ancient China exerted enormous pressure for the simplification and standardization of writing. The result was a new category of script called clerical script. The **archaic** seal script was often retained for formal titles. It was also adapted to the small seals that have been used as signatures from the Han period to the present. These small red stamps, often present on documents, letters, books, and paintings, signify either authorship or ownership.

   Find the word in the passage closest in meaning to the word **archaic**.

4. There are six general classes of map symbols: size, lightness and darkness, direction, texture, shape, and color. The mixture of these "visual variables" creates the variety that is found on maps. For example, **hue** is used on urban planning maps to show differences in land use. Different shades of the same color may be used to indicate information such as changes in elevation or population density.

   Find the word in the passage closest in meaning to the word **hue**.

5. Sleep is an intricate form of the resting state. It is observed in animals that have highly developed nervous systems. Birds and mammals, including humans, do not simply become idle and slow to react during their daily rest periods. When they sleep, their nervous systems shift into **inactive** modes that are different, but no less active, than those that they demonstrate while awake.

Find the word in the passage closest in meaning to the word **inactive**.

# Lesson 23

- analogous ■ approximately ■ compel ■ formidable
- intrusive ■ periodically ■ prone ■ prophetic
- proportions ■ readily ■ reliably ■ reluctantly
- renown ■ sacrifice ■ triumph

**analogous**      *adj.*   alike in some way

    *n.*   analogy      *syn.*   similar to

The action of light waves is *analogous* to the action of sound waves.

The *analogy* between the behavior of the bacteria in the lab and in the human body is not clear.

**approximately**      *adv.*   almost correct; not exact

   *adj.*   approximate      *syn.*   around
     *v.*   approximate
     *n.*   approximation

There are *approximately* 100 billion galaxies in the universe.

The results of this study *approximate* those of a previous study.

**compel**      *v.*   to make something happen by necessity or force

   *adv.*   compellingly
   *adj.*   compelling      *syn.*   obliged

The representatives were *compelled* to vote in favor of the legislation despite their personal opposition to it.

The lawyer's plea was made in a *compelling* manner.

**formidable**      *adj.*   difficult; causing worry or fear

   *adv.*   formidably      *syn.*   overwhelming

Their *formidable* opponents gave no sign of weakness.

The man's voice echoed *formidably* throughout the hallway.

**intrusive**

*adv.* intrusively
*v.* intrude
*n.* intrusion
*n.* intruder

*adj.* the state of being inside when not desired to be there by others

*syn.* annoying

The *intrusive* bacteria caused his condition to worsen.

The *intrusion* of the hazardous gas made it difficult to live in the house.

**periodically**

*adj.* periodic
*adj.* periodical
*n.* periodical

*adv.* happening occasionally

*syn.* sometimes

Some materials *periodically* demonstrate unusual behavior when frozen.

She has *periodic* desires to get a job.

**prone**

*adj.* likely to do something

*syn.* inclined to

Most liquids are *prone* to contract when frozen.

She is *prone* to study hard the night before her tests.

**prophetic**

*adv.* prophetically
*v.* prophesy
*n.* prophecy
*n.* prophet

*adj.* correctly telling about future events

*syn.* predictive

His *prophetic* powers were investigated by a team of psychologists.

The brilliant student fulfilled his teacher's *prophecy* that he would be a successful doctor.

**proportions**

*adv.* proportionally
*adj.* proportional
*adj.* proportionate
*adv.* proportionately

*n.* the relationship of size or importance when compared to another object or person

*syn.* dimensions

The goal of establishing a space station will take a team effort of major *proportions*.

The pilot's salary is *proportional* to that of pilots of other airlines.

**readily**      *adv.* willingly; easily

*adj.* ready
*v.* ready
*n.* readiness

         *syn.* freely

The workers *readily* complained about the food in the cafeteria.

Her *readiness* to cooperate was an important factor in the investigation.

**reliably**      *adv.* in a trusted way

*adj.* reliable
*adj.* reliant
*v.* rely
*n.* reliability
*n.* reliance

         *syn.* dependably

An appliance must perform its task *reliably* to be popular with consumers.

Satellite photos show the smallest details with great *reliability*.

**reluctantly**      *adj.* unwillingly

*adj.* reluctant
*n.* reluctance

         *syn.* hesitatingly

Although not completely satisfied with the contract, the officials *reluctantly* agreed to sign it.

The electrician was *reluctant* to estimate the cost of the repair work.

**renown**      *n.* fame

*adj.* renowned

         *syn.* prominence

This school is of great *renown*.

The *renowned* conductor made a guest appearance at the concert.

**sacrifice**      *v.* to give up something of value for the common good

*adj.* sacrificial
*n.* sacrifice

         *syn.* concession

He *sacrificed* his day off to help clean the neighborhood.

She made *sacrifices* in order to be able to attend the university.

**triumph**      *n.* a victory; a success

*adv.* triumphantly
*adj.* triumphant
*adj.* triumphal
*v.* triumph

         *syn.* achievement

His career was characterized by one *triumph* after another.

He *triumphed* over all of his difficulties.

**MATCHING**

Choose the synonym.

1. intrusive
   (A) inactive
   (B) intricate
   (C) predictive
   (D) annoying

2. obliged
   (A) distorted
   (B) dependable
   (C) compelled
   (D) settled

3. sacrifice
   (A) reliance
   (B) proportion
   (C) concession
   (D) recovery

4. formidable
   (A) predictive
   (B) overwhelming
   (C) functional
   (D) practical

5. similar to
   (A) unlike
   (B) analogous
   (C) archaic
   (D) prone

6. around
   (A) obviously
   (B) likely
   (C) entirely
   (D) approximately

7. hesitatingly
   (A) reluctantly
   (B) readily
   (C) compellingly
   (D) practically

8. achievements
   (A) triumphs
   (B) phenomena
   (C) dimensions
   (D) approximation

9. sometimes
   (A) routinely
   (B) actually
   (C) periodically
   (D) gradually

10. renown
    (A) domination
    (B) prophecy
    (C) prominence
    (D) position

## LESSON 23—MULTIPLE-CHOICE TEST QUESTIONS

1. New annual growth of trees produces growth rings. In most instances, the age of a tree can be **reliably** determined by counting the rings of a trunk's cross section. Most of the growth ring wood cells are dead. Only young xylem cells, those that grow during the current growing season, are alive. As a result, the ratio of dead to living wood cells increases as the girth of the tree increases.

   The word **reliably** in the passage is closest in meaning to

   (A)  periodically
   (B)  dependably
   (C)  approximately
   (D)  ordinarily

2. Lightships and buoys have an important function in coastal waters. They mark channels and thereby safely guide passing ships around hazards or shallow waters. Their great advantage is mobility, making them **readily** redeployable to meet changing conditions. For example, submerged hazards such as sandbars can change location rapidly under the influence of the sea. The use of buoys makes it possible to efficiently mark safe channels at all times.

   The word **readily** in the passage is closest in meaning to

   (A)  freely
   (B)  reluctantly
   (C)  repeatedly
   (D)  occasionally

3. The construction of the Saint Lawrence Seaway was an undertaking of great **proportions**. Constructing a link between the Great Lakes and the Atlantic seaboard had been proposed since 1535. Locks built in the 1800s by Canada became operational in 1901 on the upper Saint Lawrence River. But this original seaway was not deep or wide enough for modern ships. Canada and the United States constructed the new seaway, which became operational in 1959.

   The word **proportions** in the passage is closest in meaning to

   (A)  triumphs
   (B)  renown
   (C)  dimensions
   (D)  sacrifice

4. In European folklore, mermaids are mythical beings who, like sprites, have magical and **prophetic** powers. They love music and song. Though very long-lived, they are mortal and have no souls. Although sometimes kindly, mermaids are generally dangerous to man. Their gifts have typically brought misfortune, and, if offended, they have caused floods or other disasters. To see one on a voyage is an omen of shipwreck.

The word **prophetic** in the passage is closest in meaning to

    Ⓐ  formidable
    Ⓑ  intrusive
    Ⓒ  predictive
    Ⓓ  renowned

5. In Western cultures, the absence of a formal definition of responsibilities has produced an ambiguous and often conflicting set of expectations for young people. At the same time, young people are **prone** to experience problems of peer pressure. They are told to behave maturely, while being denied access to the rights and privileges of adults.

The word **prone** in the passage is closest in meaning to

    Ⓐ  obliged
    Ⓑ  positioned
    Ⓒ  cautioned
    Ⓓ  inclined

6. Among the great orchestras of the world, the Philadelphia Orchestra stands out for several reasons. One is the overall quality of its musicians, although it is especially **renowned for** its violin players. Another is the orchestra's famous recordings of nineteenth-century music, including the nine symphonies of Ludwig von Beethoven. A third is the orchestra's many international concert tours. For example, it was the first U.S. orchestra to visit China.

In saying that this orchestra is especially **renowned for** its violinists, the author means that it

    Ⓐ  has an unusual violin section.
    Ⓑ  is famous for the violin players.
    Ⓒ  has made a lot of recordings.
    Ⓓ  pays the violinists more money.

## LESSON 23—COMPUTER-BASED TEST QUESTIONS

1. The body of scales or bracts of a cone contains the reproductive organs of certain flowerless plants. The cone, a distinguishing feature of pines and other evergreens, is crudely **analogous** to the flowers of other plants. Similar cones are also found on certain mosses.

   Find the word in the passage closest in meaning to the word **analogous**.

2. Most physicians participate in continuing education to keep up with the massive amount of information being discovered each year in their fields. Many states require that physicians **periodically** prove that they have actively participated in continuing medical education in order to maintain their certification to practice medicine. Many specialty boards are now also requesting that doctors already certified in that specialty be regularly reexamined.

   Find the word in the passage closest in meaning to the word **periodically**.

3. Peace pipes are the large, ornately decorated tobacco pipes of the Indians of eastern North America. They functioned as symbols of truce and were ceremonially smoked for purposes of binding or renewing alliances. At treaties and Indian council meetings the pipe was passed around the circle, and each person present was obliged to take a puff. Peace pipes attained so much symbolic importance that it was thought that smoking the pipe with others **compelled** everyone present to be united in friendship.

   Find the word in the passage closest in meaning to the word **compelled**.

4. The Spanish conquerors attempted to replace Aztec medicine with their own. When Aztec medical personnel resisted they were killed and Spanish medicine **intruded** its way into Aztec culture. This imposed medicine became the establishment medicine among the Aztecs. However, some elements of Spanish medicine were compatible with the folk medical practice and became part of a new folk system. Mexican folk medicine thrived, yet there were many regional differences.

   Find the word in the passage closest in meaning to the word **intruded**.

5. The *Ladies Home Journal* gained prominence by instituting an advertising code to eliminate fraud and extravagant claims by advertisers. It won particular **renown** for its attention to social causes. It refused, for example, to advertise patent medicine, and the resulting campaign against those products helped bring about the passage of the U.S. Federal Food and Drugs Act in 1906.

Find the word in the passage closest in meaning to the word **renown**.

# LESSON 24

- affordable ▪ contaminated ▪ discernible ▪ flourishing
- maintain ▪ mediocre ▪ negligible ▪ parallel ▪ peculiar
- potent ▪ remarkable ▪ scattered ▪ solid ▪ somewhat
- tedious

---

**affordable**

*adv.* affordably
*v.* afford

*adj.* able to be done, usually referring to something you can do without damage or loss

*syn.* economical

The new dictionary is quite *affordable.*

He could *afford* the house because of current low interest rates.

**contaminated**

*v.* contaminate
*n.* contamination

*adj.* to make something impure by adding something dirty or a poisonous substance

*syn.* pollute

This *contaminated* water supply must be closed off to the public.

Bacteria and insects are frequently agents of food *contamination.*

**discernible**

*adv.* discernibly
*v.* discern
*n.* discernment

*adj.* noticeable; easily seen

*syn.* detectable

A feeling of anxiety was *discernible* among the members of the team.

The new student was unable to *discern* the humor of the teacher's joke.

**flourishing**

*v.* flourish

*adj.* active and growing; healthy

*syn.* thriving

Small *flourishing* companies would be harmed by an increase in the minimum wage.

A young mind will *flourish* with the proper guidance.

**maintain**        *v.* to support; to keep in good condition

*n.* maintenance      *syn.* preserve

The building had to be renovated because it was not well *maintained*.
Proper *maintenance* of a car's engine will preserve its performance and value.

**mediocre**        *adj.* of average quality; not good or bad

*n.* mediocrity      *syn.* average

This is a *mediocre* research report.
The *mediocrity* of his work was disappointing.

**negligible**        *adj.* hardly noticeable; scarcely detectable

*v.* neglect         \* to ignore; to give little attention
*adv.* negligibly
*adj.* neglected      *syn.* insignificant
*adj.* neglectful
*adj.* negligent\*
*n.* neglect\*
*n.* negligence\*

The amount of bacteria in the culture was *negligible*.

His *negligence* caused him to lose all of the work he had done on the computer.

**parallel**        *adj.* being almost of the same type or time;
*v.* parallel          comparable

              *syn.* similar

There were many *parallels* between his life and mine.
Her background *parallels* mine.

**peculiar**        *adj.* unusual; uncommon

*adv.* peculiarly     *syn.* strange
*n.* peculiarity

This plastic has a *peculiar* texture.
The puffin has many *peculiarities* not shared by other birds.

**potent**        *adj.* very strong

              *syn.* powerful

He gave a *potent* speech at the convention.
The venom of the coral snake is extremely *potent*.

**remarkable**     *adj.* worthy of mention; uncommon
*adv.* remarkably     *syn.* exceptional

The invention of the radio was a *remarkable* achievement.
The actor was *remarkably* calm before his performance.

**scattered**     *adj.* spread out or separated widely
*v.* scatter     *syn.* dispersed

Hurricane Andrew left debris *scattered* throughout Miami.
The crowd *scattered* when it began to rain heavily.

**solid**     *adj.* having good quality; being well made,
*adv.* solidly             firm; not a gas or liquid
*v.* solidify     *syn.* steady
*n.* solidification

The lawyer for the defense portrayed his client as a man of *solid* integrity.
The union attempted to *solidify* its position in the workplace.

**somewhat**     *adj.* a little
     *syn.* slight

They feel *somewhat* tired after the mile run.
Buying food at a convenience store can be *somewhat* expensive.

**tedious**     *adj.* long and tiring
*adv.* tediously     *syn.* monotonous
*n.* tedium

The *tedious* lecture bored most of the audience.
Some people become frustrated by the *tedium* of daily living.

## MATCHING

Choose the synonym.

1. discernible
   (A) exceptional
   (B) detectable
   (C) solid
   (D) negligent

2. average
   (A) ample
   (B) approximate
   (C) slight
   (D) mediocre

3. preserve
   (A) maintain
   (B) disperse
   (C) contaminate
   (D) compel

4. potent
   (A) powerful
   (B) reliable
   (C) firm
   (D) durable

5. affordable
   (A) remarkable
   (B) formidable
   (C) economical
   (D) proportional

6. similar
   (A) prophetic
   (B) substantial
   (C) parallel
   (D) varied

7. strange
   (A) peculiar
   (B) vanishing
   (C) somewhat
   (D) renowned

8. negligible
   (A) exceptional
   (B) intricate
   (C) insignificant
   (D) scattered

9. thriving
   (A) flourishing
   (B) vanishing
   (C) polluting
   (D) astounding

10. monotonous
   (A) ambiguous
   (B) hazardous
   (C) prosperous
   (D) tedious

## LESSON 24—MULTIPLE-CHOICE TEST QUESTIONS

1. The *Ceratosaurus*, a genus of large carnivorous dinosaurs found as fossils in Late Jurassic rocks of North America, was similar to, and possibly closely related to, the *Allosaurus*. *Ceratosaurus* weighed up to 2 tons. This dinosaur was **somewhat** smaller than *Allosaurus*. It had a distinctive horn on its snout, a row of bony plates down the middle of its back, and four clawed fingers rather than three.

   The word **somewhat** in the passage is closest in meaning to

   - (A) potently
   - (B) uniquely
   - (C) slightly
   - (D) peculiarly

2. The countries of Scandinavia were influenced by the spirit of improvement prevalent throughout Europe during the eighteenth century, but showed less advanced agriculture than others. Danish farmers were somewhat slowed in using new methods because of political restrictions. It was not until the end of the nineteenth century that **solid** advances in farming techniques occurred.

   The word **solid** in the passage is closest in meaning to

   - (A) sluggish
   - (B) negligible
   - (C) mediocre
   - (D) substantial

3. Tourists throng to Baltimore's Inner Harbor year-round. The Inner Harbor was built in an area that was once a **contaminated** port of the city. This area underwent rapid development in the 1980s. It is now a waterside array of high-fashion stores, new hotels, outdoor performances, moving boats, docked ships, and locales for eating and drinking.

   The word **contaminated** in the passage is closest in meaning to

   - (A) deserted
   - (B) polluted
   - (C) dangerous
   - (D) flourishing

4. The Northwest Territories are Canada's most sparsely settled area. Most settlements consist of only a few hundred people. About two-thirds of Canada's Inuit Eskimos live there, **scattered** throughout the Arctic sector. Most Europeans who live in this territory live in the Mackenzie Valley.

The word **scattered** in the passage is closest in meaning to

    Ⓐ   maintained
    Ⓑ   sheltered
    Ⓒ   organized
    Ⓓ   distributed

5. Plastics are a vast group of synthetic materials whose structures are based on the chemistry of carbon. They are also called polymers because they are made of extremely long chains of carbon atoms. An important characteristic of plastics is that they can be readily molded into finished products by the application of heat. One of its well-known properties includes **remarkable** resistance to heat.

The word **remarkable** in the passage is closest in meaning to

    Ⓐ   periodic
    Ⓑ   proportional
    Ⓒ   exceptional
    Ⓓ   practical

6. Extensive water storage is **peculiar to** a class of animals called ruminants. The class includes sheep and cattle, but the class member best known for storing water is the camel. There are two types of camel, the single-humped dromedary and the double-humped Bactrian camel found in the dry steppes of central Asia. The ability of these animals to store water makes them the ideal beasts of burden on long treks across the desert.

In saying that extensive water storage is **peculiar to** ruminants, the author means that

    Ⓐ   only these animals have this capacity.
    Ⓑ   camels have an unusual appearance.
    Ⓒ   desert life is difficult for most animals.
    Ⓓ   camels store water in their humps.

## LESSON 24—COMPUTER-BASED TEST QUESTIONS

1. As computer systems improve, databases will play an increasingly important role as sources of information for the general public. Databases will continue to expand their text and video content. As databases become more refined, the need for awareness of particular databases will become more important. Users will need to be able to **discern** where database information has come from and ascertain how reliable it is.

   Find the word in the passage closest in meaning to the word **discern**.

2. The late 1970s and 1980s were years of delirious skyscraper construction. This was found in the cities that experienced better than average economic progress, such as Dallas, Houston, and Atlanta in the southern United States, and also Hong Kong, Bangkok, and Singapore. Although New Yorkers, in particular, had reason to complain that the building of **mediocre** skyscrapers was choking Manhattan, few distinguished profiles were added to the skylines of modern cities.

   Find the word in the passage closest in meaning to the word **mediocre**.

3. The deserts of the world are distributed in a pair of **parallel** belts lying approximately 25 degrees north and south of the equator. Of these, the world's largest desert is found in the Northern Hemisphere. The Sahara and many similar but smaller deserts, forming much of the arid portion of the Middle East, are located in high-pressure regions directly influenced by global circulation of the atmosphere.

   Find the word in the passage closest in meaning to the word **parallel**.

4. The life of the Atlantic salmon is typical of all salmon. The young fish leave the streams of their origin and disperse into the feeding water of the cold seas. When they are sexually mature they return to their home streams. In early summer, vast numbers of fish can be observed in their run upstream. It is not known how the right river system and the specific nesting sites are identified, but research indicates that the fish sense a distinctive chemical code **peculiar** to their home stream.

   Find the word in the passage closest in meaning to the word **peculiar**.

5. The treadmill is a machine in which a wheel oriented with a horizontal axis of rotation is turned by persons or animals walking on boards arranged around the outside edge of the wheel. This arrangement allows the multiplication of the applied force, as in a lever. Because of the monotonous and numbing nature of working a treadmill, the name is used to describe any **tedious** work.

Find the word in the passage closest in meaning to the word **tedious**.

# LESSON 25

■ briefly ■ circulate ■ consistently ■ exhibit ■ found
■ improperly ■ impulsively ■ infrequently ■ isolated
■ overtly ■ profoundly ■ sharply ■ situated
■ subsequently ■ unmistakable

---

**briefly**

*adj.* brief
*n.* brevity

*adv.* short, usually in time

*syn.* concisely

The visiting professor spoke *briefly* at the faculty meeting.

Solar eclipses are *brief* moments when the Earth and Moon cross the Sun's fixed position in the solar system.

**circulate**

*adj.* circulatory
*n.* circulation

*v.* to cause to move along a fixed path; move freely

*syn.* distribute

The news of the president's visit *circulated* quickly throughout the city.

A dollar bill remains in *circulation* for approximately one and a half years.

**consistently**

*adj.* consistent
*v.* consist
*n.* consistency

*adv.* without changing; keeping the same principles, ideas, or quality

*syn.* dependably

The temperature must be maintained *consistently* at 75° centigrade.

The policy of the government concerning unemployment has been *consistent.*

**exhibit**

*n.* exhibit
*n.* exhibition
*n.* exhibitor

*v.* to show or demonstrate

*syn.* display

The compound *exhibits* the qualities of an acid.

It was the best *exhibition* of talent that I have ever seen.

**found**
*n.* foundation*
*n.* founder

*v.* to establish; start up
&ast; a philanthropic organization
*syn.* establish

The wealthy woman *founded* a hospital in her home town.
The *foundation* maintained a number of philanthropic activities.

**improperly**
*adj.* improper
*n.* impropriety

*adv.* not following established rules; not desirable
*syn.* inappropriately

The disappointing outcome was a result of an *improperly* prepared petri dish.
There was an *impropriety* with the way the funds were spent.

**infrequently**
*adj.* infrequent
*n.* infrequency

*adj.* almost never
*syn.* rarely

Tornados occur *infrequently* in the eastern part of the United States.
Deserts are characterized by their *infrequent* rainfall.

**impulsively**
*adj.* impulsive
*n.* impulse
*n.* impulsiveness

*adv.* acting without thinking
*syn.* capriciously

She reacted *impulsively* to the loud noise.
Many shoppers buy items on *impulse*.

**isolated**
*v.* isolate
*n.* isolation

*adj.* to keep separated from others
*syn.* secluded

The failure of the communications system left the towns *isolated*.
The doctors were unable to *isolate* the cause of the epidemic.

**overtly**
*adj.* overt

*adv.* in a way clearly seen; not done secretly
*syn.* openly

He *overtly* disregarded the regulations.
Her *overt* attempt to take control of the discussion failed.

**profoundly**

*adj.* profound
*n.* profundity

*adv.* in a deep way; showing deep knowledge of a subject

*syn.* significantly

Everyone was *profoundly* impressed by the news reports.
The Nobel Prize is a *profound* recognition of outstanding achievement.

**sharply**

*adj.* sharp
*v.* sharpen
*n.* sharpness

*adv.* showing sensitivity or quick thinking; showing a quick change in direction

*syn.* quickly

Car prices rose *sharply* over the past year.
There was a *sharp* change in the humidity after the storm.

**situated**

*n.* situation*
*v.* situate

*adj.* being found in a certain place

* a current condition

*syn.* located

The resort town of Cancun is *situated* in the northern part of the Yucatan peninsula.
They found themselves in a very difficult *situation*.

**subsequently**

*adj.* subsequent

*adv.* following; coming after something

*syn.* afterwards

The public applauded the President's actions and *subsequently* his ratings in the polls improved.
This report, and all *subsequent* reports, must be written in the appropriate style.

**unmistakable**

*adj.* unmistakably

*adj.* clearly able to be determined

*syn.* indisputable

The markings of the insect provided for an *unmistakable* identification of the species.
It is *unmistakably* clear that the report must be finished by noon.

## MATCHING

Choose the synonym.

1. consistently
   (A) dependably
   (B) significantly
   (C) readily
   (D) extremely

2. capriciously
   (A) impulsively
   (B) profoundly
   (C) reluctantly
   (D) scarcely

3. subsequently
   (A) unmistakably
   (B) around
   (C) swiftly
   (D) afterwards

4. circulated
   (A) sharpened
   (B) distributed
   (C) maintained
   (D) encircled

5. briefly
   (A) rarely
   (B) reliably
   (C) concisely
   (D) severely

6. exhibited
   (A) displayed
   (B) founded
   (C) located
   (D) highlighted

7. overtly
   (A) entirely
   (B) openly
   (C) evenly
   (D) actually

8. inappropriately
   (A) disapprovingly
   (B) approximately
   (C) improperly
   (D) unintentionally

9. secluded
   (A) situated
   (B) isolated
   (C) established
   (D) shifted

10. indisputably
    (A) severely
    (B) infrequently
    (C) significantly
    (D) unmistakably

**LESSON 25—MULTIPLE-CHOICE TEST QUESTIONS**

1. The colossal Statue of Liberty is **situated** in New York harbor on a small island park near Ellis Island. Standing 302 feet high including its base, it shows a woman holding a torch in her raised right hand. In her left, there is a tablet proclaiming liberty, bearing the date July 4, 1776. An elevator rises to the balcony level, and a spiral staircase leads to a observation platform in the statue's crown.

   The word **situated** in the passage is closest in meaning to

   Ⓐ visited
   Ⓑ exhibited
   Ⓒ isolated
   Ⓓ located

2. In its earliest forms, astrology consisted of simple omens that astrologers interpreted from the celestial bodies in the sky. In its developed form, astrology analyzes the presumed effects of the Sun, Moon, planets, and stars on the Earth for a specific time and place. Astrologists also contend that the position of constellations at the moment of your birth **profoundly** influences your future.

   The word **profoundly** in the passage is closest in meaning to

   Ⓐ subsequently
   Ⓑ significantly
   Ⓒ unmistakably
   Ⓓ consistently

3. When a language is devised as a means of communication between persons having no language in common, it is called a lingua franca. This lingua franca is native to none of those using it. A lingua franca with a **sharply** reduced grammar and vocabulary is called a pidgin. When a whole speech community gives up its former language or languages and takes a pidgin as its native tongue, the pidgin becomes a creole.

   The word **sharply** in the passage is closest in meaning to

   Ⓐ severely
   Ⓑ overtly
   Ⓒ impulsively
   Ⓓ improperly

4. Cedarwood is a light, soft, resinous, and durable wood, even when it makes contact with soil or moisture. It is an important timber used in construction in regions where it is found, but is **infrequently** used elsewhere. Many varieties of the Atlas cedar are popular ornamental trees in North America, especially along the Pacific and Gulf coasts.

The word **infrequently** in the passage is closest in meaning to

- Ⓐ rarely
- Ⓑ briefly
- Ⓒ selectively
- Ⓓ continually

5. In 1876 the Johns Hopkins University was **founded** in Baltimore as the first U.S. institution to incorporate the German ideal of university education. Since that time, graduate education has become an important aspect of many institutions. Older universities, such as Harvard and Yale, and newer ones, such as Stanford and Chicago, have embraced the aims of advanced learning conducted in a spirit of freedom and autonomy.

The word **founded** in the passage is closest in meaning to

- Ⓐ erected
- Ⓑ distinguished
- Ⓒ criticized
- Ⓓ established

6. Recent studies in psychology have explored the reasons why some purchases are made **on impulse** while others are given a significant amount of forethought. One finding is that shoppers are more likely to impulsively buy clothes than garden tools. It suggests that buying on impulse is strongly related to shoppers' attitudes about themselves and to their "self-images." Useful objects such as garden tools engage shoppers less personally than items that enhance their appearance.

In discussing purchases made **on impulse**, the author is referring to purchases that shoppers make

- Ⓐ after weighing all the plusses and minuses.
- Ⓑ on a moment's notice and without thinking.
- Ⓒ in boutiques rather than department stores.
- Ⓓ to alter the feelings of people around them.

## LESSON 25—COMPUTER-BASED TEST QUESTIONS

1. *The Adventures of Huckleberry Finn* by Mark Twain can be interpreted on several levels. On the surface, it is a picturesque novel in which young Huck Finn relates his adventures as he travels down the Mississippi River with an **impulsive** runaway slave named Jim. On another level, it is a societal satire on the constraints of civilization. Huckleberry Finn becomes a study of nature's indifference; the river, like society, is sometimes benevolent, sometimes malicious, and always capricious.

   Find the word in the passage closest in meaning to the word **impulsive**.

2. Because of New Zealand's secluded location, there was no higher animal life in the country when the Maori arrived. There were two species of lizard: the gecko, and the tuatara, a reptile that was extinct everywhere else for 100,000,000 years. There were also a few primitive species of frog and two species of bats. These are all living today, but are confined to outlying islands and **isolated** parts of the country.

   Find the word in the passage closest in meaning to the word **isolated**.

3. To solve problems by computer, all data is coded as binary numbers. This code is similar to electrical systems where only two possible values exist. A light bulb may be either on or off. The two possibilities are distinct and **unmistakable**. Binary code functions in this manner. The two binary values zero and one are used to represent the electrical ideas of off and on. These individual digits are usually referred to as bits.

   Find the word in the passage closest in meaning to the word **unmistakable**.

4. The American painter Frank Duveneck was an important influence on other American artists of his generation. In 1870 he went to Munich to study at the Royal Academy where he had a **brief** acquaintance with William Merritt Chase. Duveneck was an admirer of the realism of Gustave Courbet, but his Munich work also shows how well he had assimilated the masterful brushwork and the skill in capturing fleeting expressions of the Dutch portraitist Franz Hals.

   Find the word in the passage closest in meaning to the word **brief**.

5. A dramatic monologue is a speech of long duration made by a character to a second person. A soliloquy is a type of monologue in which a character directly displays his thoughts aloud to the audience while alone or while the other actors are silent. In fiction, an interior monologue is a type of monologue that **exhibits** the thoughts, feelings, and associations passing through a character's mind.

Find the word in the passage closest in meaning to the word **exhibits**.

# LESSON 26

■ chaotic ■ characteristic ■ controversial ■ exemplify
■ gratifying ■ interpret ■ launch ■ legitimate ■ particular
■ radiant ■ ridge ■ span ■ spontaneous ■ stream
■ striking

---

**chaotic**      *adj.* being in complete disorder and confusion

*n.* chaos      *syn.* disorganized

The traffic in Seoul is often *chaotic*.

There was complete *chaos* when the world champions arrived at the airport.

**characteristic**      *adj.* an easily recognized quality of something

*adv.* characteristically      *syn.* typical
*v.* characterize
*n.* characteristic
*n.* characterization

The markings on that butterfly are *characteristic* of the monarch butterfly.

I would *characterize* him as a diligent professional.

**controversial**      *adj.* causing disagreement or argument

*adv.* controversially      *syn.* debatable
*n.* controversy

The governor made a *controversial* decision to raise taxes.

The *controversy* was caused by the proposal to build an airport in the area.

**exemplify**      *v.* to give an example

*adj.* exemplary      *syn.* symbolize

The recent downturn in the housing industry *exemplifies* the poor economic conditions.

Her *exemplary* academic achievement is representative of most students at this institution.

**gratifying**

adv. gratefully
adj. grateful
v. gratify
n. gratification
n. gratefulness

*adj.* giving pleasure or a feeling of accomplishment; showing thanks

*syn.* satisfying

Studying abroad can be a very *gratifying* experience.

She was *grateful* for all the work he had done for her.

**interpret**

n. interpreter
n. interpretation
n. interpreting

*v.* to understand the meaning of something

*syn.* clarify

The ambiguous speech was very difficult to *interpret*.

Their *interpretation* of the story generated some interesting discussion.

**launch**

n. launch
n. launching

*v.* to cause something to begin

*syn.* initiate

The company *launched* a new program to attract more clients.

The *launching* of the first Soviet *Sputnik* created concern among the American public.

**legitimate**

adv. legitimately
n. legitimacy

*adj.* reasonable; lawful

*syn.* authentic

The engineer had a *legitimate* reason for changing the design of the building.

The *legitimacy* of the theory has yet to be determined.

**particular**

adv. particularly*

*adj.* a certain way or thing; unusual; hard to please

\* especially

*syn.* specific

The speaker has a *particular* way of persuading his audience.

That group of workers is *particularly* difficult to satisfy.

**radiant**

*adv.* radiantly
*n.* radiance
*n.* radiation
*n.* radiator

*adj.* sending out in all directions, especially heat or light

*syn.* bright

The actor's *radiant* smile captivated the audience.

The *radiance* of the fire prevented the firefighters from entering the house.

**ridge**

*n.* the top of a mountain range; a raised part of any surface

*syn.* crest

A bald eagle stood on the *ridge* of the tall office building.

The mountain *ridge* was heavily forested.

**span**

*n.* span

*v.* the length of time or distance from one limit to the other; to cross

*syn.* cover

The old man's life *spanned* two centuries.

The *span* of the bridge is three miles.

**spontaneous**

*adv.* spontaneously
*n.* spontaneity

*adj.* unplanned; uncontrolled

*syn.* instinctive

The *spontaneous* combustion inside the cylinder creates the power of the motor.

The crowd reacted *spontaneously* to the danger.

**stream**

*v.* stream

*n.* a natural flow of something; a pouring out

*syn.* river

There was a constant *stream* of information coming from the White House.

Water *streamed* from the dam as workers attempted to make the repairs.

**striking**

*adv.* strikingly

*adj.* drawing special attention to

*syn.* remarkable

His *striking* proposal saved the company from bankruptcy.

That was a *strikingly* convincing argument that the speaker delivered.

## MATCHING

Choose the synonym.

1. gratifying
   - (A) spontaneous
   - (B) thriving
   - (C) satisfying
   - (D) analogous

2. disorganized
   - (A) disrupted
   - (B) chaotic
   - (C) instinctive
   - (D) discernible

3. controversial
   - (A) conventional
   - (B) intolerable
   - (C) consistent
   - (D) debatable

4. launch
   - (A) initiate
   - (B) isolate
   - (C) compel
   - (D) stream

5. typical
   - (A) practical
   - (B) parallel
   - (C) characteristic
   - (D) mediocre

6. symbolize
   - (A) radiate
   - (B) exemplify
   - (C) span
   - (D) synthesize

7. legitimate
   - (A) peculiar
   - (B) authentic
   - (C) sharp
   - (D) subsequent

8. ridge
   - (A) crest
   - (B) current
   - (C) stream
   - (D) radiance

9. interpret
   - (A) specify
   - (B) investigate
   - (C) clarify
   - (D) initiate

10. radiant
    - (A) covered
    - (B) bright
    - (C) potent
    - (D) tedious

## LESSON 26—MULTIPLE-CHOICE TEST QUESTIONS

1. In the communications and computer fields, research in optical switching is motivated by the need to transmit data **streams** at constantly higher speeds more efficiently. At the same time, customers demand transmission and switching rates far higher than can be provided by a purely electronic system. Due to developments in semiconductor lasers and in fiber optics, transmission at higher speeds is now possible.

   The word **streams** in the passage is closest in meaning to

   - Ⓐ flows
   - Ⓑ pieces
   - Ⓒ files
   - Ⓓ particles

2. A **striking** example of a successful multiethnic country is Switzerland, where French, German, and Italian speakers from diverse religious groups live and work in harmony and prosperity. Ethnic diversity in Switzerland appears to have stimulated rather than divided the Swiss population. Studies of conditions in Switzerland demonstrate that harmony can coexist with diversity when certain characteristics are shared.

   The word **striking** in the passage is closest in meaning to

   - Ⓐ spontaneous
   - Ⓑ characteristic
   - Ⓒ legitimate
   - Ⓓ remarkable

3. In one of the most influential books on education ever written, Émile Rousseau argued that society should protect children from the corrupt nature of civilization and cautiously nurture their natural, **spontaneous** impulses, which, in Rousseau's mind were always healthy. He further maintained that it was important, to avoid premature intellectualization of emotion so that the child's intellect could develop without distortion.

   The word **spontaneous** in the passage is closest in meaning to

   - Ⓐ chaotic
   - Ⓑ gratifying
   - Ⓒ instinctive
   - Ⓓ uninterrupted

4. The water available to fulfill a **particular** need is known as the water supply. When the need is domestic, industrial, or agricultural, the water must fulfill both quality and quantity requirements. Water supplies can be acquired by several types of water resources projects, such as dams, reservoirs, or wells.

The word **particular** in the passage is closest in meaning to

     Ⓐ   critical
     Ⓑ   common
     Ⓒ   gratifying
     Ⓓ   specific

5. Joseph Haydn was undoubtedly the most prolific of all symphony writers; his works **spanned** what has been called the Classical Era. He is most celebrated for taking the established forms of the symphony and shaping them into the forceful media for musical expression through invention and experimentation. These were recognized as innovations by composers who followed.

The word **spanned** in the passage is closest in meaning to

     Ⓐ   exemplified
     Ⓑ   covered
     Ⓒ   launched
     Ⓓ   interpreted

6. Writing more than 2,500 years ago, the Greek historian Herodotus claimed that it took 100,000 people 20 years to build Khufu, one of the largest pyramids in Egypt. However, Herodotus visited Egypt almost 2,700 years *after* Khufu was built, and historical facts are **always open to interpretation** anyway. Modern Egyptologists estimate that it took as few as 5,000 men to quarry the stone, haul it to the site, and assemble the pyramid.

In stating that historical facts are always **open to interpretation,** the author means that they

     Ⓐ   are changed with the passage of time.
     Ⓑ   can be analyzed in a variety of ways.
     Ⓒ   are facts and therefore indisputable.
     Ⓓ   accumulate slowly throughout history.

**LESSON 26—COMPUTER-BASED TEST QUESTIONS**

1. An intaglio is an engraved gem that, when pressed into softened wax, produces an image in relief. This wax seal was once used to make letters and documents **legitimate**. The first authentic engraving of hard stones existed as early as about 4000 B.C. in Mesopotamia, but the style of typical intaglios, which were usually mounted on rings, was developed by the ancient Greeks.

   Find the word in the passage closest in meaning to the word **legitimate**.

2. In the late 1920s and early 1930s the trucking industry was quite disorganized. It was dominated by large numbers of itinerant owner-operators. The industry was considered to be unstable, **chaotic**, and in need of regulation. The National Industrial Recovery Act of 1933 brought together two organized groups of trucking officials to develop standards of fair competition. This action led to the formation of the American Trucking Associations.

   Find the word in the passage closest in meaning to the word **chaotic**.

3. Singapore is the only nation outside of mainland China and Taiwan where the majority of the population is ethnic Chinese. Its culture **exemplifies** this Chinese heritage, coupled with various diverse cultural influences. Its British colonial architecture and Chinese, Hindu, and Muslim shrines symbolize the cultural diversity found in this international setting.

   Find the word in the passage closest in meaning to the word **exemplifies**.

4. *De architectura*, written by Vitruvius, standardized the city plans that Roman engineers used for planning the **characteristic** fortified settlements and cities that were built throughout the empire. The typical Roman plan has traces that are still observable in many European cities. This format consisted of two perpendicular main streets running north-south and east-west with the city's main civic and business square located at their intersection.

   Find the word in the passage closest in meaning to the word **characteristic**.

5. The field of opera once belonged exclusively to the Europeans. Successful American opera seemed to be confined to Gershwin's *Porgy and Bess* and other obscure operatic works. More recently the opera world has witnessed a **gratifying** growth in successful operatic works by Americans. In addition, new opera companies and small opera groups have been established. These developments are particularly satisfying to those who favor bringing a more American flavor to the opera stage.

Find the word in the passage closest in meaning to the word **gratifying**.

# LESSON 27

- aptly ■ involuntarily ■ demonstration ■ ingredients
- marvel ■ measurable ■ moderate ■ odd ■ reflection
- supposedly ■ sustained ■ symbols ■ synthesis
- tangible ■ tightly

---

**aptly**      *adv.*   having a tendency to do something; likely

*adj.* apt      *syn.*   appropriately
*n.* aptness

It was an *aptly* timed remark.

Emotional problems are *apt* to damage personal relationships.

**involuntarily**      *adv.*   in an unthinking manner; not chosen

*adj.* involuntary      *syn.*   automatically

He *involuntarily* agreed to work overtime.

Reflexes are *involuntary* reactions to external stimuli.

**demonstration**      *n.*   a show or exhibit

*adv.* demonstrably      * overtly showing emotion
*v.* demonstrate
*adj.* demonstrative*    *syn.*   display
*adj.* demonstrable

The *demonstration* clarified the procedure for everyone.

I have never seen the politicians so *demonstrative* of their feelings.

**ingredients**      *n.*   things combined to make something; the contents of something

              *syn.*   elements

The *ingredients* of the product are kept secret.

Good style, punctuation, and grammar are the important *ingredients* of a good essay.

## marvel

*n.* something that surprises or impresses

*adv.* marvelously
*adj.* marvelous

*syn.* wonder

The Great Wall of China is one of the world's *marvels*.

The weather was *marvelous* for an afternoon get-together in the park.

## measurable

*adj.* able to determine how much or many

*adv.* measurably
*v.* measure
*n.* measurement

*syn.* assessable

Some personal characteristics, such as good teaching, are hardly *measurable*.

A yardstick is used to *measure* lengths up to three feet.

## moderate

*adj.* not too much, not too little

*adv.* moderately
*v.* moderate*
*n.* moderation

* to reduce

*syn.* medium

She made the best of her *moderate* dancing ability.

The Broadway play was *moderately* successful.

## odd

*adj.* unusual

*adv.* oddly
*n.* oddity

*syn.* strange

It is *odd* to find a person who speaks many languages.

The moon rock is an *oddity* available at the museum for all to view.

## reflection

*n.* a picture or element thrown back

*adj.* reflected
*v.* reflect

*syn.* image

His bright smile was a *reflection* of his satisfaction.

In order to perceive something visually, light must be *reflected* from the object's surface.

## supposedly

*adv.* according to reports or hearsay; widely believed or accepted

*adj.* supposed
*v.* suppose
*n.* supposition

*syn.* presumably

The new trains are *supposedly* able to reach speeds of 150 miles per hour.

The stockbroker's *supposition* is that the economy will improve.

**sustained**
*v.* sustain
*adj.* sustenance

*adj.* continuing in a constant way; remaining strong

*syn.* consistent

*Sustained* rainfall is the only hope they have for relief from the drought.

The trees could not *sustain* the attack of the locusts.

**symbols**
*adv.* symbolically
*adj.* symbolic
*v.* symbolize

*n.* signs or objects that represent something or somebody

*syn.* marks

The strange *symbols* found in Egyptian tombs have intrigued historians for centuries.

I think this painting *symbolizes* the universal themes of humanity.

**synthesis**
*adv.* synthetically*
*adj.* synthetic*
*v.* synthesize

*n.* the mixing of separate things to form a whole

* not made by nature

*syn.* combination

The language of Papiamento is a *synthesis* of Dutch and native Indian languages of Curacao.

Vitamins are *synthetically* produced.

**tangible**
*adv.* tangibly
*n.* tangibility

*adj.* real; that which can be felt

*syn.* concrete

The work of a teacher seldom produces *tangible* results until years after a student has graduated.

The solution to this problem can be *tangibly* demonstrated.

**tightly**
*adj.* tight
*v.* tighten
*n.* tightness

*adv.* being fixed in place; close, leaving no freedom

*syn.* firmly

The shirt fits too *tightly*.

The government is *tightening* the regulations on the use of seat belts.

## MATCHING

Choose the synonym.

1. marvel
   (A) ridge
   (B) chaos
   (C) wonder
   (D) combination

2. display
   (A) disperse
   (B) decline
   (C) disguise
   (D) demonstration

3. oddly
   (A) symbolically
   (B) presumably
   (C) tightly
   (D) strangely

4. appropriately
   (A) supposedly
   (B) aptly
   (C) tangibly
   (D) durably

5. moderate
   (A) sustained
   (B) medium
   (C) sharp
   (D) periodic

6. involuntary
   (A) infrequent
   (B) substantial
   (C) automatic
   (D) immeasurable

7. elements
   (A) ingredients
   (B) measurements
   (C) marks
   (D) spans

8. assessable
   (A) tangible
   (B) legitimate
   (C) accountable
   (D) measurable

9. reflection
   (A) image
   (B) synthesis
   (C) solid
   (D) tightness

10. tangible
    (A) firm
    (B) consistent
    (C) concrete
    (D) tedious

## LESSON 27—MULTIPLE-CHOICE TEST QUESTIONS

1. Mechanical traps of various carnivorous plants can been seen
   in many varieties. However, the snap traps, including Venus's-
   flytrap, are found only in the sundew family. When an animal
   touches the sensory hairs, the prey is trapped by rapid closure
   of a set of lobes around the animal. Any insect that lands on
   Venus's-flytrap will cause the trap to close **tightly**.

   The word **tightly** in the passage is closest in meaning to

   Ⓐ  completely
   Ⓑ  mercilessly
   Ⓒ  firmly
   Ⓓ  involuntarily

2. In the Western world, contemplation on art began with the
   philosophers of ancient Greece. Plato discussed proportion as
   the source of beauty, and imitation as the primary mode of art.
   Aristotle identified different kinds of imitation, and Xenocrates
   wrote technical dissertations on painting and sculpture that
   examined the ideal **synthesis** of proportion and imitation in
   terms of the lives of classical Greek artists.

   The word **synthesis** in the passage is closest in meaning to

   Ⓐ  image
   Ⓑ  symbolism
   Ⓒ  display
   Ⓓ  combination

3. Anthropologists who study human communication tend to focus
   on its central role in the survival of a society. Communication
   serves to preserve and transmit the undefined aspects of a
   culture. Society communicates culture through significant
   **symbols**. These are embodied in language and represent the
   concepts of honor, bravery, love, cooperation, and honesty.

   The word **symbols** in the passage is closest in meaning to

   Ⓐ  marvels
   Ⓑ  signs
   Ⓒ  patterns
   Ⓓ  exaggerations

4. Based on the inscriptions called codices, linguists believe that the Maya spoke a language closely related to modern Native American groups. During the classical period, the Maya also had **sustained** contact with warriors and traders from Teotihuacan in central Mexico, the largest and most powerful state of the era. There is no proof of a conquest, but the Maya embraced some foreign deities, symbols, and styles of clothing of other groups.

The word **sustained** in the passage is closest in meaning to

    Ⓐ  tangible
    Ⓑ  consistent
    Ⓒ  moderate
    Ⓓ  measurable

5. The Oregon Trail followed the Sweetwater River westward from the vicinity of Casper to South Pass. Independence Rock, a granite monolith on the north bank of the river near a reservoir, was a significant trail landmark. The river was **supposedly** named by General William Ashley in 1823 because its water tasted sweet to his trappers.

The word **supposedly** in the passage is closest in meaning to

    Ⓐ  presumably
    Ⓑ  oddly
    Ⓒ  aptly
    Ⓓ  predictably

6. At 46,000 gross tons, the *Titanic* was the largest floating object ever built. It was 853 feet long, 93 feet wide, and 61 feet high. As many people said, it was **aptly named** the *Titanic*—in ancient Greek mythology, the Titans ruled the universe until Zeus defeated and replaced them. The mighty *Titanic* was also overthrown: while carrying over 2,200 passengers, it crashed into an iceberg off Newfoundland and sank on April 14, 1912.

In stating that the *Titanic* was **aptly named,** the author means that

    Ⓐ  the ship's captain was criminally negligent.
    Ⓑ  there were too many passengers on board.
    Ⓒ  the ship's name, *Titanic,* was appropriate.
    Ⓓ  the word Titanic comes from Greek history.

**LESSON 27—COMPUTER-BASED TEST QUESTIONS**

1. The date of the earliest UFO sighting in history is unknown and the evidence for such sightings is scanty and purely speculative. The beginning of the UFO phenomenon began with the sighting of strange, dirigible-like "mystery ships" over the United States from 1896 to 1897. In 1946 people in Scandinavia, reported large-scale sightings of "ghost rockets," **odd**-looking "rockets" that made no noise. None of these phenomena has been satisfactorily explained.

   Find the word in the passage closest in meaning to the word **odd**.

2. A living cell is a **marvel** of detailed and complex structure. When examined with a microscope, this elaborate wonder gives an appearance of almost chaotic activity. On a deeper level, it is known that molecules are being synthesized at a tremendous rate. Almost any enzyme causes the synthesis of more than 100 other molecules per second. In 10 minutes, a large percentage of the total mass of a metabolizing bacterial cell has been synthesized.

   Find the word in the passage closest in meaning to the word **marvel**.

3. In the 1790s, a variety of agricultural machinery was developed. At that time, an efficient seed drill had been designed but still required **demonstrations** in the 1830s to convince farmers of its value. A few threshing machines were in use before 1800, and further displays of the machinery in the 1800s made it steadily more popular. However, in the 1830s farm laborers in England rebelled because the machines deprived them of winter employment.

   Find the word in the passage closest in meaning to the word **demonstrations**.

4. The oxygen supply in the Earth's atmosphere is a result of photosynthesis by green plants. Plants require all the essential **ingredients** of photosynthesis to build the vital compounds and structures. Water is one of the critical elements, because cell enlargement is a result of internal water pressure extending the walls. This explains why in periods of drought plants tend to have smaller leaves.

Find the word in the passage closest in meaning to the word **ingredients**.

5. The historical evolution of architectural theory is **measurable** mainly from manuscripts and published essays, from critical essays and commentaries, and from the surviving buildings of past eras. Thus, there is no way the spirit of each age can be assessable. In this respect it is similar to the history of philosophy itself. Some architectural dissertations were intended to publicize original concepts rather than to state widely accepted ideals.

Find the word in the passage closest in meaning to the word **measurable**.

# LESSON 28

- aggravating ■ amusement ■ conceivably ■ convert
- curative ■ debilitating ■ deplete ■ finite ■ perceive
- security ■ toxic ■ tranquility ■ trap ■ undeniably
- underestimated

---

**aggravating**

*n.* aggravation
*v.* aggravate

*adj.* making worse; annoying
*syn.* irritating

The *aggravating* delay was caused by road repairs.

The shortage of work *aggravated* the crisis in the small town.

---

**amusement**

*adv.* amusingly
*adj.* amusing
*v.* amuse

*n.* something that holds interest and is enjoyable
*syn.* diversion

We listened in *amusement* as he tried to convince his friend to lend him $50.

His *amusing* comment made everyone laugh.

---

**conceivably**

*adj.* conceivable
*v.* conceive

*adv.* feasibly; believably
*syn.* possibly

They could *conceivably* earn first place with their science project.

It is *conceivable* that humans will travel to distant planets one day.

---

**convert**

*adj.* convertible
*n.* conversion

*v.* to change from one form or state to another
*syn.* alter

When boiled, liquids *convert* into gases.

The *conversion* from Fahrenheit to centigrade can be easily made.

---

**curative**

*n.* cure

*adj.* being able to restore to good condition
*syn.* healing

The *curative* properties of certain plants have been well documented.

There is no simple *cure* for the ills of society.

261

**debilitating**

v. debilitate
n. debility

*adj.* weakening

*syn.* weakening

The lack of investment savings has a *debilitating* effect on the economy.

The patient's *debility* restricted him to the room.

**deplete**

*adj.* depleted
*n.* depletion

*v.* to use up; reduce greatly

*syn.* consume

She *depleted* all of her savings to buy the word processor.

The *depletion* of the Earth's oil reserves poses a threat to our current way of life.

**finite**

*adj.* of a certain amount; having an end; not infinite

*syn.* limited

There were a *finite* number of explanations for the unusual reactions.

Is there a *finite* number of stars in the universe?

**perceive**

*adv.* perceptibly
*adj.* perceivable
*adj.* perceptive
*adv.* perceptively
*n.* perception

*v.* to sense; become aware of

*syn.* observe

We *perceive* major differences between the two political parties.

Porpoises are very *perceptive* mammals.

**security**

*adv.* securely
*adj.* secure
*v.* secure

*n.* the feeling of freedom from danger, doubt, or worry

*syn.* safety

Her sense of *security* increased as her grades improved.

We *secured* all of the doors of the lab before leaving.

**toxic**

*n.* toxicity

*adj.* harmful; capable of being fatal

*syn.* poisonous

Disposal of *toxic* wastes is an ongoing problem.

This product has the highest *toxicity* of any known to science.

**tranquility**

*adv.* tranquilly
*adj.* tranquil
  *v.* tranquilize

*n.* calm; quietness

*syn.* peacefulness

The *tranquility* of the lake at sunrise inspired a profound sense of well-being.

His *tranquil* manner of expression made us all feel more secure.

**trap**

*adj.* trapped
  *n.* trap

*v.* to catch and hold onto, usually by trickery; deceive

*syn.* retain

I was *trapped* into paying for the meal.

The *trapped* animals were released after being tagged by the wildlife conservationists.

**undeniably**

*adj.* undeniable

*adv.* clearly true

*syn.* absolutely

Of all the planets in our solar system, the Earth is *undeniably* the most conducive to supporting life.

It is *undeniable* that he has skill, but he needs to show more initiative.

**underestimated**

*v.* underestimate

*adj.* guessed lower than the actual quantity

*syn.* miscalculated

The *underestimated* demand for tickets made the theater manager plan better for the next performance.

The treasurer *underestimated* the cost of the new furniture.

**MATCHING**

Choose the synonym.

1. curative
   (A) healing
   (B) gratifying
   (C) toxic
   (D) conceivable

2. limited
   (A) sustained
   (B) ample
   (C) finite
   (D) approximate

3. amusement
   (A) peacefulness
   (B) demonstration
   (C) diversion
   (D) marvel

4. security
   (A) power
   (B) safety
   (C) trap
   (D) cure

5. debilitating
   (A) convincing
   (B) formidable
   (C) accelerating
   (D) weakening

6. aggravate
   (A) irritate
   (B) convert
   (C) isolate
   (D) initiate

7. conceivably
   (A) absolutely
   (B) aptly
   (C) possibly
   (D) tranquilly

8. alter
   (A) sustain
   (B) launch
   (C) detect
   (D) convert

9. depleted
   (A) retained
   (B) consumed
   (C) polluted
   (D) inundated

10. perceive
    (A) deny
    (B) miscalculate
    (C) observe
    (D) estimate

**LESSON 28—MULTIPLE-CHOICE TEST QUESTIONS**

1.  Less than one percent of all freight cargo is carried by air, most being carried by surface methods. Nevertheless, this curious fact significantly **underestimates** the importance of air freight. In terms of value of cargo carried, air transport is greater than all other modes. By the early 1990s Tokyo's Narita Airport and New York's John F. Kennedy Airport were handling in excess of one million tons of cargo per year.

    The word **underestimates** in the passage is closest in meaning to

    Ⓐ  understands
    Ⓑ  assesses
    Ⓒ  highlights
    Ⓓ  miscalculates

2.  Margaret Mead, a well-known cultural anthropologist, was associated with the American Museum of Natural History in New York City from 1926 until her death. In the 1980s, her work, in particular her famous study of Samoa, became a subject of controversy. Her critics alleged that her belief in the predominate influence of culture in shaping personality led her to misread evidence and overgeneralize. Her defenders endorsed her **undeniably** keen observations.

    The word **undeniably** in the passage is closest in meaning to

    Ⓐ  absolutely
    Ⓑ  inconsistently
    Ⓒ  presumably
    Ⓓ  unexpectedly

3.  Ice, a nearly pure solid, contains few foreign ions in its structure. It contains particles of matter and gases, which are **trapped** in bubbles in the ice. A change in makeup of these materials over time, is recorded in the successive layers of ice. This has been used to interpret the history of the environment of Earth's surface and the influence of human activities on this environment.

    The word **trapped** in the passage is closest in meaning to

    Ⓐ  found
    Ⓑ  reflected
    Ⓒ  retained
    Ⓓ  converted

4. Wang Wei was a Chinese poet, painter, and scholar of the Tang dynasty. He left behind both a significant body of lyrical poetry and delicately depicted landscape paintings. These paintings reflected a love of nature and an inner **tranquility** derived from Buddhism and meditation. He is traditionally credited with founding the Southern school of Chinese landscape painting.

The word **tranquility** in the passage is closest in meaning to

    Ⓐ   peacefulness
    Ⓑ   amusement
    Ⓒ   fulfillment
    Ⓓ   security

5. The problem of ocean pollution has been acknowledged at national and international levels. The U.S. Congress passed an act in 1988 that phased in a complete prohibition of ocean dumping by 1991. Also in 1988, 65 nations agreed to stop burning **toxic** wastes at sea by 1994. The legality of the latter measure remains debatable and may be proven unenforceable, mirroring the experience of a 1977 law that attempted the same prohibition.

The word **toxic** in the passage is closest in meaning to

    Ⓐ   inordinate
    Ⓑ   debilitating
    Ⓒ   poisonous
    Ⓓ   dispersed

6. Before Alexander Fleming made his great discovery, he had been studying losozyme, an enzyme found in tears that prevents infection. However, he wanted to find a substance with **curative powers**, something that would keep bacteria from growing and multiplying altogether. By accident, he noticed a mold growing in one of his laboratory dishes that had this effect. It turned out to be penicillin, one of the most widely used antibiotics today.

In stating that Fleming wanted to find a substance with **curative powers,** the author means that he was looking for a medicine that would

    Ⓐ   regulate a patient's exposure to germs.
    Ⓑ   combat disease-causing bacteria.
    Ⓒ   control a patient's body temperature.
    Ⓓ   increase a patient's level of infection.

## LESSON 28—COMPUTER-BASED TEST QUESTIONS

1. Times Square, a square in midtown Manhattan in New York City, was formally known as Longacre Square. It was renamed after *The New York Times* occupied a building in the square. The news is still transmitted from the building on a band of electric lights mounted across its facade. Entertainment abounds in the square and the area around it, with theaters, cinemas, **amusement** centers, and a huge subway shopping area beneath.

   Find the word in the passage closest in meaning to the word **amusement**.

2. So-called prophetic dreams in ancient Middle Eastern cultures were often used to help the sick. In classical Greece, dreams became directly identified with the healing process; ailing people came to dream in special temples where priests and priestesses advised about their ostensible **curative** benefits. A similar practice known as dream incubation is known to have existed in the ancient cultures of Babylon and Egypt.

   Find the word in the passage closest in meaning to the word **curative**.

3. Chronic fatigue syndrome is a disorder characterized by at least six months of **debilitating** fatigue that begins abruptly and is usually accompanied by mild fever, sore throat, tender weakening of the muscles, joint pain, headache, sleep disorders, confusion, memory loss, and vision problems. Once considered as an imagined rather than a specific physical condition, chronic fatigue syndrome remains controversial. Many experts are still not in agreement about its status as a distinct disorder.

   Find the word in the passage closest in meaning to the word **debilitating**.

4. Fireworms are marine worms that inhabit warm tropical waters. They produce an **aggravating** stinging sensation if touched. One particular species, *H. carunculata,* found in the coral reefs of the Caribbean Sea, has a body covered with fine, white, brittle bristles that break if touched. Upon contact, they embed themselves in human skin and produce a substance that causes a highly irritating burning sensation.

   Find the word in the passage closest in meaning to the word **aggravating**.

5. Scientists have tried to find a way to make hurricanes less dangerous by analying their component parts and neutralizing them. A hurricane contains huge quantities of supercooled water and silver iodide. Seeding the hurricane could **conceivably** produce some changes in storm behavior. Aircraft seeding experiments have obtained some minor, short-lived changes resulting in decreased wind speeds for a few hours. This outcome could possibly be improved upon, but the effects and applications of contemporary technology for hurricane modification are inconclusive.

Find the word in the passage closest in meaning to the word **conceivably**.

# LESSON 29

- acknowledge ■ acquire ■ assimilate ■ assortment
- caliber ■ condensed ■ contradictory ■ disregard
- precious ■ prominent ■ requisite ■ unravel ■ vague
- vast ■ volume

---

**acknowledge**

*n.*  acknowledgment
*adj.*  acknowledged

*v.*  to know, remember, and accept the existence of something

*syn.*  recognize

The foreman *acknowledged* the fact that there had been a mistake in the design of the house.

The promotion he received was an *acknowledgment* of his excellent work.

---

**acquire**

*adj.*  acquisitive
*n.*  acquisition

*v.*  to gain or come to possess

*syn.*  obtain

He *acquired* two beautiful paintings during his visit to Taipei.

The office's most recent *acquisition* was a new photocopier.

---

**assimilate**

*n.*  assimilation

*v.*  to become a part of

*syn.*  incorporate

The United States of America has *assimilated* people from all parts of the world.

*Assimilation* of a new cultural environment can be difficult.

---

**assortment**

*adj.*  assorted

*n.*  a variety

*syn.*  selection

You have an *assortment* of elective courses from which to choose.

He bought a box of *assorted* books at the book fair.

---

**caliber**

*n.*  the standard of; the degree of goodness

*syn.*  quality

The high *caliber* of her work earned her a raise in pay.

Only parts of the highest *caliber* can be used to make repairs on the spacecraft.

**condensed**

*v.* condense

*adj.* made smaller; shortened; merged

*syn.* summarize

This is a *condensed* version of the original research report.

Try to *condense* the two chapters into one.

**contradictory**

*v.* contradict
*n.* contradiction

*adj.* not agreeing with the facts or previous statements made on the subject; declared wrong

*syn.* inconsistent

It is *contradictory* to say that you know French after studying it for only three months.

The expert *contradicted* himself during his presentation.

**disregard**

*n.* disregard

*v.* to pay no attention

*syn.* ignore

They *disregarded* the no parking signs and were ticketed by the police.

His *disregard* of the lab instructions caused him to make many errors.

**precious**

*adj.* having much monetary or sentimental value; beautiful

*syn.* cherished

This golden ring is my most *precious* possession.

The *precious* stone was one of a kind.

**prominent**

*adv.* prominently
*n.* prominence

*adj.* famous; having a high position

*syn.* renowned

Their talent for locating oil deposits made them *prominent* geologists in the corporation.

He gained *prominence* through his television appearances.

**requisite**

*v.* require
*n.* requirement
*n.* requisition*
*v.* requisition*

*adj.* needed for a specific purpose

* a formal request

*syn.* demanded

Here is the list of *requisite* courses for the master's degree in Biology.

The project team made a *requisition* for a new set of reference books.

**unravel**

    *n.*  unraveling

*v.*  to organize; make clear

*syn.*  separate

The detective was not able to *unravel* the mystery of the missing money.

The *unraveling* of the Soviet Union took place in the span of a few months.

**vague**

    *adv.*  vaguely
    *n.*  vagueness

*adj.*  not clear; ambiguous

*syn.*  unclear

She has only *vague* memories of her childhood.

The *vagueness* of his directions caused us to get lost.

**vast**

    *adv.*  vastly

*adj.*  very much; very large

*syn.*  huge

I have noticed a *vast* improvement in your English vocabulary.

Unfortunately, the water quality has deteriorated *vastly* since my last visit here.

**volume**

    *adv.*  voluminously\*
    *adj.*  voluminous\*

*n.*  the amount of something contained in a space

    \* holding a lot

*syn.*  quantity

The *volume* of information that a computer diskette can hold is astounding.

This *voluminous* report will erase your doubt about the financial condition of the company.

## MATCHING

Choose the synonym.

1. caliber
   - (A) volume
   - (B) marvel
   - (C) quality
   - (D) acclaim

2. ignore
   - (A) disregard
   - (B) separate
   - (C) deplete
   - (D) withstand

3. acknowledged
   - (A) exaggerated
   - (B) recognized
   - (C) exemplified
   - (D) accentuated

4. assortment
   - (A) assertion
   - (B) selection
   - (C) pattern
   - (D) ingredient

5. obtain
   - (A) acquire
   - (B) unravel
   - (C) demand
   - (D) perceive

6. precious
   - (A) cherished
   - (B) substantive
   - (C) vague
   - (D) tangible

7. condensed
   - (A) summarized
   - (B) emphasized
   - (C) legitimized
   - (D) authorized

8. assimilate
   - (A) illustrate
   - (B) incorporate
   - (C) investigate
   - (D) isolate

9. renown
   - (A) reaction
   - (B) vast
   - (C) prominent
   - (D) requisite

10. contradictory
    - (A) ambiguous
    - (B) requisite
    - (C) inconsistent
    - (D) disregarded

## LESSON 29—MULTIPLE-CHOICE TEST QUESTIONS

1. By the end of 1998, the Internet's World Wide Web had become so commonplace in the public consciousness that even nontechnical adults were likely to **acknowledge** having heard of the "Net" and the "Web." Companies large and small began including a web-site address in their advertising. Furthermore, large telecommunications firms began offering their customers Internet access services.

   The word **acknowledge** in the passage is closest in meaning to

   - Ⓐ deny
   - Ⓑ remember
   - Ⓒ concede
   - Ⓓ cherish

2. Traditionally, the South Pacific Melanesians completed the **requisite** destruction of their art objects once their ceremonial purposes were achieved. Part of the artistic tradition included the need to destroy and then recreate art objects as ritualistic or social needs arose. As a result of this behavior, the Melanesian artistic tradition existed solely as an artistic concept in the mind of the artist who often worked without models of previous works.

   The word **requisite** in the passage is closest in meaning to

   - Ⓐ required
   - Ⓑ renowned
   - Ⓒ reluctant
   - Ⓓ reliable

3. Nuclear families of the preindustrial era were bound to a set of social obligations that made the nuclear family subordinate to the wishes of the larger family. This extended family system began to **unravel** with the advent of the Industrial Revolution. Aspirations for greater personal freedom and changing economic conditions produced a slow movement toward more independent nuclear families.

   The word **unravel** in the passage is closest in meaning to

   - Ⓐ form
   - Ⓑ condense
   - Ⓒ assimilate
   - Ⓓ separate

4. In 1941 President Franklin D. Roosevelt drafted The Four Freedoms. It was a list of basic human rights: freedom of speech and expression, freedom of worship, freedom from want, and freedom from fear. Later in the same year, these were incorporated into the Atlantic Charter, a British and American statement of goals for a peaceful world. Some leaders criticized The Four Freedoms for being too **vague** to serve as a guide for prudent statesmanship.

The word **vague** in the passage is closest in meaning to

- Ⓐ contradictory
- Ⓑ prominent
- Ⓒ specific
- Ⓓ unclear

5. The earliest-known handcrafted carpet, about 2,500 years old, was discovered in ice in a tomb at Pazyryk, Siberia. Rugs were also made in Persia approximately 200 years later during the reign of Cyrus, whose tomb was covered with **precious** carpets. By the sixteenth century, rug making was a highly developed craft in Persia and Turkey.

The word **precious** in the passage is closest in meaning to

- Ⓐ fine
- Ⓑ marvelous
- Ⓒ intricate
- Ⓓ astounding

6. A bar code is a tiny cluster of vertical lines and horizontal numbers against a white field found on many products today. This electronic code is not **prominently displayed**; rather, it is usually tucked away somewhere on the backside of the packaging. The digits in the code indicate the name and price of the product; more importantly, they help merchants maintain their stock by subtracting each purchase from the store's inventory.

In saying that bar codes are not **prominently displayed,** the author means that they

- Ⓐ cover most of the packaging.
- Ⓑ can be scanned by a computer.
- Ⓒ are invisible to the naked eye.
- Ⓓ may be somewhat difficult to find.

## LESSON 29—COMPUTER-BASED TEST QUESTIONS

1.  It is not known how much time was required to accumulate the **volume** of water in the oceans. Scientists believe that the quantity of water in the oceans has not changed drastically during the last few hundred million years. This conclusion is drawn from evidence indicating that the interiors of the continents have never been covered by the oceans.

    Find the word in the passage closest in meaning to the word **volume**.

2.  The dynamic growth of communications networks after 1995, especially in the scholarly world, has accelerated the establishment of the "virtual library." At the core of this development is public-domain information. Residing in huge databases distributed worldwide, a growing portion of this **vast** resource is now accessible almost immediately through the Internet.

    Find the word in the passage closest in meaning to the word **vast**.

3.  The **caliber** of any labor force depends on education and training, physique, and health. There is evidence that physical attributes have been greatly improved because of the quality of living in the twentieth century. Due to the reduction in the size of families, this rise has been even more pronounced for children than for adults. The effects are demonstrated by the greater height and weight attained by children at a given age.

    Find the word in the passage closest in meaning to the word **caliber**.

4.  Discount stores sell products at prices lower than those found in conventional retail outlets. Some, like department stores, offer wide **assortments** of goods. Other discount chains specialize, offering wide selections of special types of merchandise such as jewelry, electronic equipment, or electrical appliances. Discount stores have become international phenomena. They have spread to western Europe, Latin America, Australia, and Japan.

    Find the word in the passage closest in meaning to the word **assortments**.

5. The major reasons for establishing a wildlife refuge are to obtain protection for a group of animals that have become significantly reduced in number and to suitably improve the habitat so that animals will breed and flourish. The process used to **acquire** the land or water for these purposes is complicated due to restrictions or prohibitions on hunting, trapping, trespassing, and fishing.

Find the word in the passage closest in meaning to the word **acquire**.

# LESSON 30

■ charisma ■ clever ■ convince ■ endure ■ forfeit
■ precarious ■ severe ■ sporadic ■ superior ■ wanton
■ weak ■ widespread ■ wisdom ■ witticism ■ woo

| | |
|---|---|
| **charisma** | *n.* a special quality that endears other |
| *adj.* charismatic | people to the person who has this quality |
| | *syn.* appeal |

She has a *charisma* that no other candidate possesses.

John F. Kennedy was known for his *charismatic* personality.

| | |
|---|---|
| **clever** | *adj.* intelligent; resourceful |
| *adv.* cleverly | *syn.* astute |
| *n.* cleverness | |

Everyone appreciated their *clever* idea.

His *cleverness* enabled him to rise quickly in the organization.

| | |
|---|---|
| **convince** | *v.* to make someone see things your way |
| *adv.* convincingly | *syn.* persuade |
| *adj.* convincing | |

They could not *convince* the girls to go to the dance with them.

The video made a *convincing* argument for the recycling of paper and plastic materials.

| | |
|---|---|
| **endure** | *v.* to last; suffer pain |
| *adj.* endurable | *syn.* perservere |
| *adj.* enduring | |
| *n.* endurance | |

How he is able to *endure* living next to the airport is beyond my comprehension.

The *endurance* displayed by the athlete gave evidence of his rigorous training.

**forfeit**
   *n.*  forfeit

*v.*  to give up; have something taken away, usually by rule or regulation

*syn.*  relinquish

Usually you must *forfeit* your native country's citizenship to become a citizen of another country.

The *forfeit* occurred because not enough players showed up.

**precarious**
  *adv.*  precariously

*adj.*  not safe, firm, or steady

*syn.*  hazardous

The diver put himself in a *precarious* situation among the sharks.

The cup was positioned *precariously* on the edge of the table.

**severe**
  *adv.*  severely
  *n.*  severity

*adj.*  extreme; harmful

*syn.*  intense

The weather service issued a *severe* storm warning for most of Michigan.

The *severity* of his condition will not be known until the test results are studied.

**sporadic**
  *adv.*  sporadically

*adj.*  not consistent; irregular

*syn.*  erratic

The radio communications were subject to *sporadic* sunspot interference.

Violent storms occur *sporadically* in the Southwest.

**superior**
  *n.*  superiority

*adj.*  excellent quality; above all the rest

*syn.*  exceptional

This is a *superior* fossil of a trilobite.

The restaurant's *superiority* was established shortly after it opened.

**wanton**
  *adv.*  wantonly

*adj.*  done without thought or consideration; grossly negligent

*syn.*  senseless

Her *wanton* disregard of the rules was unexplainable.

The jealous man was *wantonly* impolite to the winner.

**weak**      *adj.*   not strong; incapable

*adv.*   weakly      *syn.*   ineffective
  *v.*   weaken
  *n.*   weakness

The *weak* light was inadequate for reading.

Most people have at least one area of *weakness*.

**widespread**      *adj.*   found everywhere

                *syn.*   extensive

There is a *widespread* rumor that there will be no class next Thursday.

The political influence of the developed countries of the world is *widespread*.

**wisdom**      *n.*   knowledge and understanding

*adv.*   wisely      *syn.*   insight
*adj.*   wise

It is often said that *wisdom* is the product of experience.

It was a *wise* decision for you to buy a car.

**witticism**      *n.*   a joke; a funny story

*adv.*   wittily      *syn.*   humor
*adj.*   witty
  *n.*   wit
  *n.*   wittiness

His *witticisms* captivated the audience.

Mark Twain was famous for his sharp *wit*.

**woo**      *v.*   to make efforts to attain or gain something

                *syn.*   attract

The directors tried to *woo* the support of the union.

The opponents of the proposed highway *wooed* nearby residents to defend their position.

## MATCHING

Choose the synonym.

1. astute
   - (A) acknowledge
   - (B) extensive
   - (C) clever
   - (D) weak

2. sporadic
   - (A) prophetic
   - (B) intrinsic
   - (C) erratic
   - (D) archaic

3. relinquish
   - (A) recover
   - (B) disperse
   - (C) forfeit
   - (D) deplete

4. perservering
   - (A) enduring
   - (B) ineffective
   - (C) secure
   - (D) sincere

5. superior
   - (A) prosperous
   - (B) sustained
   - (C) superficial
   - (D) exceptional

6. appeal
   - (A) wit
   - (B) charisma
   - (C) impression
   - (D) wisdom

7. precarious
   - (A) peculiar
   - (B) dangerous
   - (C) widespread
   - (D) aggravating

8. persuade
   - (A) convince
   - (B) conform
   - (C) confirm
   - (D) conceal

9. wisdom
   - (A) acceleration
   - (B) insight
   - (C) caution
   - (D) marvel

10. intense
    - (A) instant
    - (B) hazardous
    - (C) severe
    - (D) robust

**LESSON 30—MULTIPLE-CHOICE TEST QUESTIONS**

1. The circulation war of the tabloids that took place in New York City in the 1920s was copied in Britain in the 1930s. This brought numerous circulation-boosting schemes. Prizes for readers were introduced in the 1890s and had become popular measures to **woo** new subscribers by the 1900s. Although the practice was condemned by the Newspaper Proprietors' Association, gift schemes grew along with the number of newspapers for many years. They continue today.

   The word **woo** in the passage is closest in meaning to

   Ⓐ forfeit
   Ⓑ attract
   Ⓒ convince
   Ⓓ deceive

2. Intensity, intimacy, and omnipresence have been identified as the distinctive characteristics of the motion-picture image. Its intensity stems from its power to capture the complete attention of the theatergoer. Outside the theater, a person's attention is usually divided among the elements of the limitless reality around him or her, except for **sporadic** moments of concentration on what is selected for closer examination.

   The word **sporadic** in the passage is closest in meaning to

   Ⓐ occasional
   Ⓑ charismatic
   Ⓒ recurrent
   Ⓓ splendid

3. Established in 1942, the Voice of America is the international radio network of the U.S. Information Agency. Its charge is the **widespread** decree of a favorable understanding of the United States abroad. It achieves this task with a wide range of programs, including news, editorials, features, and music. The VOA has established a long-term modernization plan to increase its number of broadcasting languages from 42 to 60.

   The word **widespread** in the passage is closest in meaning to

   Ⓐ unlimited
   Ⓑ discernible
   Ⓒ extensive
   Ⓓ alluring

4. Jellyfish feed on organisms like plankton, fish, and other jellyfish. They capture their prey by using nematocysts, small stinging organs found on their tentacles. Their movement is produced through rhythmic contractions of the bell's perimeter surface, which discharges water. This causes water to move the animal forward by jet propulsion. Some varieties of jellyfish are able to swim well, but most are **weak** swimmers that drift with sea currents.

The word **weak** in the passage is closest in meaning to

    Ⓐ   ineffective
    Ⓑ   chaotic
    Ⓒ   harmful
    Ⓓ   agile

5. During his administration, Thomas Jefferson pursued a policy of expansion. He seized an opportunity when Napoleon Bonaparte decided to **forfeit** French ambitions in North America by offering the Louisiana territory for sale. This remarkable acquisition, purchased for a few cents per acre, more than doubled the area of the United States. Jefferson had no constitutional right to complete the transaction. Nevertheless, he made up the rules as he went along, broadly interpreting the Constitution.

The word **forfeit** in the passage is closest in meaning to

    Ⓐ   accelerate
    Ⓑ   restrain
    Ⓒ   relinquish
    Ⓓ   postpone

6. In some countries, high-speed driving is **severely punished**, while in others speed is ignored, tolerated, or encouraged. For example, French police fine drivers as much as 380 euros on the spot for driving more than 110 kilometers per hour, while the famous German expressway known as the "Autobahn" has no speed limit, although sections of it may have recommended limits. The lack of a speed limit and lighter police surveillance turn many drivers into skillful competitors.

In stating that high-speed driving is **severely punished**, the author means that

    Ⓐ   offenders are sure to be arrested at once.
    Ⓑ   exceeding the limit carries the death penalty.
    Ⓒ   authorities impose a large fine.
    Ⓓ   speeding is officially encouraged.

## LESSON 30—COMPUTER-BASED TEST QUESTIONS

1. As a U.S. congressman, Davy Crockett won a reputation as a **witty**, shrewd, and outspoken backwoodsman. It was in Washington that the legend of this man as a coonskin-hatted bear hunter and humorous tall-tale teller was created. There, his political allies promoted this image so he could compete with President Jackson's image as a democrat.

   Find the word in the passage closest in meaning to the word **witty**.

2. The volcanic areas of southern Guatemala contain some of the nation's most richest soils. However, the northern parts of this region are particularly subject to erosion encouraged by steep slopes and senseless deforestation. Within the Sierra region, heavier rainfall combined with thinner soils on the steep slopes and the **wanton** destruction of forests have led to widespread erosion.

   Find the word in the passage closest in meaning to the word **wanton**.

3. Seasonal droughts exist where wet and dry seasons regularly alternate. Farming, if conducted during the dry season, must rely on irrigation. Contingent, or unpredictable, droughts exist where normally expected rainfall fails to occur. This most commonly occurs in humid or semi-humid areas. These droughts tend to be most intense when they are combined with the increased water needs of the growing season. They are the most **severe** of the physical threats to farming.

   Find the word in the passage closest in meaning to the word **severe**.

4. In all the Apache groups, the central family structure was matriarchal. The women cared for the children, gathered plant food, and collected firewood and water. The men of the family hunted, fought, raided, and made weapons and shields. The head of the family had special appeal in the Apache society. The most persuasive, tenacious, and successful of the family heads became Apache leaders. Those in authority were chosen because they had personal **charisma** and success in warfare.

   Find the word in the passage closest in meaning to the word **charisma**.

5. Bishop Wright profoundly influenced the lives of his children. Wilbur and Orville, like their father, were independent thinkers. They had deep confidence in their own talents and an unwavering faith in the soundness of their judgment. They were taught to **endure** difficulties and persevere in the face of disappointment. Those qualities, when combined with their unique talents, help to explain the accomplishments of the Wright brothers as inventors.

Find the word in the passage closest in meaning to the word **endure**.

# ANSWERS TO EXERCISES

|  | MATCHING | MULTIPLE-CHOICE TEST QUESTIONS | COMPUTER-BASED TEST QUESTIONS |
|---|---|---|---|

## LESSON 1

| MATCHING | MULTIPLE-CHOICE TEST QUESTIONS | COMPUTER-BASED TEST QUESTIONS |
|---|---|---|
| 1. A  6. C | 1. **D** autonomous—independent | 1. actually—truly |
| 2. A  7. D | 2. **C** persistent—constant | 2. abrupt—sudden |
| 3. C  8. B | 3. **A** haphazardly—carelessly | 3. acceptable—permissible |
| 4. A  9. D | 4. **A** disruptive—disturbing | 4. acclaim—praise |
| 5. C  10. B | 5. **D** adverse—unfavorable | 5. abroad—overseas |
|  | 6. **B** condemn or oppose their use |  |

## LESSON 2

| MATCHING | MULTIPLE-CHOICE TEST QUESTIONS | COMPUTER-BASED TEST QUESTIONS |
|---|---|---|
| 1. C  6. B | 1. **C** celebrated—renowned | 1. advent—arrival |
| 2. A  7. A | 2. **A** energetic—vigorous | 2. agile—nimble |
| 3. D  8. C | 3. **C** distribution—dispensing | 3. allowed—permitted |
| 4. B  9. C | 4. **A** contemporary—current | 4. albeit—although |
| 5. C  10. D | 5. **D** appealing—alluring | 5. advanced—progressive |
|  | 6. **D** view city life as advantageous |  |

## LESSON 3

| MATCHING | MULTIPLE-CHOICE TEST QUESTIONS | COMPUTER-BASED TEST QUESTIONS |
|---|---|---|
| 1. C  6. B | 1. **D** intolerable—unbearable | 1. analysis—examination |
| 2. B  7. A | 2. **B** enrich—enhance | 2. altered—changed |
| 3. D  8. D | 3. **A** vital—indispensable | 3. annoying—bothersome |
| 4. A  9. C | 4. **A** ongoing—current | 4. ancient—old |
| 5. C  10. D | 5. **D** revitalize—restore | 5. anticipated—predicted |
|  | 6. **D** looks the same as its environment |  |

## LESSON 4

| MATCHING | MULTIPLE-CHOICE TEST QUESTIONS | COMPUTER-BASED TEST QUESTIONS |
|---|---|---|
| 1. C  6. B | 1. **B** deceptive—elusive | 1. asserted—declared |
| 2. B  7. A | 2. **C** petition—appeal | 2. arbitrary—haphazard |
| 3. A  8. D | 3. **B** forbidden—banned | 3. apparently—visibly |
| 4. D  9. A | 4. **B** tempt—entice | 4. authorized—empowered |
| 5. A  10. D | 5. **A** astounding—astonishing | 5. astute—perceptive |
|  | 6. **C** insist on reducing them |  |

## LESSON 5

| MATCHING | MULTIPLE-CHOICE TEST QUESTIONS | COMPUTER-BASED TEST QUESTIONS |
|---|---|---|
| 1. B  6. B | 1. **C** shed—discarded | 1. cautioned—warned |
| 2. D  7. D | 2. **A** brilliance—radiance | 2. bright—brilliant |
| 3. A  8. A | 3. **D** unique—rare | 3. blurred—clouded |
| 4. B  9. B | 4. **A** persuade—convince | 4. bears—produces |
| 5. C  10. C | 5. **A** replacement—substitute | 5. baffle—puzzle |
|  | 6. **A** interests a lot of scientists |  |

## LESSON 6

| MATCHING | MULTIPLE-CHOICE TEST QUESTIONS | COMPUTER-BASED TEST QUESTIONS |
|---|---|---|
| 1. C  6. B | 1. **A** immense—massive | 1. complex—intricate |
| 2. C  7. B | 2. **C** conventional—traditional | 2. comparatively—relatively |
| 3. A  8. A | 3. **A** routinely—ordinarily | 3. commonplace—standard |
| 4. C  9. D | 4. **B** curious—peculiar | 4. coarse—rough |
| 5. A  10. A | 5. **B** rigid—stiff | 5. chiefly—mostly |
|  | 6. **B** some have less of a hold on a user's attention |  |

| MATCHING | | MULTIPLE-CHOICE<br>TEST QUESTIONS | COMPUTER-BASED<br>TEST QUESTIONS |
|---|---|---|---|

## LESSON 7

| | |
|---|---|
| 1. **B** | 6. **A** |
| 2. **D** | 7. **B** |
| 3. **A** | 8. **B** |
| 4. **C** | 9. **C** |
| 5. **C** | 10. **A** |

1. **B** reveals—discloses
2. **D** purposefully—deliberately
3. **C** distort—deform
4. **C** diverse—different
5. **B** prosperous—thriving
6. **A** is entirely interested only in itself

1. core—central
2. convenient—practical
3. constant—continuous
4. confirms—proves
5. concealed—hid

## LESSON 8

| | |
|---|---|
| 1. **C** | 6. **B** |
| 2. **D** | 7. **A** |
| 3. **D** | 8. **C** |
| 4. **A** | 9. **A** |
| 5. **B** | 10. **D** |

1. **B** flaws—defects
2. **B** reflect—mirror
3. **D** settle—colonize
4. **A** distinguish—discriminate
5. **D** fragments—particles
6. **D** kept ballooning from becoming more popular

1. cultivated—grown
2. crush—grind
3. creep—crawl
4. created—produced
5. cracks—fractures

## LESSON 9

| | |
|---|---|
| 1. **C** | 6. **D** |
| 2. **B** | 7. **B** |
| 3. **A** | 8. **A** |
| 4. **B** | 9. **A** |
| 5. **A** | 10. **D** |

1. **B** vibrant—brilliant
2. **D** enduring—lasting
3. **C** gigantic—enormous
4. **A** impressive—imposing
5. **D** depth—thoroughness
6. **C** population is the largest per square kilometer

1. display—exhibit
2. dim—faint
3. dense—thick
4. deep—thorough
5. currency—money

## LESSON 10

| | |
|---|---|
| 1. **C** | 6. **C** |
| 2. **B** | 7. **A** |
| 3. **A** | 8. **C** |
| 4. **D** | 9. **C** |
| 5. **A** | 10. **D** |

1. **D** rudimentary—basic
2. **D** superficial—shallow
3. **A** prime—chief
4. **B** hazardous—dangerous
5. **C** phenomenal—exceptional
6. **C** the most talented are few in number

1. dramatic—emotional
2. drab—colorless
3. dormant—inactive
4. dominant—major
5. distinct—definite

## LESSON 11

| | |
|---|---|
| 1. **B** | 6. **A** |
| 2. **A** | 7. **A** |
| 3. **B** | 8. **D** |
| 4. **B** | 9. **C** |
| 5. **D** | 10. **C** |

1. **C** encircles—surrounds
2. **C** eliminated—deleted
3. **D** elementary—primary
4. **B** element—component
5. **A** dwellings—abodes
6. **B** are more numerous than compacts

1. erratic—inconsistent
2. piers—docks
3. prevalent—commonplace
4. exaggerates—embellishes
5. dispersed—scattered

## LESSON 12

| | |
|---|---|
| 1. **C** | 6. **A** |
| 2. **C** | 7. **D** |
| 3. **D** | 8. **B** |
| 4. **A** | 9. **A** |
| 5. **B** | 10. **A** |

1. **D** evaporated—disappeared
2. **D** eroded—deteriorated
3. **C** entirely—completely
4. **B** benefit—assistance
5. **B** endorsed—supported
6. **B** were alleged to exist

1. burgeoning—thriving
2. broaden—enlarge
3. shifts—switches
4. recovered—retrieved
5. enormous—tremendous

| MATCHING | MULTIPLE-CHOICE TEST QUESTIONS | COMPUTER-BASED TEST QUESTIONS |
|---|---|---|

## LESSON 13

| | |
|---|---|
| 1. **B** | 6. **B** |
| 2. **D** | 7. **C** |
| 3. **B** | 8. **B** |
| 4. **A** | 9. **D** |
| 5. **C** | 10. **A** |

1. **A** suitable—appropriate
2. **C** crucial—critical
3. **A** inaccessible—remote
4. **D** predicted—anticipated
5. **B** heroes—philanthropists
6. **B** in front of each other

1. evident—apparent
2. exhausted—depleted
3. extremely—highly
4. face—confront
5. facets—aspects

## LESSON 14

| | |
|---|---|
| 1. **C** | 6. **A** |
| 2. **C** | 7. **D** |
| 3. **A** | 8. **D** |
| 4. **B** | 9. **D** |
| 5. **A** | 10. **A** |

1. **B** ample—abundant
2. **C** arid—dry
3. **C** defying—resisting
4. **D** avert—avoid
5. **B** spacious—expansive
6. **A** basically well designed and built

1. fundamental—basic
2. functions—roles
3. freshly—recently
4. fertile—rich
5. feigning—pretending

## LESSON 15

| | |
|---|---|
| 1. **B** | 6. **C** |
| 2. **D** | 7. **B** |
| 3. **B** | 8. **D** |
| 4. **D** | 9. **A** |
| 5. **A** | 10. **C** |

1. **B** halt—stop
2. **A** substantially—significantly
3. **D** mysterious—baffling
4. **A** rejects—refuses
5. **C** boosts—promotes
6. **D** was nearly entirely eliminated

1. perilous—dangerous
2. harmful—unhealthy
3. harbor—shelter
4. handle—manage
5. gained—attained

## LESSON 16

| | |
|---|---|
| 1. **C** | 6. **D** |
| 2. **C** | 7. **B** |
| 3. **A** | 8. **D** |
| 4. **B** | 9. **B** |
| 5. **B** | 10. **B** |

1. **D** systematically—methodically
2. **A** recover—retrieve
3. **D** meticulous—conscientious
4. **D** encompass—include
5. **B** unlikely—doubtful
6. **B** more conscious of the situation

1. infancy—beginnings
2. inadvertent—unexpected
3. inevitable—unavoidable
4. emphasizes—highlights
5. heighten—intensify

## LESSON 17

| | |
|---|---|
| 1. **A** | 6. **B** |
| 2. **B** | 7. **D** |
| 3. **A** | 8. **A** |
| 4. **A** | 9. **A** |
| 5. **D** | 10. **B** |

1. **A** involve—include
2. **B** inundated—overwhelmed
3. **A** intrinsic—inherent
4. **D** intentionally—deliberately
5. **C** instantly—immediately
6. **B** occurs slowly over time

1. agitated—disturbed
2. nominal—moderate
3. confidential—secret
4. documented—proven
5. inordinate—excessive

## LESSON 18

| | |
|---|---|
| 1. **B** | 6. **B** |
| 2. **A** | 7. **B** |
| 3. **A** | 8. **A** |
| 4. **A** | 9. **B** |
| 5. **D** | 10. **C** |

1. **C** narrow—thin
2. **B** means—method
3. **A** absurd—ridiculous
4. **A** limber—flexible
5. **C** lack—shortage
6. **B** information for and against

1. feasible—possible
2. robust—strong
3. swift—rapid
4. fallacy—misconception
5. preconception—bias

| MATCHING | | MULTIPLE-CHOICE TEST QUESTIONS | COMPUTER-BASED TEST QUESTIONS |
|---|---|---|---|

## LESSON 19

| | | |
|---|---|---|
| 1. **B** | 6. **D** | |
| 2. **C** | 7. **C** | |
| 3. **A** | 8. **C** | |
| 4. **A** | 9. **C** | |
| 5. **A** | 10. **D** | |

1. **A** antiquated—outmoded
2. **A** novel—original
3. **B** notion—concept
4. **D** notice—observe
5. **D** normally—typically
6. **D** are against its continuation

1. unbiased—objective
2. suspect—speculate
3. investigate—probe
4. coherent—logical
5. recorded—registered

## LESSON 20

| | |
|---|---|
| 1. **B** | 6. **C** |
| 2. **D** | 7. **A** |
| 3. **B** | 8. **D** |
| 4. **C** | 9. **A** |
| 5. **A** | 10. **B** |

1. **A** pass—approve
2. **A** partially—somewhat
3. **B** overcome—conquer
4. **B** outlandish—bizarre
5. **C** omit—neglect
6. **A** play in an offensive way

1. disguise—concealment
2. initiation—launching
3. narrate—relate
4. innovative—inventive
5. accentuate—emphasize

## LESSON 21

| | |
|---|---|
| 1. **A** | 6. **B** |
| 2. **D** | 7. **C** |
| 3. **B** | 8. **D** |
| 4. **B** | 9. **C** |
| 5. **D** | 10. **B** |

1. **B** plentiful—abundant
2. **D** sheltered—protected
3. **C** philanthropic—humanitarian
4. **D** phenomena—occurrences
5. **A** decrease—decline
6. **A** combines chemically with the acid

1. placid—calm
2. reactions—responses
3. scenic—picturesque
4. patterns—habits
5. vanish—disappear

## LESSON 22

| | |
|---|---|
| 1. **B** | 6. **D** |
| 2. **D** | 7. **B** |
| 3. **C** | 8. **A** |
| 4. **B** | 9. **C** |
| 5. **A** | 10. **D** |

1. **A** predominant—principal
2. **C** disregarded—overlooked
3. **A** practical—functional
4. **D** hasten—accelerate
5. **A** polls—surveys
6. **C** explain what causes them

1. induces—prompts
2. positions—locations
3. archaic—ancient
4. hue—color
5. inactive—idle

## LESSON 23

| | |
|---|---|
| 1. **D** | 6. **D** |
| 2. **C** | 7. **A** |
| 3. **C** | 8. **A** |
| 4. **B** | 9. **A** |
| 5. **B** | 10. **C** |

1. **B** reliably—dependably
2. **A** readily—freely
3. **C** proportions—dimensions
4. **C** prophetic—predictive
5. **D** prone—inclined
6. **B** is famous for the violin players

1. analogous—similar
2. periodically—regularly
3. compelled—obliged
4. intruded—imposed
5. renown—prominence

## LESSON 24

| | |
|---|---|
| 1. **B** | 6. **C** |
| 2. **D** | 7. **A** |
| 3. **A** | 8. **C** |
| 4. **A** | 9. **A** |
| 5. **C** | 10. **D** |

1. **C** somewhat—slightly
2. **D** solid—substantial
3. **B** contaminated—polluted
4. **D** scattered—distributed
5. **C** remarkable—exceptional
6. **A** only these animals have this capacity

1. discern—ascertain
2. mediocre—average
3. parallel—similar
4. peculiar—distinctive
5. tedious—monotonous

| MATCHING | MULTIPLE-CHOICE TEST QUESTIONS | COMPUTER-BASED TEST QUESTIONS |
|---|---|---|

## LESSON 25

| | | | |
|---|---|---|---|
| 1. A | 6. A | 1. **D** situated—located | 1. impulsive—capricious |
| 2. A | 7. B | 2. **B** profoundly—significantly | 2. isolated—secluded |
| 3. D | 8. C | 3. **A** sharply—severely | 3. unmistakable—indisputable |
| 4. B | 9. B | 4. **A** infrequently—rarely | 4. brief—fleeting |
| 5. C | 10. D | 5. **D** founded—established | 5. exhibits—displays |
| | | 6. **B** on a moment's notice and without thinking | |

## LESSON 26

| | | | |
|---|---|---|---|
| 1. C | 6. B | 1. **A** streams—rivers | 1. legitimate—authentic |
| 2. B | 7. B | 2. **D** striking—remarkable | 2. chaotic—disorganized |
| 3. D | 8. A | 3. **C** spontaneous—instinctive | 3. exemplifies—symbolize |
| 4. A | 9. C | 4. **D** particular—specific | 4. characteristic—typical |
| 5. C | 10. B | 5. **B** spanning—covering | 5. gratifying—satisfying |
| | | 6. **B** can be analyzed in a variety of ways | |

## LESSON 27

| | | | |
|---|---|---|---|
| 1. C | 6. C | 1. **C** tightly—firmly | 1. odd—strange |
| 2. D | 7. A | 2. **D** synthesis—combination | 2. marvel—wonder |
| 3. D | 8. D | 3. **B** symbols—signs | 3. demonstrations—displays |
| 4. B | 9. A | 4. **B** sustained—consistent | 4. ingredients—elements |
| 5. B | 10. C | 5. **A** supposedly—presumably | 5. measurable—assessable |
| | | 6. **C** the ship's name, *Titanic*, was appropriate | |

## LESSON 28

| | | | |
|---|---|---|---|
| 1. A | 6. A | 1. **D** underestimates—miscalculates | 1. amusement—entertainment |
| 2. C | 7. C | 2. **A** undeniably—absolutely | 2. curative—healing |
| 3. C | 8. D | 3. **C** trapped—retained | 3. debilitating—weakening |
| 4. B | 9. B | 4. **A** tranquility—peacefulness | 4. aggravating—irritating |
| 5. D | 10. C | 5. **C** toxic—poisonous | 5. conceivably—possibly |
| | | 6. **B** combat disease-causing bacteria | |

## LESSON 29

| | | | |
|---|---|---|---|
| 1. C | 6. A | 1. **C** acknowledge—concede | 1. volume—quantity |
| 2. A | 7. A | 2. **A** requisite—required | 2. vast—huge |
| 3. B | 8. B | 3. **D** unravel—separate | 3. caliber—quality |
| 4. B | 9. C | 4. **D** vague—unclear | 4. assortments—selections |
| 5. A | 10. C | 5. **A** precious—fine | 5. acquire—obtain |
| | | 6. **C** are invisible to the naked eye | |

## LESSON 30

| | | | |
|---|---|---|---|
| 1. C | 6. B | 1. **B** woo—attract | 1. witty—humorous |
| 2. C | 7. B | 2. **A** sporadic—occasional | 2. wanton—senseless |
| 3. C | 8. A | 3. **C** widespread—extensive | 3. severe—intense |
| 4. A | 9. B | 4. **A** weak—ineffective | 4. charisma—appeal |
| 5. D | 10. C | 5. **C** forfeit—relinquish | 5. endure—persevere |
| | | 6. **C** authorities impose a large fine | |

# CHAPTER 7

# THE PRACTICE TEST (COMPUTER-BASED FORMAT)

## GENERAL DIRECTIONS

*Essential Words for the TOEFL* provides you with a 60-item TOEFL practice test for Section 3, which tests reading comprehension, including specific vocabulary items and whole phrases or words in combination. The paper and pencil TOEFL contains 50 items in the Reading Comprehension section, while the computer-based TOEFL contains 45–55 items in this section. However, we have included a longer passage (775 words), like the kind of passage that is likely to be found in the new version of TOEFL that will appear in 2005. This passage is followed by 10 questions (numbers 51–60). The practice test is on the pages that follow. It uses the computer-based format. The computer-based version contains the same kinds of items found on the paper version, plus some additional item formats. Thus, this test will be helpful to you regardless of which version of TOEFL you plan to take.

After you have studied the vocabulary lessons in this book, take the test in a single sitting. Using a watch or a clock, time yourself when taking the test. Write down on a piece of paper your start time and the time at which you will stop. Allow yourself 65 minutes to take the test. Use the full 65 minutes. If you finish early, go back and check your work, following the helpful strategies and hints for test takers covered in Chapter 1 and Chapter 2 of this book.

When taking the test, follow the directions for each question. For multiple-choice questions, circle the correct answer in your book. For vocabulary questions, circle the correct word or words in the passage. For other types of questions, do as indicated. Although this test is not administered on a computer, every effort has been made to make it like the computer-based version.

After you take each test, score it using the answer key provided on page 313 of this book. For each vocabulary item you answer incorrectly, look up the word tested in this book. Try to understand why you made the mistake so you won't make it again. If necessary, look up the tested word or the options in your English dictionary. This will provide you with additional information on the meaning of the word in different contexts, and perhaps another example sentence demonstrating its usage.

For information on interpreting your performance and converting it to the TOEFL scale, follow the directions in Scoring Your TOEFL Practice Test at the end of this chapter.

Now, review Chapters 1 and 2; then write down your starting time, and take the TOEFL Practice Test, Reading section.

## SECTION 3: READING

In this section of the TOEFL you will read six passages. Each passage is followed by 10 questions. You should answer all questions on the basis of what is stated or implied in the passage. You will be asked to perform a variety of tasks in this section. Read and follow the directions for each test question carefully before you answer. After you have completed this test, you may refer to the Score Conversion Table to determine your approximate TOEFL score for the Reading Comprehension section of the TOEFL.

## Questions 1–10

Learning, remembering, and forgetting have traditionally been considered separate processes. However, contemporary research regarding the differences between long- and short-term memory blurs the distinction between the three
(5) processes. Evidence to support the theory that these are just separate steps in the learning process is provided by observations of how learners remember information over a period of time. Today, most scientists believe that there are three stages of memory: immediate, short-term, and long-term. Immediate
(10) memory seems to last more than a second or so. For example, subjects may be asked to remember the location of specific objects within a complicated arrangement that they have just seen. Their performance shows that considerable information is remembered briefly. Then it is rapidly forgotten unless it is
(15) given special attention.

Short-term memory lasts about 15 to 30 seconds, such as after looking up a telephone number. One makes the call, discovers that he or she has forgotten the number (perhaps in the midst of dialing), and has to look it up again. Nevertheless,
(20) such short-term memory makes information available long

enough to be rehearsed. If the learner repeats it internally, the number could be transferred to some sort of long-term storage.

(25) Thus, by repeating information, one can transfer information from short-term to long-term memory. Once present in long-term memory, it is available for recall for a long time. While any memory can be abruptly erased when specific parts of the brain are injured or removed, in most cases, long-term memories undergo little or no forgetting over periods of months or years.

1. What is the main topic of the passage?
   Ⓐ Short term memory allows us to perform tasks without remembering the information.
   Ⓑ Learning, remembering, and forgetting are different stages of the same process.
   Ⓒ Repetition is an important factor in retaining information for immediate or long-term use.
   Ⓓ The way people retain information varies.

2. What does the author suggest in order to remember information for long periods of time?
   Ⓐ Concentrate while you are reading or listening to the information.
   Ⓑ Repeat the information to yourself.
   Ⓒ Pay attention to details.
   Ⓓ Be sure to pass through all three stages of learning.

---

(25) Thus, by repeating information, one can transfer information from short-term to long-term memory. Once present in long-term memory, **it** is available for recall for a long time. While any memory can be abruptly erased when specific parts of the brain are injured or removed, in most cases, long-term memories undergo little or no forgetting over periods of months or years.

---

3. Find the word "**it**" in line 25 of the passage above. Circle the word in the text that refers to "**it**."

4. The following sentence can be added to paragraph 1.

**Thus, activation of immediate memory is the first stage in learning.**

Where would it best fit in the paragraph: **(A), (B), (C), (D), (E), (F), (G), (H), or (I)?**

Paragraph 1 is marked with →

→ **(A)** Learning, remembering, and forgetting have traditionally been considered separate processes. **(B)** However, contemporary research regarding the differences between long- and short-term memory blurs the distinction between the three
(5)   processes. **(C)** Evidence to support the theory that these are just separate steps in the learning process is provided by observations of how learners remember information over a period of time. **(D)** Today, most scientists believe that there are three stages of memory: immediate, short-term, and long-term. **(E)** Immediate
(10)   memory seems to last more than a second or so. **(F)** For example, subjects may be asked to remember the location of specific objects within a complicated arrangement that they have just seen. **(G)** Their performance shows that considerable information is remembered briefly. **(H)** Then it is rapidly forgotten unless it is
(15)   given special attention. **(I)**

Learning, remembering, and forgetting have traditionally been considered separate processes. However, contemporary research regarding the differences between long- and short-term memory blurs the distinction between the three
(5)   processes. Evidence to support the theory that these are just separate steps in the learning process is provided by observations of how learners remember information over a period of time. Today, most scientists believe that there are three stages of memory: immediate, short-term, and long-term.

5. Look at the word **stage**s in line 8 of the passage above. Circle the word in the passage that is closest in meaning to the word "**stages.**"

> Short-term memory lasts about 15 to 30 seconds, such as after looking up a telephone number. **One** makes the call, discovers that he or she has forgotten the number (perhaps in the midst of dialing), and has to look it up again. Nevertheless,
> *(20)* such short-term memory makes information available long enough to be rehearsed. If the learner repeats it internally, the number could be transferred to some sort of long-term storage.

6. Look at the word "**One**" in line 17 of the passage above. Circle the word or phrase in the text that refers to "**One.**"

7. In which of the following lines does the author explain how a long-term memory could be erased?
   Ⓐ Lines 7–9
   Ⓑ Lines 9–12
   Ⓒ Lines 13–17
   Ⓓ Lines 20–22

8. About how long can a typical immediate memory last?
   Ⓐ 1½ seconds
   Ⓑ 20 seconds
   Ⓒ 3 months
   Ⓓ 2 years

9. What is the order of the stages of memory?
   Ⓐ long-term, short-term, immediate
   Ⓑ immediate, short-term, long-term
   Ⓒ short-term, immediate, long-term
   Ⓓ short-term, long-term, immediate

Learning, remembering, and forgetting have traditionally been considered separate processes. However, **contemporary** research regarding the differences between long- and short-term memory blurs the distinction between the three
*(5)* processes. Evidence to support the theory that these are just separate steps in the learning process is provided by observations of how learners remember information over a period of time. Today, most scientists believe that there are three stages of memory: immediate, short-term, and long-term.

10. The word **"contemporary"** in the passage above is closest in meaning to which of the following words?

   Ⓐ current

   Ⓑ persuasive

   Ⓒ worthwhile

   Ⓓ independent

## Questions 11–20

Most communication satellites are not launched from ideal sites located on the equator, the imaginary line that separates the Northern and Southern Hemispheres. This presents scientists with the challenge of adjusting the orbit of satellites
*(5)* during their launch. This adjustment is made in several stages.

Many satellites are launched in stages by vehicles that are discarded after their use. The adjustments are made in a specific order. The first stage, known as the boost, lifts the satellite
*(10)* out of the atmosphere and gives the vehicle the high speed necessary to leave the atmosphere. When this stage burns out, it separates from the rocket, falls to the Earth, and is destroyed as it passes through the atmosphere. The fairing, which protects the satellite and associated final stages of the rocket as it
*(15)* passes through the atmosphere, is also eliminated.

After the fairing is eliminated, the second stage is ignited. It places the satellite into a circular low-Earth "parking" orbit, where it is kept at an altitude of between 100 and 200 miles. After the second stage is discarded, the satellite is maintained
*(20)* in this "parking" orbit for some time.

The third stage, known as the perigee thrust stage, is fired and then eliminated. The perigee thrust sends the satellite into an orbit with the shape of an ellipse. In this type of orbit, there are two important locations scientists must consider

(25)  when making adjustments to send the satellite into an orbit above the equator. These are the perigee, the closest point to Earth, and the apogee, the farthest point from Earth. While the satellite is in this transfer orbit, tests are performed, and the satellite is positioned for the ignition of the apogee motor,
(30)  which is the final stage of the launch process. The apogee motor puts the satellite into a circular orbit in the area of the equator. Then antennas and solar panels are deployed and the satellite begins operating.

11. Look at the drawings of the Earth. Use the information in the passage to choose the launch site, marked with an "X," from which a geostationary orbit could most probably be most easily and quickly achieved.

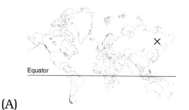

(A)

(B)

(C)

(D)

Many satellites are launched in stages by vehicles that are discarded after their use. The adjustments are made in a specific order. The first stage, known as the boost, lifts the satellite (10) out of the atmosphere and gives the vehicle the high speed necessary to leave the atmosphere. When this stage burns out, it separates from the rocket, falls to the Earth, and is destroyed as **it** passes through the atmosphere. The fairing, which protects the satellite and associated final stages of the rocket as it (15) passes through the atmosphere, is also eliminated.

12. Find the word "**it**" in line 13 of the passage above. Circle the word or phrase in the text that refers to "**it**."

After the fairing is **eliminated,** the second stage is ignited. It places the satellite into a circular low-Earth "parking" orbit, where it is kept at an altitude of between 100 and 200 miles. After the second stage is discarded, the satellite is maintained (20) in this "parking" orbit for some time.

13. Look at the word "**eliminated**" in the passage above. Circle the word or phrase in the passage that is closest in meaning to the word "**eliminated**."

14. Which of the following is NOT mentioned as part of the satellite launch process?
    Ⓐ the perigee thrust
    Ⓑ the boost stage
    Ⓒ the variable stage
    Ⓓ the ignition of the apogee motor

15. In which paragraph does the author identify the means by which the parking orbit is achieved?
    Ⓐ paragraph 1
    Ⓑ paragraph 2
    Ⓒ paragraph 3
    Ⓓ paragraph 4

> After the fairing is eliminated, the second stage is **ignited**. It places the satellite into a circular low-Earth "parking" orbit, where it is kept at an altitude of between 100 and 200 miles. After the second stage is discarded, the satellite is **maintained**
> (20) in this "parking" orbit for some time.
>
> The third stage, known as the perigee thrust stage, is fired and then eliminated. The perigee thrust sends the satellite into an orbit with the shape of an ellipse.

16. Look at the word "**ignited**" in line 16 of the passage above. Circle the word or phrase in the passage that is closest in meaning to the word "**ignited**."

17. The word "**maintained**" in the passage is closest in meaning to which of the following words?
    (A) converted
    (B) accelerated
    (C) preserved
    (D) enhanced

18. What is the apogee?
    (A) the farthest point from the Earth
    (B) the low-Earth altitude orbit
    (C) the geostationary altitude
    (D) the transfer orbit altitude

19. At what point are the antennas and solar panels deployed?
    (A) at the apogee of the transfer orbit
    (B) at the geostationary orbit at the equator
    (C) at the perigee of the transfer orbit
    (D) at the boost stage of the launch sequence

20. Which of the following statements should NOT be included in a summary of the passage?
    (A) The launch site location is an important consideration of the launch procedure.
    (B) The launching process is a complex series of maneuvers.
    (C) A geostationary orbit is required for communication satellites.
    (D) A satellite's length of service depends on its size and orbit.

## Questions 21–30

Early humans probably settled all the continents except Antarctica within the short span of about 50,000 years. Initially, humans lived in tropical areas, which contained diseases and parasites. As populations spread outward from the
(5)  tropical areas, mortality rates declined, causing fast population growth. Over a long period of time this resulted in a large population that could no longer be supported simply by finding additional hunting grounds. Thus began a transition from migratory hunting and gathering to migratory agriculture,
(10)  causing a swift spread of crops across the Middle East and all of Eurasia within only 5,000 years.

About 10,000 years ago a new and more resourceful way of life, involving static agriculture practices, became the primary life style of human societies. These new practices permitted a
(15)  greater investment of labor and technology in crop production, which substantially increased the food supply. Despite this development, occasional migrations persisted.

The next wave of migration began around 4000 B.C. It was encouraged by the development of seagoing boats using sails,
(20)  and by innovative farming practices. The Mediterranean Sea was the center of a maritime culture that settled the offshore islands and inspired the development of long-distance trade. At the same time, creative farming practices altered animals, which were tamed for human use. These changes allowed
(25)  humans to use animals for physical tasks and to consume the meat of most male newborn animals and the milk produced by the females.

Both sea merchants and farmers were inherently migratory, and both struggled for power over vast regions. The farmers
(30)  were able to populate the extensive grasslands of the Eurasian Steppe and Middle Eastern savannas. Yet the influence of the merchants was also expanding quickly. Their superior nutrition and mobility gave them clear military advantages over the farmers they encountered.

21. What does the passage mainly discuss?
   Ⓐ How human populations spread throughout the world.
   Ⓑ How agriculture influences human development.
   Ⓒ Why human populations grew so fast.
   Ⓓ How technologies facilitated population growth.

> Early humans probably settled all the continents except Antarctica within the short **span** of about 50,000 years. Initially, humans lived in tropical areas, which contained diseases and parasites. As populations spread outward from the
> (5) tropical areas, mortality rates declined, causing fast population growth. Over a long period of time **this** resulted in a large population that could no longer be supported simply by finding additional hunting grounds. Thus began a transition from migratory hunting and gathering to migratory agriculture,
> (10) causing a **swift** spread of crops across the Middle East and all of Eurasia within only 5,000 years.

22. Look at the word **"span"** in line 2 of the passage above. Circle the word or phrase in the passage that is closest in meaning to the word **"span."**

23. Look at the word **"this"** in line 6 of the passage above. Circle the word in the text that refers to **"this."**

24. The word **"swift"** in the passage above is closest in meaning to which of the following words?
    Ⓐ fast
    Ⓑ profound
    Ⓒ partial
    Ⓓ spontaneous

25. What caused the change from a hunter-gatherer migratory society to an agricultural migratory society?
    Ⓐ the spread of human populations from the tropics
    Ⓑ the need to secure an adequate food supply
    Ⓒ the growth of maritime trade
    Ⓓ the domestication of animals

26. With which of the following statements would the author most ·probably agree?
    Ⓐ Human populations moved out of the tropics when food supplies were not sufficient.
    Ⓑ The growth of maritime trade caused migration to cease.
    Ⓒ The domestication of animals encouraged populations to migrate to offshore islands.
    Ⓓ The merchant class had superior nutrition and mobility.

> The next wave of migration began around 4000 B.C. It was encouraged by the development of seagoing boats using sails, (20) and by **innovative** farming practices. The Mediterranean Sea was the center of a maritime culture that settled the offshore islands and **inspired** the development of long-distance trade. At the same time, creative farming practices altered animals, which were tamed for human use.

27. Look at the word "**inspired**" in line 22 of the passage above. Circle the word or phrase in the passage that is closest in meaning to the word "**inspired**."

28. The word "**innovative**" in the passage above is closest in meaning to which of the following words?
    Ⓐ erratic
    Ⓑ creative
    Ⓒ striking
    Ⓓ practical

29. The following sentence can be added to paragraph 4 below.

    **The former were able to settle previously uninhabited lands or to control less mobile populations.**

    Where would it best fit in the paragraph: **(A)**, **(B)**, **(C)**, or **(D)**?

> Both sea merchants and farmers were inherently migratory, and both struggled for power over vast regions. **(A)** The farmers (30) were able to populate the extensive grasslands of the Eurasian Steppe and Middle Eastern savannas. **(B)** Yet the influence of the merchants was also expanding quickly. **(C)** Their superior nutrition and mobility gave them clear military advantages over the farmers they encountered. **(D)**

30. What factor contributed to the development of a larger, more stable source of food?
    Ⓐ the use of static agriculture practices
    Ⓑ the continuation of occasional migrations
    Ⓒ the growth of sea trade
    Ⓓ the development of migratory hunting methods

## Questions 31–40

The presence of natural radioactive carbon, or carbon 14, in the atmosphere presents a unique opportunity to establish the age of fossils up to 50,000 years old. The carbon 14 technique of dating organic materials relies on its gradual decay
(5)  over a certain period of time.

The discovery of natural carbon 14 by Willard Libby of the United States began with the realization that the same special process that had produced radiocarbon in the laboratory also takes place in the earth's upper atmosphere. This process
(10) creates carbon 14 atoms that react with oxygen to form carbon dioxide. Because it is formed in the air, radioactive carbon can enter any place atmospheric carbon dioxide is absorbed. It is found in plants, in animals that feed on plants, in marine waters and fresh waters as a dissolved component,
(15) and in aquatic plants and animals. All these living organisms are invaded by carbon 14 atoms.

Invaded is probably not the proper word to describe the action of an element that Libby calculated to be present only to the extent of about one atom in one trillion. So low is the
(20) quantity of carbon 14 in the atmosphere that no one had detected it until Libby set out to measure it. He created methods to measure two factors, the degree to which carbon 14 is uniform throughout life forms, and the extent to which today's level of carbon 14 has remained constant over the years.
(25)   First, Libby demonstrated that carbon 14 exists in uniform quantities in living material. Subsequently, he determined the second factor by measuring the radiocarbon level in 5,000-year-old organic samples from places such as Egyptian tombs. He found that the half-life of carbon 14 is 5,700 years. Thus,
(30) he created a standard for a new method of dating organic materials.

31. Why had no one detected carbon 14 before Libby?
    Ⓐ No one had recognized carbon 14's importance.
    Ⓑ No one had ever looked for carbon 14.
    Ⓒ No one had ever tried to solve the relationship between carbon 14 and carbon dioxide.
    Ⓓ No one had thought that carbon 14 was uniform throughout the plant and animal kingdoms.

32. Why does the author make the statement "**Invaded is probably not the proper word**," in line 17?

Ⓐ Because carbon 14 is found only in minuscule quantities.

Ⓑ Because carbon 14 does not actually attack life forms.

Ⓒ Because carbon 14 is uniform throughout the plant and animal kingdoms.

Ⓓ Because carbon 14 has always been present in life forms.

---

The presence of natural radioactive carbon, or carbon 14, in the atmosphere presents a **unique** opportunity to establish the age of fossils up to 50,000 years old. The carbon 14 technique of dating organic materials relies on **its gradual** decay
(5) over a certain period of time.

The discovery of natural carbon 14 by Willard Libby of the United States began with the realization that the same special process that had produced radiocarbon in the laboratory also takes place in the earth's upper atmosphere.

---

33. Look at the word "**its**" in line 4 of the passage above. Circle the word in the text above that refers to "**its**."

34. Look at the word "**unique**" in line 2 of the passage above. Circle the word or phrase in the passage that is closest in meaning to the word "**unique**."

35. The word "**gradual**" in line 4 of the passage above is closest in meaning to which of the following words?

Ⓐ observable

Ⓑ steady

Ⓒ reliable

Ⓓ significant

> Invaded is probably not the proper word to describe the action of an **element** that Libby calculated to be present only to the extent of about one atom in one trillion. So low is the (20) quantity of carbon 14 in the atmosphere that no one had detected it until Libby set out to measure it. He created methods to measure two factors, the **degree** to which carbon 14 is uniform throughout life forms, and the extent to which today's level of carbon 14 has remained constant over the years.

36. Look at the word "**element**" in line 18 of the passage above. Circle the word or phrase in the passage that is closest in meaning to the word "**element**."

37. The word "**degree**" in the passage above is closest in meaning to which of the following words?
    Ⓐ appeal
    Ⓑ uniqueness
    Ⓒ intensity
    Ⓓ extent

38. In which of the following would carbon 14 be least likely to be found?
    Ⓐ water
    Ⓑ inorganic rocks
    Ⓒ starfish
    Ⓓ human hair

39. Circle the sentence in paragraph 3 that explains what Libby did after discovering carbon 14.

40. Which of the following is NOT a method by which carbon 14 is absorbed by fish?
    Ⓐ by absorbing the carbon 14 present in ocean waters
    Ⓑ by ingesting other marine animals
    Ⓒ by absorbing the carbon 14 in the atmosphere
    Ⓓ by eating plants in the ocean

# Questions 41–50

The process by which public or private lands are transformed into park areas is complex. The ecological balance of a park cannot be easily controlled. This is evidenced in Florida's Everglades National Park, which protects only the lower end of
(5)   a massive watershed. It is difficult to maintain and protect the Everglade's resources because of the growing degradation of the park's ecology. Throughout its history, the park has tried to control water and land use in areas outside the park, mainly because its future existence depends on the flow and
(10)  quality of water from those areas. In contrast, Mount Kinabalu on the island of Borneo, and Glacier National Park in Montana, both of which have enormous mountain reserves, are immune to such difficulties, simply because of their remote locations, far from population centers.
(15)      And not all parks are for public recreational use. Parks can be designated for scientific research. These parks are known as "strict nature reserves." They are reserved for scientific purposes, since their  use for recreation or other purposes could upset the natural character. The public is often unaware of
(20)  their designation and trespasses without knowledge that they are in violation of the law.

It is important that park boundaries be clearly marked and identifiable in order to prevent accidental trespassing that could damage the park. The use of these reserves is regulated
(25)  by scientists. Usually a scientific advisory panel controls any proposed research and determines if a research project itself may disturb the ecology of the park.

The decision to protect a natural area for scientific purposes is a complex one, especially in developing countries. In
(30)  addition to the factors discussed above, in most cases the less affluent countries, which possess neither money nor technical expertise, find it virtually impossible to establish strict reserves and maintain them, except in the most remote areas. Usually, international monetary or manpower assistance is
(35)  required if they are to be established and maintained properly.

41. Why does the experience of the Everglades National Park illustrate the problems many parks have in protecting their resources?
   Ⓐ Factors outside park boundaries influence its ecology.
   Ⓑ Scientific research disturbs the area's ecology.
   Ⓒ The park is in need of monetary assistance.
   Ⓓ There is accidental intrusion and modification of the ecology of the park.

---

**(A)** The process by which public or private lands are transformed into park areas is complex. **(B)** The ecological balance of a park cannot be easily controlled. This is evidenced in Florida's Everglades National Park, which protects only the lower end of
(5) a massive watershed. It is difficult to maintain and protect the Everglade's resources because of the growing degradation of the park's ecology. **(C)** Throughout its history, the park has tried to control water and land use in areas outside the park, mainly because its future existence depends on the flow and
(10) quality of water from those areas. **(D)** In contrast, Mount Kinabalu on the island of Borneo, and Glacier National Park in Montana, both of which have **enormous** mountain reserves, are immune to such difficulties, simply because of their remote locations, far from population centers. **(E)**

---

42. The following sentence can be added to paragraph 1.

   **Political realities play a role in decision making.**

   Where would it best fit in the paragraph: **(A)**, **(B)**, **(C)**, **(D)**, or **(E)**

43. The word "**enormous**" in the passage above is closest in meaning to which of the following words?
   Ⓐ celebrated
   Ⓑ prominent
   Ⓒ massive
   Ⓓ tangible

44. Why does the author mention Mount Kinabalu and Glacier National Park?
   Ⓐ to give examples of parks largely unaffected by human activity
   Ⓑ to illustrate that mountain parks also have problems
   Ⓒ to demonstrate that parks can be regulated too much
   Ⓓ to contrast the two enormous mountain reserves

> It is important that park boundaries be clearly marked and identifiable in order to prevent accidental trespassing that could damage the park. The use of these reserves is regulated
> (25) by scientists. Usually a scientific advisory panel controls any proposed research and determines if a research project itself may **disturb** the ecology of the park.

45. Look at the word "**disturb**" in line 27 of the passage above. Circle the word or phrase in the passage above that is closest in meaning to the word "**disturb**."

46. For what purpose are strict nature reserves created?
    Ⓐ advisory panel use
    Ⓑ scientific research
    Ⓒ ecological educational purposes
    Ⓓ governmental use

47. Who is responsible for regulating the use of a strict nature reserve?
    Ⓐ government officials
    Ⓑ the closest city or town
    Ⓒ the scientific community
    Ⓓ forestry experts

> The decision to protect a natural area for scientific purposes is a complex one, especially in developing countries. In
> (30) addition to the factors discussed above, in most cases the less affluent countries, which possess neither money nor technical expertise, find it virtually impossible to establish strict reserves and maintain them, except in the most remote areas. Usually international monetary or manpower assistance is
> (35) required if **they** are to be established and maintained properly.

48. Look at the "**they**" in line 35 of the passage above. Circle the word or phrase in the text above that refers to "**they**."

49. In which paragraph does the author describe the obstacles that poorer nations have in establishing parks?
    Ⓐ paragraph 1
    Ⓑ paragraph 2
    Ⓒ paragraph 3
    Ⓓ paragraph 4

50. With which one of the following statements would the author most probably agree?

    Ⓐ The decision to protect natural areas should always be made by scientists.

    Ⓑ The public is generally aware of restrictions on the use of park land.

    Ⓒ Parks located near population centers are difficult to maintain and preserve.

    Ⓓ Advisory panels should be established to determine the location of parks.

## Questions 51–60

The skyscraper was born in the late nineteenth century, but it wasn't born in that astounding city best known for iconic skyscrapers, New York City, home of the Empire State Building. Rather, it was much farther west, along the western edge
(5)   of Lake Michigan, that modern urban architecture's most striking innovation first took shape.

Prior to the 1870s, U.S. architects looked to Europe for their models and inspiration. For decades, their styles derived from European history. Townhouses, churches, and banks that
(10)  resembled European temples, cathedrals, and castles were the norm. These structures were typically made of stone and built from the ground up like the Pyramids, block by block. Meanwhile, advances in engineering, and particularly in the use of tough, flexible steel structures called skeletal frames, were
(15)  opening a radical alternative—namely, the possibility of putting the skeleton up first and *hanging* a building's exterior sheath on the frame like a coat draped on a hanger. Once that design breakthrough had been achieved, it was possible to imagine structures that could grow taller because their weight
(20)  was suspended and distributed across a framework. It made an entirely different cityscape imaginable.

Chicago was incorporated as a city in 1837, but it was the railroad that eventually joined the east and west coasts and put the city on the map economically. The railroad made it
(25)  possible to transport beef cattle from the remote plains lying to the west via the stockyards in Chicago to the slaughterhouses and kitchens in heavily populated eastern cities. Despite a fire that gutted the city's downtown in 1871, it soon became a boomtown again, home to big business and interna-
(30)  tional banking, and commercial buildings constructed on a revolutionary principle.

Economic conditions and social attitudes in Chicago favored the birth of a new, assertive architecture. At the city's commercial core, land was at a premium: property values had
(35) soared after the downtown was rebuilt and westward expansion continued unrelentingly to fuel the city's robust economy. Thus, any plan to get more office space out of less acreage—build taller, more narrow buildings—was bound to attract capital investment. Many refugees fleeing hard times, unrest, and
(40) economic uncertainty in Europe and elsewhere had flocked to Chicago to find work, and bigger buildings meant more work and a demand for more workers. Taller buildings also appealed to Chicago's energetic business community. The city had grown up quickly, it had recovered from a fire, it had
(45) proven itself to be a tough survivor, and now the time had come to declare its preeminence. It was time for Chicago to claim the heights.

Skeletal framing was first used in the Western Union Telegraph Building in 1873, but it really took off as a structural
(50) principle once Louis Sullivan arrived in Chicago in 1875. Louis Henri Sullivan was a Bostonian who had studied architecture at the Massachusetts Institute of Technology (MIT) and in Paris. In the next 40 years, he would design dozens of buildings, primarily in the Midwest—the Auditorium Building
(55) (1889), the Wainwright Building (1891), the Carson Pirie Scott Department Store (1904), the National Farmers' Bank (1908). Though many were only a few stories high, Sullivan's design approach clearly showed that taller buildings were now possible. By distributing a building's weight across its steel under-
(60) pinning, he was able to build a more solid structure that could support a much greater height. Later, his famous axiom—"form follows function"—would be adopted by many architects. It means that architects should start with the function of a building in mind, not its decorative potential, and repre-
(65) sent that function honestly in the building's design. Instead of smothering buildings in a lot of historical detail, architects after Sullivan would proudly reveal how they were constructed and what was going on inside. By the time he died in 1924, he had replaced a nineteenth century preference for disguised
(70) and horizontal buildings with the belief that building height is mainly limited by a lack of imagination. The Sears Tower, erected 100 years after the Western Union Telegraph Building, and a for a time the world's tallest building, was part of his legacy.

*(75)*     Today, skyscrapers are found all over the world. By the end of the twentieth century, the tallest one was no longer in Chicago, or even the United States. The tallest in the world, at 452 meters, was the Petronas Tower in Malaysia. But the skyscraper had started more modestly a long time before that in
*(80)*  a tough, enterprising city on a lake. It sprang from the insight that buildings didn't have to rise slowly, stone by stone, from the bottom up. Instead, they could be hung on powerful steel frames and thereby soar to unimagined heights.

51. What is the main topic of the passage?

   Ⓐ Chicago was a powerful U.S. business hub in the late 1800s.

   Ⓑ Engineering and economics led to the rise of the skyscraper.

   Ⓒ The skyscraper derived from European styles of architecture.

   Ⓓ Louis Sullivan was an important architect in the nineteenth century.

52. In which paragraph does the author explain Chicago's role in the emergence of the skyscraper as a building type?

   Ⓐ paragraph 1

   Ⓑ paragraph 2

   Ⓒ paragraph 3

   Ⓓ paragraph 4

53. Look at the word "**striking**" in line 6 of the passage below. Circle the word or phrase in the passage that is closest in meaning to the word "**striking**."

>     The skyscraper was born in the late nineteenth century, but it wasn't born in that astounding city best known for iconic skyscrapers, New York City, home of the Empire State Building. Rather, it was much farther west, along the western edge
> *(5)* of Lake Michigan, that modern urban architecture's most **striking innovation** first took shape.

54. The word "**innovation**" in the passage above is closest in meaning to which of the following word combinations?

   Ⓐ new concept, principle, or method

   Ⓑ a tall building hanging on a frame

   Ⓒ rapid growth in commercial wealth

   Ⓓ an improvement in building design

55. Which of the following is NOT mentioned in the reading as a factor in the emergence of the skyscraper as a building type in the nineteenth century?

    Ⓐ The railroad gave Chicago a big economic boost.

    Ⓑ Skeletal framing was used in building cathedrals.

    Ⓒ Sullivan took advantage of structural innovations.

    Ⓓ Funds were available for real estate investment.

---

had grown up quickly, it had recovered from a fire, it had *(45)* **proven itself to be** a tough survivor, and now the time had come to declare its preeminence. It was time for Chicago to claim the heights.

---

56. In stating that Chicago had **proven itself to be** a tough survivor in the passage above, the author of the reading means that Chicago

    Ⓐ caught fire and nearly disappeared in 1871.

    Ⓑ thrived because of favorable circumstances.

    Ⓒ came through or passed some difficult tests.

    Ⓓ lost jobs as the railroad reached completion.

---

Economic conditions and social attitudes in Chicago favored the birth of a new, assertive architecture. At the city's commercial **core,** land was at a premium: property values had *(35)* soared after the downtown was rebuilt and westward **expansion** continued unrelentingly to fuel the city's robust economy. Thus, any plan to get more office space out of less acreage—build taller, more narrow buildings—was bound to attract capital investment.

---

57. The word "**core**" in the passage above is closest in meaning to which of the following words?

    Ⓐ architecture

    Ⓑ business

    Ⓒ economy

    Ⓓ center

58. The word "**expansion**" in the preceding passage is closest in meaning to which of the following word combinations?

&#9398; the presence of a skilled immigrant workforce

&#9399; improvement in engineering and architecture

&#9400; movement that extends the size of an entity

&#9401; gradual rebuilding after the city's fire in 1871

> **"form follows function"**—would be adopted by many architects. It means that architects should start with the function of a building in mind, not its decorative potential, and repre-
> (65) sent that function honestly in the building's design.

59. In stating that "**form follows function**," the author means that the design of a building should

&#9398; hide or disguise its true purpose.

&#9399; stress purpose over appearance.

&#9400; stress appearance over purpose.

&#9401; reveal the architect's personality.

60. With which of the following statements would the author of the passage most probably agree?

&#9398; Innovation always stems from a single cause.

&#9399; Engineering can sometimes inspire architects.

&#9400; Chance is the primary motivation for change.

&#9401; Architects always follow popular preferences.

## ANSWERS TO TOEFL PRACTICE TEST

1. B
2. B
3. information
4. I
5. steps
6. he or she
7. D
8. A
9. B
10. A
11. B
12. this stage
13. discarded
14. C
15. C
16. fired
17. C
18. A
19. A
20. D
21. A
22. period of time
23. fast population growth
24. A
25. B
26. D
27. encouraged
28. B
29. A
30. A
31. B
32. A
33. carbon 14

34. special
35. B
36. atom
37. D
38. B
39. He created methods to measure two factors, the degree to which carbon 14 is uniform throughout life forms, and the extent to which today's level of carbon 14 has remained constant over the years.
40. C
41. A
42. B
43. C
44. A
45. damage
46. B
47. C
48. reserves
49. D
50. C
51. B
52. D
53. astounding
54. A
55. B
56. C
57. D
58. C
59. B
60. B

## SCORING YOUR TOEFL PRACTICE TEST (READING)

*Essential Words for the TOEFL* contains a Practice Test. This test is provided so you may determine what effect the study of this book has had on your knowledge of TOEFL vocabulary and on your ability to answer vocabulary questions in the TOEFL format. The tests will also provide you with a fairly accurate estimate of how you would do on Section 3 of the TOEFL.

Remember Section 3 consists of Reading Comprehension, Vocabulary, and Cohesion questions. Thus, your performance on the Vocabulary items will contribute one-third of your score on this section. Reading Comprehension questions make up 60 to 65 percent of the items on this section.

To score your TOEFL Vocabulary Practice Tests please follow the procedures described below.

1. Go to the key (list of correct answers) for the test. It is located on the previous page.
2. Score the test using the key. Place a C next to each correct answer on the book.
3. Count the number of correct answers and write that number in the space called Number Right below.

| Number Right Score | Paper TOEFL Scale Score | Computer-Based TOEFL Scale Score |
|---|---|---|
| _____ | _____ | _____ |

4. Now, go to the Score Conversion Table on pages 316 and 317. Find your Number Right Score in the left column. Using a ruler or straight edge, draw a line under your score and across to the center and right columns.
5. Now, in the center column, find the Paper TOEFL Scale Score that corresponds to your Number Right Score. Write that number in the space above, next to your Number Right Score.
6. Now, in the right column, find the Computer-Based TOEFL Scale Score that corresponds to your Number Right Score. Write that number in the space above, where it says Computer-Based TOEFL Scale Score.

Now let's practice these procedures in order to verify that you are following them correctly.

Suppose on the Practice TOEFL you answered 35 questions correctly. Your Paper TOEFL Scale Score would be 48 and your Computer-Based Scale Score would be 17.

When you take the TOEFL at an official administration, if your score on Section 3 is different from your Scaled Score on the TOEFL Practice Test, the difference is probably due to the fact that on any given day and on any given set of items your performance will vary slightly. However, your Scaled Score will probably not vary by more than 3 points from the score you got here. So, you can feel some degree of confidence that the score you obtained here is similar to the score you would obtain on the real TOEFL, if you took it today, after using this book.

## TOEFL SECTION 3 SCORE CONVERSION TABLE

| Number Right Score | Paper TOEFL Scale Score | Computer-Based TOEFL Scale Score |
|:---:|:---:|:---:|
| 60 | 67 | 30 |
| 59 | 66 | 29 |
| 58 | 65 | 29 |
| 57 | 64 | 28 |
| 56 | 63 | 28 |
| 55 | 62 | 27 |
| 54 | 62 | 27 |
| 53 | 61 | 26 |
| 52 | 60 | 26 |
| 51 | 60 | 25 |
| 50 | 59 | 25 |
| 49 | 58 | 24 |
| 48 | 57 | 24 |
| 47 | 57 | 23 |
| 46 | 56 | 23 |
| 45 | 55 | 22 |
| 44 | 55 | 22 |
| 43 | 54 | 21 |
| 42 | 53 | 21 |
| 41 | 53 | 20 |
| 40 | 52 | 20 |
| 39 | 51 | 19 |
| 38 | 50 | 19 |
| 37 | 49 | 18 |
| 36 | 48 | 18 |
| 35 | 48 | 17 |
| 34 | 47 | 17 |
| 33 | 46 | 16 |
| 32 | 45 | 16 |
| 31 | 44 | 15 |
| 30 | 44 | 15 |
| 29 | 43 | 14 |
| 28 | 42 | 14 |
| 27 | 43 | 13 |
| 26 | 41 | 13 |
| 25 | 40 | 12 |
| 24 | 39 | 12 |
| 23 | 38 | 11 |
| 22 | 37 | 11 |

| Number Right Score | Paper TOEFL Scale Score | Computer-Based TOEFL Scale Score |
|---|---|---|
| 21 | 37 | 10 |
| 20 | 36 | 10 |
| 19 | 36 | 9 |
| 18 | 35 | 9 |
| 17 | 34 | 8 |
| 16 | 34 | 8 |
| 15 | 33 | 8 |
| 14 | 32 | 7 |
| 13 | 31 | 7 |
| 12 | 30 | 6 |
| 11 | 29 | 6 |
| 10 | 28 | 5 |
| 9 | 28 | 5 |
| 8 | 27 | 4 |
| 7 | 27 | 4 |
| 6 | 25 | 3 |
| 5 | 24 | 3 |
| 4 | 23 | 2 |
| 3 | 23 | 2 |
| 2 | 22 | 1 |
| 1 | 21 | 1 |
| 0 | 20 | 0 |

# INDEX

This index is a list of all the key TOEFL words introduced and taught in this book. You may use the list to determine which words you have not mastered. Identify the location of each whose meaning you do not know. Then, learn the key word, the words related to it, and the synonym associated with it.

# NOTES